The Spirit of International Law

The Spirit of the Laws

Alan Watson, General Editor

The *Spirit of the Laws* series illuminates the nature of legal systems throughout the world. Titles in the series are concerned less with the rules of the law and more with the relationships of the laws in each system with religion and moral perspectives; the degree of complexity and abstraction; classifications; attitudes to possible sources of law; authority; and values enshrined in law. Topics covered in the series include Roman law, Chinese law, biblical law, Talmudic law, canon law, common law, Hindu law, customary law, Japanese law, and international law.

THE SPIRIT OF
INTERNATIONAL
LAW

David J. Bederman

The University of Georgia Press
Athens & London

© 2002 by the University of Georgia Press
Athens, Georgia 30602
All rights reserved
Designed by Walton Harris
Set in Trump 9.5/14 by Bookcomp, Inc.
Printed and bound by Thomson-Shore, Inc.

The paper in this book meets the guidelines for permanence
and durability of the Committee on Production Guidelines
for Book Longevity of the Council on Library Resources.

Printed in the United States of America
06   05   04   03   02   C   5   4   3   2   1

Library of Congress Cataloging-in-Publication Data

Bederman, David J.
The spirit of international law / David J. Bederman.
p.   cm. — (The spirit of the laws)
Includes bibliographical references and index.
ISBN 0-8203-2404-3 (hardcover : alk. paper)
1. International law. I. Title. II. Spirit of the laws (Athens,
Georgia)
KZ3410 .B433 2002
341—dc21   2001008257

British Library Cataloging-in-Publication Data available

*For my mother
and her love of books and learning*

CONTENTS

PREFACE

It is right and proper that a volume on international law appears in this series on the "Spirit of the Laws," and I am grateful to Professor Alan Watson for extending me an invitation to essay such a project. Polymath and eclectic as he was, Charles Louis Montesquieu opined about many legal systems in his *Spirit of the Laws*, and international law (or, as he called it, the "law of nations") did not escape his encyclopedic attention. He observed, "The law of nations is naturally founded on this principle[:] that different nations ought in time of peace to do one another all the good they can, and in time of war as little injury as possible, without prejudicing their real interests."[1] Elsewhere in his treatise, Montesquieu considered the role of international law in domestic legal systems[2] but nowhere returned to this elliptical comment made in the opening pages of his book.

This volume answers Montesquieu's rhetorical challenge and distills the essence of international law as a legal system, its "true principles."[3] This book offers a broad thematic conspectus of the structure, characteristics, and main features of the international legal system. I do not attempt to provide a doctrinal review of the rules of international law, preferring to leave that to other writers.[4] I recognize, moreover, that there are many blind spots in this volume. Some doctrinal pockets of international law are glossed over or ignored altogether. Most significantly, aspects of the incorporation of international law into domestic legal systems are purposefully sublimated here. I have regarded my charge in writing this book as requiring that I accept international law on its own terms.

Indeed, some readers may regard the structure of this book as strange and counterintuitive. Part intellectual history, part contemporary review, this book reflects on the nature of international law as a unique legal system—nonterritorial but secular, cosmopolitan, and traditional. The relevant unit of exposition in this volume is a series of meditations on different aspects of my subject. Moving from almost philosophical concerns in chapter 1 (on the nature of authority and obligation in international law), I consider the sources and methods of international lawmaking in the successive chapters. Chapter 4 canvasses the roster of legal actors in the international system as well as the permissible scope of international legal regulation (what I call the subjects and objects of the discipline). I then take a step back and reflect on the primitive character of international law and its ability to remain coherent. Chapter 6 undertakes the delicate task of divining the essential objectives of international legal order as well as possible tensions among those values. In sharp contrast, the following chapter explores how the discipline is bounded by considerations of domesticity, privity, and politics. Toward the end of the book I finally reflect on the nature of international law rules: the extent to which they are either formal or pragmatic (chapter 8), are enforced and respected (chapter 9), and have reflected both conservative anachronisms and progressive achievements (chapter 10). The last chapter muses on the inquiry of whether we are justified in feeling either cynical or enthusiastic about international law.

In writing these reflections, I have emphasized what I regard as "canonical" documents of international law: famous cases (whether decided by international or domestic tribunals), significant treaties, important diplomatic correspondence, serious international incidents, and weighty scholarly commentary. Again, my purpose in discussing these texts is not to knit together a doctrinal review of international law. Rather, I felt that because international law has a reputation as being aridly theoretical in its self-understanding, the best antidote was to ground the points I was making in materials that reflected the realities of international law practice. In a similar vein, while there is much international legal history in this volume, I have chosen to give substantial attention to the very contemporary problems and prospects of international life.

I incurred many debts in writing this book. Particular thanks go to Anthony Clark Arend, Harold J. Berman, Richard B. Bilder, Curtis A.

Bradley, Thomas M. Franck, W. Michael Reisman, Alfred P. Rubin, and Alan Watson. I am grateful to the participants in Emory Law School's Faculty Colloquium Series and Emory University's Halle Faculty Seminar on Globalization for their helpful comments on earlier drafts. I am also indebted for the superb research assistance of Ian J. Popick and Kurt R. Hilbert. As always, any errors and omissions are my own responsibility.

ABBREVIATIONS

AJIL	American Journal of International Law
Ann. Dig.	Annual Digest of Public International Law Cases
BYBIL	British Year Book of International Law
CITES	Convention on International Trade in Endangered Species
CJTL	Columbia Journal of Transnational Law
EEZ	exclusive economic zone
GATT	General Agreement on Tariffs and Trade
GYBIL	German Yearbook of International Law
HILJ	Harvard International Law Journal
ICC	International Criminal Court
ICCPR	International Covenant on Civil and Political Rights
ICJ	International Court of Justice
ICLQ	International and Comparative Law Quarterly
ICTFY	International Criminal Tribunal for the Former Yugoslavia
IDIA	Institut de Droit International Annuaire
ILC	International Law Commission
ILM	International Legal Materials
ILR	International Law Reports
LNTS	League of Nations Treaty Series
NAFTA	North American Free Trade Agreement
NGO	nongovernmental organization

NIEO   New International Economic Order

Oppenheim   Sir Robert Jennings and Sir Arthur Watts eds., *Oppenheim's International Law* (Vol. 1: *Peace*) [9th ed., London, 1996]

PCIJ   Permanent Court of International Justice

RCADI   Recueils des Cours de l'Academie de Droit International de la Haye

RIAA   UN Reports of International Arbitration Awards

UN   United Nations

UNTS   UN Treaty Series

VCLT   1969 Vienna Convention on the Law of Treaties, 1155 UNTS 331

VJIL   Virginia Journal of International Law

WTO   World Trade Organization

Y.B. Int'l L. Comm'n   Yearbook of the UN International Law Commission

YJIL   Yale Journal of International Law

The Spirit of International Law

1 Authority and Obligation

International law is those rules of conduct that are binding on international actors in relations, transactions, and problems that transcend national frontiers. As a legal system, international law has been present, in some form, at all times in which an authentic system of self-aware polities has existed in human history.[1] A hundred years ago, a writer considering this subject would have called it the "law of nations"—that body of law governing relations between sovereign states. But public international law can also be the law applied to individuals, relationships, and transactions across national boundaries. International law is also the basis of international business and trade. It dictates the uses of international common resources and the management of common transnational problems. In short, international law has come to exercise a significant role not only in international politics but also in the affairs of a striking array of individuals, enterprises, and institutions.

Why, then—if international law is so historically legitimate and ethically relevant, so doctrinally robust and functionally necessary—do so many people (including lawyers, policy makers and scholars) believe it does not exist? Why does it seem to be the stepchild of legal studies, a discipline in search of its own reality? No other area of law is compelled to justify its very ontology and existence, and yet international law seems condemned perpetually to do so.

Public international law is its own legal system, with unique ways of making and enforcing rules. But because of its sense of separation from municipal or domestic legal systems, international law has been criticized as not being law at all. International law still labors under what might be called the Austinian critique and other forms of extreme skepticism. John Austin observed in 1832 that "the duties which [the law of nations] imposes are enforced by moral sanctions" only and that because international law lacks a supreme legislator, a coercive sovereign, and an authoritative law interpreter, it can only be regarded as "positive international morality."[2] This attack on international law has undergone many permutations, most recently with H. L. A. Hart's challenge that international law lacks two features he deemed central to a concept of law: first, "a unifying rule of recognition, specifying 'sources' of law and providing general criteria for the identification of its rules," and second, "the secondary rules of change and adjudication which provide for legislatures and courts."[3]

Reduced to their essentials, both Austin's and Hart's jurisprudence regard international law as devoid of the elements that confer order, predictability, structure, and validity on any legal system. The apparent lack of authority and legitimacy in international legal process and in the substantive rules of international law gives rise to a special problem for scholarship in this area, one that cuts to the quick any attempt to fashion an identity for international law as a discipline. Identifying a basis of obligation in international law—and answering the seemingly simple inquiry of why states and other transnational actors obey international law rules—is thus essential for capturing the spirit of international law.

POSITIVIST AND NATURALIST BASES IN HISTORICAL CONTEXT

Discussing the bases of international law obligation has become a sort of rite de passage for international law commentators (known more formally as publicists), whether traditional or contemporary. In almost all of international law discourse over the past half millennium, consideration of the nature of obligation in interstate relations has always been anterior to an explication of what law matters (the sources of international law, discussed in chapter 2), the participants in the legal system (the subjects of international law rights and duties, in chapter 4), and the legitimate topics of international legal regulation (the permissible confines of those rules, in chapter 7). So, too, in this book.

The entire construct of international law theory and practice depends on some coherent explanation of why international actors should obey a body of law that may be at variance with their interests. The nature of international obligation has thus become a proverbial Rorschach test for international lawyers. Depending on what they make of the "inkblots" that characterize the reasons why international actors obey international legal rules, lawyers draw important conclusions as to the sources, processes, and doctrines of international law. Theory thus has a place of prominence in international legal analysis that might otherwise seem undeserved. This discussion of the bases of international obligations also tends to give the law of nations an arid, surreal feel. Moral philosophical inquiries ("Why should states follow international law?") merge with empirical observations ("Why do states obey international law?") and definitional quandaries ("What is international law?"). These disquisitions are part of international law's spirit as well, and one must confront this debate in any consideration of the contours of the international legal system.

It is then no surprise that publicists have, in a cyclical fashion, returned to the questions of authority and obligation. This is so particularly at times (such as these) of significant doctrinal change in international law rules and profound alterations in the way that those rules are made. Most traditional accounts of the bases of international obligation have located these periodic transformations in a Manichaean struggle between natural law and positive law. Such might be essayed with the following historic narrative.

Whether because of historical serendipity, or (more likely) Western ethnocentrism, the date that is commonly given as the birth of international law is one of peculiarly European significance. The year is 1648, the end of what has come to be known as the Thirty Years War (1618–48). This was a period of ferocious and bloody religious conflict in Europe, a war that resulted in the decimation of close to 20 percent of Europe's population. These events—culminating in the Peace of Westphalia, a comprehensive peace treaty signed by virtually all European nations—led to two significant observations about the development of international law.

The first is that international law needs states to grow and develop. More than that, it needs states with strong internal institutions and a profound self-awareness that we would today call nationalism. It just so happens that the Thirty Years War saw the rise of modern nation-states such as Great Britain, France, Spain, Portugal, Sweden, and Russia. The Thirty Years War also provided the ultimate intellectual and political justification for nation-states: they needed to be sovereign to confront the challenges that war and domestic upheaval brought.

So was born the notion of sovereignty in the writings of such political theorists as Jean Bodin (writing in his 1576 volume *Six Livres de la Republique*), Thomas Hobbes, and (later) John Locke and Jean-Jacques Rousseau. Sovereignty became the linchpin of the notion that states are independent and autonomous and accountable only to the whim of their rulers or (in what was then the exceptional case) the popular will. States thus owed no allegiance to a higher authority—not to God, to a moral order, or to an ideological ideal. States answered to nothing but themselves, and a rule of law was possible between nations only to the extent that they had specifically consented to be bound by such rules.

The Peace of Westphalia heralded a second phenomenon: the defining moments for international law of the last three and a half centuries have come only after periods of intense global conflict. One can almost linearly chart the progress of new international organizations, new substantive rules of international conduct, and new procedures of dispute settlement between international actors by the dates that mark the end of cataclysmic wars: the 1763 Definitive Peace (concluding the Seven Years War or Great War for Empire), the 1815 Final Act at Vienna (ending the French Revolution and Napoleonic Wars, 1791–1815), the 1919 Treaty of Versailles and Covenant of the League of Nations (completing World War I, 1914–18), and the 1945 Charter of the United Nations (marking the end of World War II, 1939–45). It thus appeared that international law was the stepchild of war and destruction, offering a utopian hope of order and moral renewal.

So far, this historical narrative is pretty grim: international law has prospered only by extolling state power and sovereignty and as an antidote to national conflict. Before one gets too discouraged by this doubtful pedigree of international law rules, it would be useful to chart other influences on norms of international conduct. One such consideration is that the notion of sovereignty—and its handmaiden of positivism (that states are subject to no moral authority above them)—has not always been ascendant and is not so today. Indeed, international law was seen in the Middle Ages as an outgrowth of universal values and norms, largely derived from Roman law (the *ius civile*, or civil law), religious institutions (the law of the Roman Catholic Church, or canon law), and common European customs involving such transnational issues as trade and control of conflict (the *ius commune*).

The earliest, "classic" scholars of international law, writing before and during the Thirty Years War, were often reacting to the excesses of sovereignty and positivism. Commentators such as Francisco de Vitoria (1486–1546), Francisco Suarez (1548–1617), Hugo de Groot ("Grotius") (1583–1645), and Christian von Wolff (1679–1754) tended to emphasize the moral imperatives of law between nations and were part of a larger natural law tradition—a "common law" of states backed up by religious and philosophical principles of good faith and goodwill between men and nations. By the late 1600s, however, publicists were starting to consider that the actual experience of state relations was the real basis of obligation in international affairs. This is the positivist tradition, reflected in the works of Alberico Gentili (1552–1608), Richard Zouche (1590–1660), Samuel Pufendorf (1632–94), Cornelius van Bynkershoek (1673–1743), Johan Jacob Moser (1701–55), and Emmerich de Vattel (1714–69).

Of these great writers, Grotius and Vattel represented the best attempts at a naturalist and positivist synthesis of rules for international actors. Grotius has earned the title "father of international law," largely on the reputation of his volume *De Jure Belli ac Pacis*

(On the Laws of War and Peace), first published in 1625. But Vattel probably had greater practical influence. His treatise, *Le Droits
des Gens* (The Law of Nations), published in 1758, was widely read
in European capitals and was admired both by the founders of the
United States (in 1776 and 1787) and by the Jacobin leaders of France
(in 1789). Vattel's positivism was the favored instrument of international relations in the age of revolutions and was followed by the leading nineteenth-century American writers on the subject: Chancellor
James Kent, Professor Henry Wheaton, and Justice Joseph Story.

There was bound to be a collision between positivist and naturalist
approaches to international law. It came in the early 1800s and was
waged over the most compelling social issue of the day: the institution of slavery and the slave trade. The practical problem for international lawyers of that time was whether a small group of states (Great
Britain and the United States) could unilaterally seek to suppress the
international traffic in slaves. That question turned on whether the
slave trade violated international law. For those who believed in natural law principles—that state conduct was subordinated to moral
values—the answer was easy: slavery was an abomination. Indeed, a
handful of judges so ruled. Justice Joseph Story, in his 1822 decision
in *La Jeune Eugénie,* observed that

> it may be unequivocally affirmed, that every doctrine, that may
> be fairly deduced by correct reasoning from the rights and duties
> of nations, and the nature of moral obligation, may theoretically
> be said to exist in the law of nations; and unless it be relaxed
> or waived by the consent of nations, which may be evidenced
> by their general practice and customs, it may be enforced by a
> court of justice, whenever it arises in judgment. And I may go
> farther and say, that no practice whatsoever can obliterate the
> fundamental distinction between right and wrong, and that ev-
> ery nation is at liberty to apply to another the correct princi-
> ple, whenever both nations by their public acts recede from such
> practice, and admits the injustice or cruelty of it.[4]

Under Story's reasoning, states and other international actors (including the slave traders at issue in that case) were subject to a natural

overlaw unless there had been some manifest opting out by contrary state practice.

For positivists, who embraced state sovereignty and the necessity of ascertaining state consent for new rules of international conduct, the issue was more difficult. In a series of cases decided by English and U.S. courts, the positivist view ultimately prevailed: slavery and the slave trade could only be suppressed if states explicitly agreed that their nationals could not legally engage in it. As Chief Justice John Marshall wrote in 1825, in a pointed riposte to his friend and colleague Story, "The Christian and civilized nations of the world with whom we have most intercourse, have all been engaged in [the slave trade]. However abhorrent this traffic may be to a mind whose original feelings are not blunted by familiarity with the practice, it has been sanctioned in modern times by the laws of all nations who possess distant colonies, each of whom has engaged in it as a common commercial business which no other could rightfully interrupt. It has claimed all the sanction which could be derived from long usage, and general acquiescence."[5] Indeed, Marshall had earlier observed, "This argument [advancing a particular rule of international custom] must assume for its basis the position that modern usage constitutes a rule which acts directly upon the thing itself by its own force, and not through the sovereign power. This position is not allowed. This usage is a guide which the sovereign follows or abandons at his will. The rule, like other precepts of morality, of humanity, and even of wisdom, is addressed to the judgment of the sovereign; and although it cannot be disregarded by him without obloquy, yet it may be disregarded."[6] Decisions such as this sounded the death knell for the effective application of natural law principles to derive concrete international legal rules.

Positivism reigned supreme in international relations from 1848 to 1919. Gone were the days of nation-state building and the popular revolutions in Europe and the Americas. In their place was a period of colonialism and imperialism during which explicit (and exclusionary) European political and value systems were forcibly transmitted to Africa and Asia. Among these was a peculiarly European notion of a law of nations for "civilized" nations. Despite the fact that China,

Japan, and India had their own historic conceptions of international rules of behavior, in the face of overwhelming European military and economic power, the price of Asian admission into the global order was acceptance of Western international law.

The European domination of international law ultimately collapsed in the charnel house of World War I. Four empires (the Austrian Hapsburg, German Hohenzollern, Russian Romanov, and Ottoman Turkish) disintegrated into new ethnic states. Only the British Empire remained, and three new powers entered the international scene: Japan, the United States, and the Soviet Union. The 1919 Treaty of Versailles and the Covenant of the League of Nations (history's first attempt at an organization for global peace and security) were probably doomed to failure. With the United States remaining outside the league, the Soviet Union disengaged, and Britain and France morally and physically exhausted, the world was powerless to respond to the aggressions of new totalitarian powers (Germany, Italy, and Japan). The League ultimately was unable to do the primary task it had set for itself—keep the peace.

The cataclysm of World War II remade the globe. First, the war accelerated the process of decolonization. The British and French colonial empires collapsed by the early 1960s, and by the 1980s there remained no part of the world that was under unwilling European colonial domination. This meant that the international community—the family of nations—grew into a large, rowdy clan. Before 1945, the group of "civilized" nations had never numbered more than 50. By 1960, it had increased to 100, and in 2000 the number has topped out at 195 states. The sheer increase in state entities (quite apart from other international actors) has changed the face of international law in fundamental and irreversible ways.

World War II and the Cold War rivalry that followed also set in motion a host of technological, social, environmental, and economic phenomena that we now identify as "globalism." Whether it is the integrated international economy and trade disciplines, nuclear power and proliferation, space exploration and computer applications, environmental pollution and habitat degradation, or intellectual properties and entertainment, we are gradually living in a shrinking, inter-dependent world. International law has been compelled to respond to the functional demands of the international community.

Finally, the end of World War II brought a vision of world order that had only been incompletely realized by the League of Nations. Enshrined in the UN Charter, this dream created an organizational architecture for the international community. With the UN's political organs at its center, this system has reached out into every aspect and spectrum of human cooperation. It has created progressively more complicated and supple legal and regulatory regimes for virtually all functional areas of international concern.

At the same time, this world order has managed to place state values (including sovereignty and maintaining international peace and security) side by side with the principle of protecting and extending the dignity of individual human beings. Thus, this vision is not exclusively one of state power and a positive grant of rights by nations to people. Instead, it is at least partly premised on a natural law notion of the inherent worth of human beings and is manifested in the creation of rules by which a state must treat its own citizens. Therefore, the pendulum of natural and positive approaches to international obligation has swung back to a more neutral position in which the international community recognizes values separate and apart from state sovereignty.

This correction in the balance between natural and positive sources of international legal obligation is illustrated by an event as momentous as the battle to end the slave trade a century before: the Nuremberg and Tokyo trials of the top German and Japanese military and political leadership after World War II. Indicted under the London Charter, one of the crucial counts against some of the defendants was the "planning, preparation, initiation or waging of a war of aggression."[7] But it was by no means clear that at the outbreak of hostilities in Europe in September 1939, a firm international consensus had developed against aggressive war—at least through the traditional sources of international obligation (what Chief Justice Marshall called "long usage, and general acquiescence"). The London Charter thus had rather the flavor of an ex post facto law, and (in the only credible argument made by the German and Japanese defendants before both the International Military Tribunals and occupation courts) the Charter was challenged.

Nevertheless, the Nuremberg and Tokyo tribunals brushed this objection aside. Some judgments took a positivist approach by suggesting that a prohibition against aggression was well enough established by 1939 to give fair notice to the defendants. But another panel took a very different tack, denying the very relevance of positivism: "the maxim nullum crimen sine lege is not a limitation of sovereignty, but is in general a principle of justice. To assert that it is unjust to punish those who in defiance of treaties and assurances have attacked neighbouring states without warning is obviously untrue, for in such circumstances the attacker must know that he is doing wrong, and so far from it being unjust to punish him, it would be unjust if his wrong were allowed to go unpunished."[8] Likewise, another bench ruled that "the specific enactments for the trial of war criminals which have governed the Nuremberg trials, have only provided a machinery for the actual application of international law theretofore existing. [Criminals] are amenable to punishment . . . without any prior designation of tribunal or procedure."[9]

The Nuremberg and Tokyo trials—and the human rights revolution they spawned—may well have been the signal international law development of the twentieth century. But the irony should not be lost that a criminal judgment that purported to affirm fundamental human rights values was nevertheless condemned as "victor's justice" and was criticized by at least one dissenting judge as lacking in legal validity.[10] Nuremberg should not necessarily be seen as a morality play extolling the virtues of natural law. After all, a natural law principle seen as indispensable to fairness and right can just as easily perpetrate injustice. Nevertheless, the abolition of the slave trade, the withdrawal of legitimacy for aggression, and the humanization of warfare are among international law's most profound achievements (as considered in chapter 10). That they occurred at times of momentous change in the shifting bases of international obligation is itself quite significant.

POSITIVIST AND NATURALIST ACCOUNTS
OF OBLIGATION

The antinomies presented by the abolition of the slave trade in the early nineteenth century and the war crimes prosecutions in the mid-twentieth bracket the period of "high positivism" in international law. Both before and after that time, positive and naturalist bases of international obligation mixed with and suffused each other. However, neither naturalism nor positivism could provide a definitive theory as to why states and other international actors did, or should, obey international law.

The *ius naturae* was ultimately derived from a combination of divine and reasoned sources.[11] Religion, morality, and ideology have always exercised an important influence on the development of international law. The Roman law vision of *ius gentium* (a law of peoples), a body of rules recognized by and applied to citizens and non-Romans alike, supplied a significant historical pedigree for the notion that there were common principles of conduct for all peoples in all places at all times. Religious values have been drawn from many faith-based traditions,[12] although Christianity (and a peculiarly Thomist vision of natural law) has tended to dominate in Eurocentric international law. Finally, contemporary political and social ideologies—as diverse as socialism, liberation theology, sexual and reproductive freedom, postmodernism, postcolonialism and globalism—also have come to exercise important influences on the formation of naturalist rules. As a consequence, natural law has been properly seen as a surrogate for "some more concrete conception such as reason, justice, utility, the general interests of the international community, necessity, and religious dictates."[13] Nevertheless, naturalism in international law has suffered from an association of the law of nature with platitudes and assumptions that "were so vague as to become practically meaningless."[14] And natural law as applied to the law of nations has always been an attractive target for positivists who assert that rights and duties presuppose the existence of a legal system established by direct human volition and lawmaking.[15]

The exogenous character of natural law rules has always posed difficult problems for identifying a basis of international obligation. Social-contract theorists (such as Jean-Jacques Rousseau, Roscoe Pound, H. Krabbe, and Leon Duguit),[16] who were able to fashion credible (if not entirely coherent) theories of obligation and law observance in domestic legal systems, were not able to replicate the feat for the law of nations. Although some early publicists emphasized the "necessity of law" as an adjunct of any community (drawing from the maxim *ubi societas, ibi jus*),[17] the difficulty is characterizing international life as an authentic society, with the requisite elements of civil community and social solidarity. The British "international society" school and the new American international relations approach of constructivism attempt such an argument,[18] but it still founders on the supposition that a real "social bond" or "social contract" can exist between autonomous and sovereign states, much less other kinds of transnational actors.

Closely related to social-contract theories but now largely discredited is the notion that every nation, by virtue of its statehood and capacity as a member of the international community, is endowed with certain essential, inherent, or natural rights. The fundamental-rights-of-states doctrine thus locates a naturalist basis of obligation for international law in the idea that polities are really like individuals, endowed with certain inalienable dignities and prerogatives. These fundamental rights are exogenous in the sense that they are antecedent to other sources of international law; they preexisted and conditioned the international legal system itself.[19] The notion of fundamental rights has, however, been transformed into the idea of fundamental *duties* of states. These are the *jus cogens* obligations (such as prohibition of genocide) that nations are not free to contract out of.

The obvious difficulty with this fundamental-rights approach is its strong statist flavor. To the extent that states are no longer the only kind of entity that can bear international rights and duties and thus no longer the sole subjects of international law, this theory cannot really account for reasons why other types of actors obey international law rules. Quite apart from that, this conjecture lumps different kinds of states, with potentially divergent political, social, and legal cultures, into one monolithic category. It also reflects an overweening atavism and sense of individualism among states. That international polities are in a proverbial "state of nature" seems almost to be a negation of the sense of community argued by other natural law theorists.[20] Likewise, the naturalist conception that states are restricted in their actions by fundamental obligations, particularly in a human rights context, can be attacked as vague and incoherent.

Natural law theories of international obligation seem to be internally conflicted as to whether states (and other transnational actors) are more like atomistic individuals or participants in a community. Positivist bases suffer from similar difficulties. The Machiavellian principle of "reason of state" as a justification for princes breaking their promises was Grotius's primary foil in *De Jure Belli ac Pacis.* Grotius's recourse to the natural law principle of good faith was one antidote to this unbridled view of state sovereignty.[21] Other early positivist writers like Zouche, Bynkershoek, and Vattel sought to make a clean break with natural law theories, and those publicists tended to mix different explanations for why states obeyed international law. Although theories of sovereignty existed in early modern political thinking (such as that of Jean Bodin), it remained until the early nineteenth century (and the dawn of what I have called here "high positivism") to establish a linkage between sovereignty and a positivist basis of international law.

This was provided in the writings of Georg Wilhelm Friedrich Hegel (1770–1831), which emphasized the "sovereign will of the state."[22] Under this theory, while states are supreme within their own spheres and can only be limited by the laws they issue, international law can exist as "external public law," in Hegel's expression. There is an obvious problem here: how can otherwise supreme states be subject to some exogenous law? Later writers, such as Heinrich Triepel[23] and Hans Kelsen, attempted to explain that the sovereign will of states had some manifest limits. In one well-reasoned example, Kelsen noted that newly created states enter international life with some rights and duties already specified, without the necessity of adoption or ratification.[24] "Just as the individual does not submit [himself] voluntarily to the domestic law of [his] state which is binding upon him without and even against his will," Kelsen wrote, "a state does not submit voluntarily to international law, which is binding upon it whether it does recognize international law or does not recognize it."[25] Other scholars have noted that it really was not possible to speak of a "collective will" of states, dismissing such a notion as they would a naturalist basis of social contract or fundamental rights.

One of the leading conjectures for a positivist basis for international legal obligation is consent. Under this theory, the rules of international law become positive law when the will of the state consents to being bound by them either expressly or by implication. The doctrine of consent generally teaches that the common consent of states voluntarily entering the international community gives international law its validity. States—and presumably other international actors—are said to be bound by international law because they have given their consent. The notion of consent is supposed to be applicable, irrespective of the particular source of an international legal obligation. Consent positivists have sharply disagreed on this point. Alf Ross, for example, observed that the "positivist theory takes it for granted that all International Law is conventional [treaty] law . . . and that all validity of International Law is in the last instance derived from a union of the wills of sovereign states."[26] But the majority view, dating as far back as Vattel and Bynkershoek,[27] is that state consent to international law norms need not be made in reference to written treaties but may be also manifested in regard to customary obligations. According to the proponents of this approach, because consent can be either express or tacit, a broader range of obligations can be made binding on states.

Consent certainly has been regarded as the most intelligible of positivist theories of obligation in international law. Nevertheless, it suffers from many of the same analytic failings as its competitors. Charles Fenwick raised the same kind of chicken-and-egg paradox as previously described: Do states, at the beginning of their international life or at the commencement of an authentic international community, really consent to certain basic principles of international law? The consent theory, according to Fenwick, is "inadequate to explain the assumption upon which governments appear to have acted from the beginning of international law."[28] Likewise, James Brierly suggested that to believe that international law consists only of rules to which states have consented does not account for the reality and complexity of the international system. At a bare minimum, he said, consent has difficulties explaining the integrity of norms drawn from nonexpress sources, such as custom.[29] Another difficulty, also noted by Brierly, is that if consent becomes the benchmark for international obligation, what happens when an international actor withdraws its approval of a particular legal norm (whether reflected in a treaty, custom, or another manifestation of consent)?

In response to this critique, traditional positivism developed an idea known as voluntarism or "autolimitation." Under this idea, states voluntarily derogate their sovereignty in the act of accepting norms of international behavior and thereby limit their subsequent ability to release themselves from those obligations. Writers like Georg Jellinek offered an important caveat: a state's willingness to limit its authority went only as far as the rules it embraced did not interfere with its essential sovereignty. In short, when push came to shove, a state could reassert its sovereignty and reject a rule that had previously bound it. Needless to say, this qualification drew sharp criticism. Brierly pungently noted that a voluntarily self-imposed limitation "is no limitation at all."[30] Lassa Oppenheim suggested that while states could individually consent to new norms of international conduct, only the "common consent" of the wider international community could release them from those obligations.[31] In a similar vein, Dionisio Anzilotti explained that the duty to respect obligations otherwise consented to—the *pacta sunt servanda* principle—was an absolute postulate of the international legal system.[32] This variation on the consent theme essentially recognized one natural law precept (the duty to respect promises) and combined it with a positivist thrust that states need follow only those rules they have accepted.[33]

Both naturalist and positive accounts of international obligation have been invigorated by post–World War II publicists and, perhaps more importantly, in the application of international law rules by transnational actors, tribunals, and institutions. Natural law theories

underwent a renaissance with renewal of interest in human dignity
and the protection of human rights, particularly after the horrors of
the Holocaust and other crimes perpetrated in World War II. Certain
kinds of codification efforts for international law (including the 1943
London Charter, the 1948 Universal Declaration of Human Rights,
and the 1949 Draft Declaration on the Rights and Duties of States)
also required a return to first principles. Religious values (particularly
an enhanced role for just-war theory, prevention of nuclear conflict,
and social-justice principles) were also significant in the postwar era.

With the acceleration of developments in international law after
1945—the creation of more states, the conclusion of more treaties,
the resolution of more disputes under customary principles, and the
availability of more international legal literature (whether arbitral or
case decisions or publicist writings)—positivism had the opportunity
to prevail in finally establishing a coherent basis of international obligation. Alas, it did not. Hans Kelsen's "normativist school" or "pure
science of law," although a complete rejection of naturalism, nevertheless embraced certain *grundnormen* at the top of a pyramid of
normative rules.[34] Kelsen's theory was later critiqued as being too
abstract, too detached from the realities of international society.[35]

Likewise, the policy-oriented approach of Myres McDougal and
Harold Lasswell of the "New Haven school," despite its laudable emphasis on world public order issues and the value-dependent policies
and wide range of behavioral factors used by international decision
makers, tended to diminish the role played by actual legal rules.[36]
The New Haven school consistently argued that international law
was not a body of rules but a process of authoritative decision making.[37] By emphasizing the sociological influences on those decision
makers, the New Haven school was often faulted as being apologetic
toward states that chose not to obey international law rules.

Some "neopositivist" theories of international legal obligation after World War II took a decidedly antilegal turn. Realist international
relations commentators, including Hans Morgenthau and George
Kennan, regarded international law as being merely "epiphenomenal," having no real impact at all on state behavior.[38] Different forms
of skepticism in the international relations discipline—including

forms of both descriptive and prescriptive realism—savaged international law. Within the international law academy itself, a postmodernist turn of "New Stream" scholarship has suggested that international law is intellectually incoherent and is a mere cover for power politics.[39]

A number of theoretical counterweights to these antilegalist approaches to international relations have recently emerged. These include new strands of liberal international relations theories for compliance with international legal standards.[40] In addition, the international legal process school attempts to define a role for law, lawyers, and legal institutions in various aspects of international life.[41] Drawing from Louis Henkin's famous observation that "almost all states observe almost all principles of international law and almost all of their obligations almost all of the time,"[42] the working assumption for these writers is that nations observe legal rules for many different reasons, some utilitarian and rational, others sociological and political. Law compliance, according to these publicists, was an objective fact subject to empirical testing through observation of the behavior of states and other international actors.

ORGANIZING PRINCIPLES OF INTERNATIONAL AUTHORITY

This discussion of natural and positive theories of international legal obligation has been quite extended because the naturalist-positivist dualism has been regarded as the crucial dialectic of international law.[43] The ongoing battle between positive and natural bases of obligation and authority in international relations provides a sensible historic narrative of international legal history. But it does not otherwise explain the structure of current discourse about why states and other transnational actors obey rules of conduct that emanate from a system that is, to some degree, separate and distinct from the polities themselves. Assuming that the international community is not anarchic (and thus has some order), not hegemonic (has an authentic system of states), and not world government (and so does not yet possess the Austinian indicia of society), can it still be governed by a rule of law? The tensions apparent in modern international life, expressed in a series of oppositions, help to explain the basis of authority and obligation in international law.

Autonomous of, or Dependent on, International Politics?

International law is a special kind of legal system because it serves a unique community of states and other kinds of polities, institutions, and individuals that act in international relations (see chapter 3). But is international law really autonomous of international relations? If a primary function of international law is to serve the needs of an international community, does that mean that it can be successful only insofar as it is a manifestation of the international political system? Structural realists among international relations theorists, as well as critical New Stream jurists, answer this set of inquiries by asserting that international law depends on international politics and lacks any legitimacy or authority apart from it. Indeed, this claim of dependence appears to be entertained more seriously for international law than for any other modern, non-faith-based legal system.

Despite the political function of rules in an international community (as in any other), it is certainly fair to refer to an international legal system. I would go even further and assert that international law is, to a growing degree, becoming more autonomous and independent of state behavior. Some doctrinal aspects of international law seem well settled and are largely impervious to change by the whim of particular international actors. Apart from those situations, international law has proven itself adept at incorporating state expectations and translating them into rules that are neutral and objective in application.

That international norms track state behavior and expectations is a signal strength of the international legal system. As long as international law does not, in Martti Koskenniemi's turn of phrase, become too "apologetic" for aberrant or atavistic state behavior, that kind of dependence is acceptable.[44] Even so, Koskenniemi's opposite fear that international law will become too "utopian"—too removed from international realities—seems less likely to materialize. Under these circumstances, international law would do better to err on the side of being more autonomous of international politics.

Consent or Principle as the Basis of Rules?

This opposition is my preferred way of describing the polemic between natural and positive sources of international obligation. The debate today is not so much about the historic pedigree of these ideas. Rather, the issue is whether law for the international community is exclusively the product of consent by the participants in the system (however manifested) or also includes enduring truths that somehow reflect the fundamental values of that community. Put another way, are all rules in a legal community internally generated by means and institutions chosen by the participants, or is there also a metaphysic of first principles that govern the system?

As I have already indicated, one of the primary features of international law as a legal system is its historic embrace of both internal and exogenous bases of obligation. What makes contemporary international law so distinctive is the reemergence of naturalist, value-based positions that compete in prominence with the vastly expanding institutions and principles of positive lawmaking. This development is not confined to obvious areas such as human rights protections but also permeates many other doctrinal pockets of the discipline (including international environmental law, state responsibility, and treaty law).

Sovereignty or Cooperation as the Paradigm for State Relations?

How an international decision maker or commentator views sovereignty and the necessity of cooperation in international life says much about his or her attitude toward international law.[45] Those who view sovereignty as an immutable characteristic of the international system—and believe that states and state-based values (considered in chapter 6) will continue to predominate in international life—are less likely to view cooperation between states as being substantively meaningful or likely to change deeply held state policies or significant behavior. Realists (of whatever stripe) will tend to regard international law as merely epiphenomenal, acting only on the margins of state action and usually only in reference to peripheral matters of concern for international actors.

In contrast, I take the view that functional cooperation between states and international actors is conditioned largely by forces that have nothing to do with law. These might include developments in the international economy; movements of people, goods, and services; and the globalization (homogenization?) of culture and intellectual life. (The values and paradoxes of these functional concerns will be explained in chapter 6.) The phenomenon of functional legal cooperation between states has been overwhelmingly responsive or reactionary. International law has acknowledged the demands of international life rather than anticipating or directing them. That is not entirely a bad circumstance; some of the signal failings of international law have arisen when lawyers and diplomats have moved ahead of the needs of the international community (see chapter 10). International law is doctrinally most vulnerable—and most illegitimate—when it loses touch with its constituencies and function.

Obedience or Compliance with International Law Rules?

The ultimate realist critique of international law and relations is that states do not really obey international legal rules. This assertion depends on a utilitarian and rationalist attitude that states and other international actors conduct themselves only out of self-interest. When that self-interest coincides with community norms of behavior, the realist might say, then international law will be obeyed. However, when the law conflicts with national self-interest, the law will be ignored. The realist concludes that any law that can be followed or not at the whim of the legal actor is no law at all.

My response would be that states and other international actors do indeed follow international law norms out of self-interest. That self-interest is expressed as more than a situational observance of a particular rule at a particular time. Instead, nations have a self-interest in promoting a systemic rule of law in international relations, a "culture" of law observance. And while the handful of examples of violations of international law norms are extraordinarily well publicized, the literally thousands of instances of law compliance go unnoticed and unheralded. Countries have a self-interest in the predictability and stability that law and legal relations bring to the international community. Whether law observance in the international community has any causal link with the legal system itself (and some international relations game theorists have suggested that it is merely coincidental)[46] seems hardly to matter.

Does that mean that states never disobey international law? Of course not. But that cannot be the operating standard for any "real" legal system. Even in the most highly advanced domestic legal systems, lawlessness may well be rife. Whether it is traffic infractions, tax evasion, or violent crime, all legal systems recognize that unlawful behavior does occur. The question for international law and the international legal system is whether unlawful conduct is flagrant by the wrongdoer and tolerated by everyone else. If it were, that might raise the specter that the law is but a fiction to be observed or ignored at whim. That is not the case for international relations today. (This subject will be considered fully in chapter 9.) Protests to actions that are regarded as violating international law are quick and vociferous. Even when states engage in legally dubious conduct, they will still attempt to justify or rationalize their behavior on legal grounds. These defenses might be spurious and the avenues for effective relief from unlawful behavior limited, but the attitude and culture of international law is still that actors may not justify bad behavior by expediency or strength.

Separate or Distinct from Domestic Law?

Is international law its own, separate, and distinct legal system? As already indicated, international law began as a "law of nations," where states were the only relevant actors in international affairs and only countries had rights and duties in that legal system. That notion radically changed in the twentieth century, to the point that institutions, individuals, business associations, and other entities were also capable of being actors under international law.

One consequence of this development is that international law has come to exhibit many features of "mature" domestic legal systems, even as it remains a fairly primitive or youthful regime. There is a rough (very rough) correlation between doctrinal areas in international law and those in most domestic (or "municipal") legal systems. For example, the law of treaties shows many common structural similarities with contract law. Likewise, there is a strong flavor of property law in the international law of territory, tort law in the international law of state responsibility, constitutional law in the operation of international organizations, and civil rights law in the international law of human rights. All of this is no coincidence. International law has consistently borrowed from domestic legal systems as it has sought to fill in doctrinal gaps.

It would be a profound mistake to believe that domestic law has not been affected by the development of international rules of conduct. That is the myth in thinking that international law is "separate and apart" from domestic legal systems. By various means, international law has been incorporated and applied into domestic law. It is fair to say, though, that this process has been long and slow. Although at one point in the Middle Ages, all European legal systems were substantially influenced by an international *ius commune*, as modern nation-states developed, they tended to be more and more exclusionist of "foreign" law, and (to some degree) international law was regarded as not being quite domestic. Some areas of domestic law (including maritime commerce and international trade) have always been influenced by international norms and expectations. However, only in the late 1800s and early 1900s did technological developments (like communications and transport) start to make the world smaller and allow for the acceleration of economic integration, a phenomenon that continues apace. Domestic legal systems have been obliged to transform themselves in the face of this process of globalization.

The separation of international and municipal law has had a variety of significant consequences. It has affected the "confines" of the international legal system, the permissible boundaries of its application (see chapter 7). It certainly has impacted enforcement of international law norms (see chapter 9). Finally, it has influenced the extent to which international law is conservative or progressive and the manner in which it has reached or fallen short of its objectives of serving the international community (see chapter 10).

Is International Law about Rules or Process?

Participants in any legal system will always disagree about the nature of norms and the rules that are supposed to govern participants. That is, I suppose, part of being in a civil society. Because there is no agreement about the fundamental nature of the international legal system—and certainly no conclusive answer about the oppositions I have described here—it is tempting to build consensus about international law by deflecting the debate from rules to something else. If we cannot agree about law, then there is always process.

Scholarship about international legal process has taken many forms, whether the New Haven school's emphasis on authoritative decision making and policy values; rationalist institutionalist writing in international relations theory; or examinations of legitimacy in state relations.[47] The tendency of much of this writing has been to reject a rules-based jurisprudence—or at least to downplay its significance—and, to some degree, that may lead to helpful contributions about the nature of international legal rules and their practical enforcement.

Taken too far, however, process thinking inexorably empties international law of content. By way of contrast, international actors tend to live process rather than to reflect on it. Process is merely a means to an end of some individual or collective objective. Process discourse has been seen as a way to move international law to a higher and more abstract, but more philosophically defensible, plane. But doing so risks alienating international law from its constituency. And given the robust relevance of international law as rules of international conduct today, that would appear to be a most unwise course to pursue.

IS INTERNATIONAL LAW "LAW"?—
AND WHY IT MATTERS

International law historically has been enriched by religious values, moral philosophy, political attitudes, and international relations theory. Much of domestic law has been similarly influenced by such "nonlegal" or "outside" notions, and no one suggests that it is theory bound and thereby lacks practical application. To talk about the "theory" of international law is nothing more than asking how someone (whether policy maker or attorney) actually uses that law. Understanding the historic nature and uses of legal rules in international relations helps one to identify appropriate and useful *sources* of international legal obligation. Having engaged in the lawyerly task of collecting the sources and materials that describe international law, one can then offer an intelligent opinion of the *doctrines* or *rules* of international conduct and behavior. Only then can a lawyer or policy maker provide helpful advice—suggesting a course of diplomatic action, structuring a business transaction, framing arguments in a legal proceeding, or deciding an international dispute.

Thus, to criticize international law as being "too theoretical" is really no criticism at all. Theory is just one of the tools in the international lawyer's tool chest (see chapter 5), and there certainly is plenty of "practice" for international law and international lawyers. The resolution of many international law disputes has turned on the decision makers' attitudes toward bases of obligation for international actors. The ICJ, the judicial organ of the UN, has relied on an unstated teleology for a constitutional document (the UN Charter),[48] a sense of rightness in the interpretation of a custom,[49] humanitarian values in the construction of a treaty,[50] economic necessity as support for a state practice,[51] and the rejection of "self-preservation" as a ground for violating international law.[52] All of these are examples of consent-based obligations mixing with enduring truths, or sovereignty giving way to cooperation, or legal norms being delinked from political expediency. What is manifest in this handful of examples drawn from international judicial decisions is replicated in the everyday work of foreign ministries, treaty negotiators, international businesses, human rights and environmental advocates, and other transnational actors.

I will now summarize my position on the basis of obligation in international law. I conceive of an international legal system that is becoming autonomous from international politics, but its primary function is to serve the needs of an international community that includes an authentic state system. Cooperation is the chief paradigm of state relations, necessitated by globalism and the need to confront common problems and challenges. The rule content of international law is derived largely from consensual (positive) means by international actors themselves but is significantly supplemented by enduring (natural law) principles that are not subject to the whim of the constituents or necessarily even to internal lawmaking processes. International law relies on a number of mechanisms to enforce its norms and is not hermetically sealed from domestic legal systems. By necessity, international law interpenetrates municipal law on many different levels. Finally, international law is both a normative system (a framework for making law) and a body of rules. A theory of international law—one that accounts for the basis of obligation for international legal rules—will simply make no sense if the content of paradigmatic rules for international conduct is ignored.

Inevitably, I return to answer the Austinian critique of international law: that it is not really "law" at all. This statement is the heart of darkness for detractors of this discipline, and, I must admit, it is a pernicious myth, exceedingly difficult to debunk. It takes elements of the previous propositions (that international law is not like domestic law, is too dependent on international politics, and is confined by sovereignty) and conflates them into an awesomely broad condemnation of this area of legal pursuit. Repeated enough times, it becomes the proverbial big lie.

If this myth was articulating only that international law does not have the characteristic features of mature domestic legal systems, I would have no quarrel with it. Although hardly an original sentiment, it is still true that the international legal system does not have a supreme "lawmaker" or legislature (like Congress or Parliament), a commanding "law enforcer" or executive, or an authoritative "law interpreter" or judiciary (like the Supreme Court or a Constitutional Court). Indeed, if there were a world parliament (capable of making law binding on the whole globe) and a world police force, the face of international relations would be utterly different. In fact, it would not be international relations at all: it would be world government. And world government (like anarchy or hegemony) is the antithesis of international law for a world of many separate and independent political entities.

International law remains a primitive legal system. It makes its law through a combination of consensual and coercive means. Enforcement is often through unilateral "self-help" rather than through multilateral action. As the next chapter will consider, the practices of the international community (known as customary international law) are an actual source of law—and an exceedingly effective one. Likewise, the network of bilateral and multilateral treaties that not only adjust potential disputes between nations but also prescribe rules for the future is also terribly significant. At the same time, international law is certainly evolving toward an administrative and regulatory model for prescribing rules of conduct for such areas of functional cooperation as the operation of the international economy, protection of the global environment, and management of common resources.

Thus, to say that international law is "unreal" because it does not exhibit the characteristic features of what we take to be "real" legal systems is both false and misleading. It is false in the sense that international doctrines and institutions are evolving to replicate the successful forms of lawmaking in domestic legal systems. Much more than that, however, because international law serves the interests of a special constituency (the global community) and a special value (the rule of law in international relations), it is unreasonable and unfair to expect it precisely to mimic domestic legal systems to be labeled a "real" kind of law.

More than any other modern legal system, international law needs to be secure in its historical and intellectual traditions, confident of its role in international affairs, and certain of the bases of authority and obligation for its rules. Considering these questions—as I have done in this chapter—is not an empty, theoretical exercise. It is central to a vision of international law that has relevance and purpose in today's complex world.

2 Sources

Most international lawyers have accepted that any discussion of the bases of international obligation is likely to be inconclusive. No similar concession has been made for determining the sources of international law. Essential to understanding the nature of international law as a legal system is comprehending the sources of international legal rules. It would be hard to practice within any legal system without knowing, quite literally, where to find the law, and international law is no exception. This is true whether one believes in the positivist nature of international law, that the sources of international law are a neutral and objective means of providing rules of conduct in international relations, or that these sources are readily accepted by all international actors.

Because identifying the sources of international law is such a crucial exercise for the legitimacy and credibility of this legal system, elaborate thought has been dedicated to the effort. Serious consideration of international law sources dates back to such publicists as Grotius and Pufendorf, who both wrote long passages concerning the formation of unwritten customary rules between nations and of the methods of treaty interpretation. During the period of high positivism described in the last chapter, jurisprudential discourse was obviously focused on sources of law that had strong consensual credentials and likewise rejected anything with a naturalist or inchoate flavor.

One of the difficulties in considering the basic structure of the sources of international law today is that it has been codified, or even "constitutionalized," in one of the key documents of world order: the UN Charter, which includes as a constituent part the Statute of the International Court of Justice (ICJ), or World Court. The ICJ is the judicial organ of the UN, and the relevant language of the statute is nearly verbatim that of the ICJ's predecessor, the Permanent Court of International Justice (PCIJ), derived from a provision drafted by a League of Nations Commission of Jurists in 1920. In other words, what is regarded today as the most reliable guide to the sources of international law was conceived by lawyers and diplomatists whose mind-set and attitudes reflected the high positivism of nearly a century ago. The ICJ statute's articulation of sources thus may not be entirely authoritative or relevant today.

Article 38, paragraph 1 of the statute indicates that in disputes submitted to the Court, the law the Court will apply will be

> a. international conventions, whether general or particular, establishing rules expressly recognized by contesting states;
> b. international custom, as evidence of a general practice accepted as law;
> c. the general principles of law recognized by civilized nations;
> d. . . . judicial decisions and the teachings of the most highly qualified publicists of the various nations, as a subsidiary means for the determination of rules of law.[1]

One favorable aspect of this provision is its clear sentiment that it is enunciating *legal* sources of norms in resolving disputes between states (the only parties that can appear before the World Court). Another clause of article 38 bars the Court from deciding cases "ex aequo et bono" (what is just and good) unless the parties expressly agree to that. This suggests to many international law scholars and practitioners that the Court is a judicial institution and is thus bound to decide controversies on the basis of respect for a rule of law. By implication, this is supposed to confer also on the sources mentioned in article 38 the unalloyed status of international law.

Substantial methodological confusion continues to surround even the basic structure of international law sources. Except in one (admittedly important) respect, there is no hierarchy established among the sources. Indeed, in reading article 38 one might believe that the sources mentioned may not even have an obvious interrelationship: they are separate and distinct, hermetically sealed in practical application. The one caveat is the distinction made in reference to the

last category of materials—judicial decisions and publicist writings—
as being a "subsidiary means for the determination of rules of law."
These subsidiary means are often called "evidences" of international
legal rules, as distinct from the primary "sources." The list of secondary evidences of international law in article 38(1)(d) appears to be
woefully inadequate, perhaps reflecting the relative lack of richness
of such materials in 1920.

Taking the analytic structure of Statute article 38 at face value,
one is left with two categories of international law materials: the essential sources of rules and the subsidiary evidence of those norms.
The classic sources of international law include treaties, custom, and
general principles (the order in which they are described in article 38)
and will be considered in this chapter. Subsidiary means of ascertaining the content of international legal rules will be deferred until the
next chapter to canvass them in the wider context of methods and
approaches for the dynamic of international lawmaking.

GENERAL PRINCIPLES

The last curious aspect to the statement of international law sources
in article 38 of the ICJ Statute is that they are revealed in precisely
the opposite order in which one might intuitively expect. International conventions (treaties), "establishing rules expressly recognized
by contesting states," are detailed first. This may be the product of
the high positivism that produced this formulation or (just as likely) a
recognition that international tribunals will first consult any written
agreements between "contesting" nations in a litigation before examining other sources. As a wider assertion of how international law is
formed, this seems wrong. Not all norms of international conduct are
made through express, written agreements. Indeed, many rules begin
in any legal system as unwritten practices, perceived to be binding as
law. This is called custom.

Even before the customary practices of international actors begin
a process of establishing legal rules, it is possible to imagine certain
norms that figure in almost all legal systems and are thus either coa-

lesced into international law at its inception or later incorporated to fill gaps in practice or agreements. These are known as general principles. As already mentioned in the last chapter, there is a strong correlation between general principles (whether derived from municipal legal systems or other sources) and a naturalist vision of international obligation. Lord Asquith, in a 1951 arbitral decision, had occasion to regard this as "the application of principles rooted in good sense and common practice of the generality of civilised nations—a sort of 'modern law of nature.'"[2]

Article 38, paragraph 1(c) of the ICJ Statute refers to "general principles of law recognized by civilized nations." It does not say "general principles of *international* law." These are not, as some commentators have suggested,[3] metaphysical "first principles" of international legal order. Rather, the emphasis is on general principles of domestic law (sometimes called municipal law), as recognized in the legal systems of "civilized nations." The point here is that the international legal system remains primitive and unformed and that often recourse must be had to "borrowing" legal rules from domestic law. General principles of law are the ultimate seedbed and gap filler of international law rules.

How does a legal rule become a general principle? The process by which a principle is "elevated" from domestic law to the realm of international law is subtle and complex. The language of article 38 suggests that a principle would have to be "recognized" not just in one legal system but rather in most of the world's legal cultures. So when article 38 problematically speaks of "civilized nations"—a residuum of nineteenth-century legal and cultural chauvinism[4]—it should today eclectically be taken as referring to jurisdictions embracing the common law tradition, the civil law, significant religious legal cultures (including Islamic law), and ideological legal systems (including socialist law as practiced in China and elsewhere).

To argue that a general principle is a binding rule of international law, it would be necessary to canvass all of the world's great legal systems for evidence of that principle and to reference manifestations of that principle in the domestic law of as many nations as possible. This is no easy task. Simply citing a few domestic court decisions or quoting a Latin legal maxim will not do the trick. Nevertheless, it is often imagined that there is something obvious and transparent in identifying a general principle in domestic legal systems and elevating it to the international plane.

There is also a bit of a paradox in the incorporation of general principles as international legal rules. The more abstract the principle, the greater consensus of legal systems but also the less useful the rule. Some general principles of this sort include a rule of good faith in international obligations (known as *pacta sunt servanda*) and the doctrines of necessity and self-defense. These are expedient doctrines, typically deduced by analogizing states to juristic persons and imagining certain "fundamental" rights of such entities. Yet these general principles are short on specifics. The less abstract (and more concrete) the principle, the greater meaning it has but also the more difficult it is to find a consensus among domestic legal systems.

A good example of this paradox at work is the rather prosaic notion that there should be a period of repose for international claims. Every domestic legal system has this principle. In common law it would be called a statute of limitations, repose, or laches; in civil law it is known as extinctive prescription. But is it a general principle applicable in international law? In 1903 an international arbitral tribunal ruled that there was sufficient consensus to make it a rule of international claims practice (and thus to bar a nearly thirty-year-old claim). The tribunal could not say definitively whether the international statute of limitations was ten years, thirty years, or fifty years.[5] The abstract principle of prescription was thus recognized, but no specific rule or time limit was set. Such are the pitfalls of general principles.

Nevertheless, general principles continue to exert a strong influence on the sources of international law, even as the international legal system has grown and matured.[6] General principles have been developed on such issues as good faith in the exercise of international rights (including the abuse-of-right doctrine),[7] due process issues before international tribunals (especially on evidentiary questions and burdens of proof),[8] and the rules of state responsibility (like rules of contributory or comparative fault).[9] For example, the World Court, in the *Chorzów Factory* case, observed that "it is a principle of international law, and even a general conception of law, that any breach of an engagement involves an obligation to make a reparation."[10] Why the Court even bothered to justify this self-evident assertion, it did not explain. General principles can thus be resorted to by international tribunals (and other decision makers) not so much as a gap filler but as a belaboring of the obvious.

It would be a mistake to think that international tribunals will invariably resort to general principles to fill a gap, or lacuna, in international law. The ICJ declined, for example, to apply domestic rules of easements or servitudes in a case involving the right of military access to areas subject to decolonization and refused to elevate municipal law trust principles in cases involving areas under international trusteeship or custodianship.[11] In a recent cause célèbre involving the use of force by countries in Central America, the World Court emphasized that the general principle of good faith, although one of the basic tenets governing the creation and performance of legal obligations, was not itself a source of obligation where none would otherwise exist.[12]

In spite of these caveats, one is well advised not to ignore general principles as a source for binding rules of international conduct. These principles are sometimes forgotten altogether as a primary source of international law or are inadvertently lumped in with secondary "evidences" of international law rules. Nevertheless, general principles not only constitute international law's link with its naturalist bases of obligation but also serve a significant function as both gap filler and paradigm shifter.

CUSTOM

Custom is a source unique for public international law, and it presents special problems of interpretation and method. Most of these problems stem from the fact that in most mature legal systems, it is typically assumed that the only binding rules are those made by legislatures (or, by delegation, administrative agencies or bureaucrats) or by courts. We tend to forget that law can also be made by the consent of communities of people, without any formal enactment by governmental entities. Such customs or practices are sometimes not even written down. Custom is rooted not in the high positivism that only formal legal organs (courts and legislatures) can make law[13] but rather in a historicist insight that law resides in the spirit of a people and community, and custom is the expression of that will.[14]

So, custom remains a powerful, if subliminal, source of law, even in "mature" legal systems. Public international law is not a mature legal system at all—it remains strikingly primitive. And customary international law is a source of signal durability and flexibility for international law. It allows international legal players to informally develop rules of behavior without the necessity of resorting to more formal and difficult means of lawmaking (such as treaties).[15] Custom "tracks" or follows the conduct of such actors as states, international institutions, transnational business organizations, religious and civic groups, and individuals involved in international matters.

There are two key elements in the formation of a customary international law rule. They are elegantly and succinctly expressed in article 38 of the ICJ Statute. Custom is "evidence of a general practice accepted as law." To show a rule of customary international law, one must prove to the satisfaction of the relevant decision maker (whether an international tribunal, domestic court, or government or intergovernmental actor) that the rule has (1) been followed as a "general practice" *and* (2) has been "accepted as law."

The first part of the equation (the general-practice element) is an objective inquiry: Have international actors really followed the rule? Has the practice been consistent? Has the practice been followed for a sufficient period of time? The second part of the equation (the "accepted as law" element) has often been called a subjective, or even psychological, inquiry. It asks *why* an international actor has observed a particular practice. This is specifically known as *opinio juris sive necessitatis* (or just *opinio juris*), and it attempts to ascertain whether a practice is observed out of a sense of legal obligation or necessity or merely out of courtesy, neighborliness, or expediency.

There is an inherent tension between these two elements, and practicing international lawyers (as distinct from legal academics) suspect that the two parts are deliberately redundant. The tendency has been, in proving whether something is a rule of customary international law, to simply satisfy oneself that a particular practice is followed by states and other international actors and to forget about *why* the rule is observed.[16] Nonetheless, there really is a need to have an extra element, an additional ingredient for the recipe that makes customary international law. Otherwise, international players will be bound to follow practices that may not really reflect their expectations of lawful international conduct or, worse yet, may be unreasonable or anachronistic. Thus, whether one thinks of an *opinio juris* requirement or instead focuses on the reasonableness and utility of a rule of custom,[17] something in addition to the bare fact that states and other actors follow the practice is necessary.

How, then, is it proven that a norm of international conduct is really a "general practice" that qualifies it as a binding rule of customary international law? States rarely oblige by disclosing and handily collecting all of their relevant international practices in one location, and customary practices often are not formally recorded at all. Furthermore, what states do should matter a lot more than what they say. International lawyers necessarily rely on written evidence of state practice (such as diplomatic correspondence, official manuals, or newspaper accounts of contemporary events). While customary international law is very much a struggle between competing positions, no international lawyer would desire that, in their exuberance to demonstrate their positions, states more readily resort to muscular and violent means of asserting rights. But it is vital for customary international law's legitimacy that it be based on empirically observed state practice and not merely on the aspirations of policy makers and commentators or an elaborate charade of *de lege ferenda.*

One of the best examples of the hard work of lawyering evidence of state practice is shown in *The Paquete Habana*, a case decided by the U.S. Supreme Court in 1900.[18] The facts and issues presented in the case were deceptively simple. Two Cuban fishing boats had been captured by U.S. naval forces in the Spanish-American War and condemned as prizes of war. The question was whether small coastal fishing boats were immune from capture under customary international law. Drawing from sources as varied as medieval English royal ordinances, agreements between European nations, orders issued to the U.S. Navy in earlier conflicts, and the opinions of treatise writers, the Supreme Court held that custom barred the capture of small fishing boats.

The boat owners' victory was not only a demonstration of an eclectic and scholarly collection of evidence of state practice. It was also a tour de force of argument insofar as it persuaded a majority of the justices that the immunity granted to coastal fishing boats was grounded in humanitarian concerns as well as supported by legal obligation. The United States had particularly relied on one earlier case, *The Young Jacob*, decided by the English High Court of Admiralty in 1798.[19] That case had held that the practice of immunizing fishing craft was not a rule at all but instead was only "comity" or courtesy. The English court had ruled that the practice was not supported by *opinio juris*, and the United States (a century later) seized on this as a basis for arguing that protecting enemy fishing boats was only a matter of "grace." The boat owners persuaded the Court, however, that within the intervening century the practice had become obligatory: it was no longer optional and was indeed binding on the United States.

The boat owners had the advantage, of course, of proving a customary usage that was supported by an impeccable evidentiary pedigree: nearly two centuries of consistent and well-documented state practice. And although this conclusion has been doubted in some new scholarly literature,[20] it is generally regarded that the *Paquete Habana* Court properly distinguished between a rule of binding custom and a mere courteous practice.

Must all evidence of a general practice be confirmed by this high threshold of uniformity, consistency, and longevity of usage? The ICJ has indicated that uniformity need not be perfect and that minor inconsistencies in the observance of the practice are acceptable.[21] Likewise, the ICJ has held that for a norm to be established as customary, the corresponding practice need not be in absolutely rigorous conformity with the rule. Instead, the conduct of states in such situations should be consistent with such rules, and, to the extent they are not, such inconsistencies should be treated as breaches of the norm, not as an indication of the emergence of a new rule.[22]

There also is no requirement that a practice necessarily be observed for a long time before it will be confirmed as a binding custom. Unlike customary obligations in many domestic legal systems, there is no necessity that a usage be followed "from time immemorial." The history of international law is replete with examples of state practice that enjoyed such immediate popularity and around which formed such a complete consensus of the international community that they were recognized almost as "instant custom." One well-known example was the development of state claims to offshore oil and gas deposits under a theory of continental shelves that took barely fifteen years to become binding law.[23] It is not the age of a practice that makes a custom. Rather, it is the high degree of consistency and uniformity of observance by most (if not all) of the international community that satisfies the objective element of confirming it as a "general practice."

Therefore, it is by no means an easy task even to establish the "objective" prong of a custom as a general practice. But it is the "subjective" element of *opinio juris* that remains the most problematic for international lawyers. The most obvious difficulty with this vision of the binding nature of custom—that nations obey a practice out of a sense of legal obligation—is that it cannot explain the psychology of "first movers": the handful of international actors that follow a new practice or the attitudes of states in opposing a currently accepted usage. In this regard, international tribunals have not been helpful. They have adopted lax standards of *opinio juris* in some cases (making it almost self-proving), while in others imposed a demanding test that was all but impossible to satisfy.[24] Nothing necessarily distinguishes the disputes save the cynical view that the World Court was desirous in one instance of accepting a rule as a custom and not so obliging in the other matters.

It has been suggested that the real binding force behind a custom is not the tautological "sense of legal obligation" that international actors may or may not espouse (and which we will never know, of course). Rather, it must be that actors follow a custom out of a sense that it is reasonable or functional for the international community.[25] This approach tends to substitute a naturalist test of reasonableness, utility, fairness, or justice for every emerging or conflicting custom, at least in the absence of the express evidence of state consent to be bound to a legal custom (which is often lacking).

All of this may beg the larger question of how exactly customary international law gets made. This problem is particularly acute when one realizes that for most evolving rules of international behavior or conduct, there is no consensus. Instead, as I have suggested already, there is a dynamic struggle for law in which countries actively compete in a marketplace of rules. A country might, by both its words and deeds, attempt to build support for a new custom. Other nations might join this bid. Another group of countries might actively resist the creation of a new norm. They might lodge diplomatic protests, and—in extreme circumstances—undertake affirmative steps to block the formation of a new practice or, at a minimum, deny that new usage the legitimacy of *opinio juris*, reasonableness, or functional utility.

That leaves the question of how states can effectively opt out, or block the application of a customary rule. While the formation of customary obligations can be foiled by a lack of duration or consensus in the practice or the occasional denial of *opinio juris*, once a usage has gained momentum it is hard to stop. The general presumption is that unless a state has persistently objected during the process of crystallizing a customary norm, the state will be held to that rule.[26] This is perhaps the decisive feature of the customary regime in international law. This means that states are obliged to protest loud and often if they wish to avoid being bound by a norm of emerging global custom. (A different rule has been developed for customs on a regional level, a matter considered in the next chapter.)

This general presumption for global custom seems unfair. After all, it somehow expects that all countries in the world have hordes of international lawyers in their employ with nothing better to do than closely monitor what other nations are "bidding" and "claiming" as new rules of custom and then effectively protest them. The reality of legal staffing for foreign ministries around the world is quite different. Nevertheless, it has always been understood that customary international law could never really develop if it required the affirmative and express consent of nations to produce a binding state practice. Hence, the general assumption is that for global custom, silence means acceptance of a new rule.

The structure of customary law is thus skewed in favor of rule formation, at least once a magic threshold has been crossed. Persistent objection is difficult to sustain. Tribunals will occasionally allow states to silently abstain from a usage (or to substitute another rule), and if other interested nations themselves fail to object, that lack of "opposability" might have the same effect as a successful persistent objection.[27]

If one regards this pattern of assumptions and presumptions about the formation of customary international law as troublesome, one would be correct to be concerned. It would seem that fortune favors those states that aggressively stake out new rules and hope that other nations simply do not notice or fail to act in a timely or compelling manner. Aside from the basic question of what constitutes an effective protest of an emerging custom, how can one know whether a new practice is successfully supplanting an old usage? One could, I suppose, look at the extent, frequency, and consistency of departures from old customs and tally the number of states that adhere to one rule or the other or try to trace a linear progression as states shift from one practice to another.

Another question that needs to be considered is the role of new states in the process of customary international law formation. Are newly independent countries bound to the existing rules of custom, almost as the price of admission to the community of nations, even though they have had no role in making those rules? This seems to be the preferred approach. The international community does not give new states the alternative of opting out of customs they do not like. Instead, if a new state dislikes a rule of custom, it can compete in the global marketplace and struggle to change it.

If this dynamic and consensual model of customary international law appeals, bear in mind that some rules of international conduct have become so important that the international legal system will not let any state opt out of them, even if they have loudly and conscientiously protested. For example, the former minority white government of South Africa persistently objected to the development of customary international law condemning that government's practice of apartheid, or racial separation. But to no avail: the international legal consequences of South Africa's failure to observe that custom were notable.[28] Similarly, rules against genocide (systematic destruction of groups of people based on ethnic, cultural, or linguistic identity), war crimes, and aggressive war have come to acquire special status.

For example, there are some rules of custom that are so significant—including those just mentioned—that the international community will not suffer states to "contract" out of them by treaty. For example, two states may not conclude a treaty reciprocally granting themselves the right to commit genocide against a selected group or to engage in aggressive war.[29] These are called peremptory, or *jus cogens*, norms.[30] Likewise, some customary international law duties are so portentous that the international community will permit any state to claim for their violation, not just the countries immediately affected. These are *erga omnes* obligations.[31]

So some principles of customary international law appear to transcend state consent, seemingly immune from the bidding process of objection. How these particular rules of "supercustom" are designated and achieve the exceptionally high level of international consensus they require is a bit of a mystery. This enigma should not detract from what would otherwise be the conclusion that custom is a unique source of strength for international law, precisely because it ensures that rules of international conduct are current with the needs and expectations of the international community. Likewise, the methods for finding the evidences of state practice are very supple and require substantial imagination and skill in investigating. The last element of the customary international law equation—whether *opinio juris* or the reasonableness or utility of a rule—brings into sharp focus the essential question of why states (and other international players) choose to obey international law.

At a time when customary international law is coming under simultaneous attack both from extreme positivists (who suggest that its processes are illegitimate and nontransparent)[32] and from those of a naturalist bent (who regard it as merely advancing state interests),[33] it might be useful to recall that in some ways custom is the most positive and progressive of international law sources. It is certainly the most likely to track (although, admittedly, a bit inelastically) the behavior of international actors. The market aspect of customary norm creation largely ensures that. Custom may, however, suffer from a "democracy deficit" in the sense that powerful nations (larger "market players") are more likely to exercise substantial influence over the processes of its formation and revision than smaller nations. That may be no different for other sources and might be a systemic concern with all international lawmaking.

TREATIES

Along with general principles and custom, treaties are an essential source of international law. Indeed, it is easy to think of written agreements between countries as being *the* source of international legal rules. This view was widely embraced in the attitudes of nations that felt alienated from the process of customary international lawmaking, particularly socialist countries and those in the decolonized, developing world. Although customary international law and general principles remain an important part of the dynamic of international law formation, treaties and treaty making are gradually becoming the dominant source of rules for international conduct.

International law academics have spilled much ink in trying to distinguish various kinds of treaties, depending on some essential characteristics or subject matter. This has largely been futile. Most international agreements defy easy categorization. Some writers have tried to differentiate treaties that purport to crystallize existing rules of customary international law ("codification"), as opposed to freshly legislating rules of international conduct ("progressive development"). This distinction is supposed to explain whether a new treaty really reflects existing international law and assumes the status of general conventional law. It rarely does. Treaty projects that "merely" codify existing law have been among the most contentious in modern diplomatic history. (One example is the UN International Law Commission's fifty-year attempt to fashion draft articles on state responsibility, the consequences that follow when one nation injures another.) Conversely, the international community can often mobilize substantial support for entirely novel forms of lawmaking—if the circumstances are compelling enough.

Using another distinctive trope, some scholars have attempted to identify treaties that are more like contracts between nations and those that have more the flavor of legislation, definitively establishing rules of conduct between countries. Many international agreements have aspects of both properties: they try to settle relations between nations while ordaining future rules. The contracts-legislation duality is significant and explains the peculiar problems that international lawyers face in interpreting and applying treaties. Unfortunately, it does not serve as a reliable guidepost for categorizing international agreements.

One reason is that many contractual metaphors for treaties are downright misleading.[34] For example, must all international agreements be written, in satisfaction of some international version of the Statute of Frauds or Civil Code requirement? To be covered by the "default" rules of the 1969 Vienna Convention on the Law of Treaties (VCLT)—quite literally a treaty on treaties—the answer is yes. That does not, however, invalidate oral agreements concluded between nations or even countries' unilateral declarations. In a number of cases, the World Court has enforced such verbal agreements or unilateral declarations. For example, the PCIJ in the *Eastern Greenland* case enforced an oral promise by the Norwegian foreign minister to renounce Norwegian claims to Greenland, especially when the promise was motivated by the quid pro quo of Denmark's forgoing claims to Norwegian territory elsewhere.[35] The same goes for unilateral declarations made by states, even without consideration. The French president's announcement of his nation's termination of atmospheric nuclear testing in the South Pacific was held to be legally binding on France.[36]

The key factor in deciding the binding character and enforceability of unilateral declarations is whether the declaring state intended to create a legal obligation or induce reliance on the part of other states. If this sounds circular, it probably is, but it is increasingly important to distinguish between binding and nonbinding agreements. The latter—sometimes called gentlemen's agreements, aspirational texts, or soft law—are intended by their parties not to be legally obligatory.[37] That does not mean they are purely political or hortatory. A nonbinding accord might start the process of forming a state practice that, when accompanied by *opinio juris*, would make a custom. An aspirational text might later mature into a fully enforceable and binding treaty. I believe the inevitable trend is that soft law hardens into legal obligation, and in any rules-standards typology for norms, there is an asymmetric dynamic at work. Rules rarely dissolve into standards, but standards (my surrogate for soft law in an international context) will usually solidify into legal rules.[38]

As has already been intimated, profound tensions can arise between rules based on treaties and those based on custom. The first is presented by the question of whether treaties can bind nonparties. The straightforward answer should be no: agreements should never bind nonparties. There are, however, situations where an international agreement might confer benefits on a nonparty, and, once conferred, such benefits cannot be withdrawn without the consent of the beneficiary. Treaties that are conceived as largely contractual in their force should not, therefore, be binding or legally enforceable against states that decline to participate. This is known as the principle of *ius tertii.*[39]

This all seems standard contracts "black-letter," and (for the most part) it is a correct statement of international law. Nonetheless, there are some notable exceptions where duties in international agreements can be applied to nonparties. There are a handful of "objective regimes," treaties that have been understood to be binding even on nonparties. The ICJ has found that the UN Charter—the constitution of the post–World War II international order—creates rights and duties for nonmembers.[40] Some newer environmental regimes, including the 1959 Antarctic Treaty, have also been found to have this objective character, as have some aspects of regional economic integration (including the European Union).[41]

A more complicated problem is presented where a state deliberately does not become party to a treaty, but it is nevertheless asserted that the state has become bound to a custom codified or progressively developed in the agreement. This was the situation in the *North Sea Continental Shelf* cases,[42] where Denmark and the Netherlands asserted that the Federal Republic of Germany was bound to a rule of equidistance in delimiting their respective continental shelves, even though Germany had purposefully not signed the 1958 Convention on the Continental Shelf. Needless to say, Germany had declined to sign that instrument precisely because adoption of the equidistance rule would have had disastrous consequences for its legal claim to offshore oil and gas in the North Sea.

The ICJ ruled that the equidistance rule—unlike the basic concept of a nation's claim to a continental shelf—was a progressive development, not a codification of existing custom. Holland and Denmark could not, therefore, assert that the equidistance rule contained in the 1958 convention had quickly matured into a custom (the dispute arose in the mid-1960s and was decided in 1969). This saved Germany from proving that it had persistently objected to the new custom, as distinct from merely rejecting the treaty.

The important thing to remember here is that a rule can develop through a parallel evolution in both treaties and custom. Even though a country rejects a treaty provision containing a rule, if it fails to object as that same norm is renewed in state practice, the country will later become bound to the rule. If treaty rules and custom can converge, they can also clash. Despite the fact that more and more areas of international law are being governed by rules contained in international agreements, it would be profoundly mistaken to believe that in case of conflict, custom will be trumped by treaty.

A number of diplomatic incidents and tribunal decisions have given customary international law norms precedence over treaty rules. In diplomatic correspondence between the United States and United Kingdom just before America's entry into World War I, the United States successfully protested the British practice of stopping American vessels and arresting German nationals.[43] Britain justified this practice based on an extensive network of treaties, but the United States relied on a customary rule granting immunity to neutral vessels. Absent an explicit agreement between Britain and the United States sanctioning such arrests, the United States was correct to rely on custom.

In the SS *Wimbledon* case, the World Court (in its first decision)[44] was faced with a collision between customary principles of neutrality and treaty-based rules of access to an international canal. The PCIJ opted for the treaty and compelled Germany to grant passage through the Kiel Canal to a vessel carrying munitions to Poland (then engaged in a war with the Soviet Union). Germany was thus whipsawed. By satisfying its obligations under the Treaty of Versailles, it was violating its customary international law obligation of neutrality to the Soviets (who were not a party to Versailles). What I call the Wimbledon Paradox reveals a troubling aspect to the relationship between custom and treaty: international actors can be placed in the awkward position of having to breach a rule emanating from one source of legal obligation in order to satisfy another.

A similar if even more intractable problem arises in the context of informal mechanisms for treaty modification. Modification arises when some (but not all) of the parties to a treaty subsequently agree to a material change. VCLT article 41 sets out an elaborate regime in which, as long as a treaty does not bar modification, selected states can give notice of a modification, provided the change does not derogate the rights of other parties and does not affect a provision the performance of which is essential. Interestingly, in drafting the VCLT, the International Law Commission had included a provision recognizing that customary international law could modify the terms of a treaty. This provision was later dropped, however, as being inappropriate and problematic for treaty law.

Thus, the interaction between treaties and custom can be subtle and is by no means clearly understood. International lawyers realize that they must assess both treaty-based and customary sources for a particular rule. It is not enough to assume that if a duty is contained in an international agreement, it will necessarily trump a contrary custom. Nor can it always be supposed that a treaty rule will never bind a nonparty.

SYNERGIES AMONG SOURCES

More significantly, there is no established hierarchy among the three core sources of international law—general principles, custom, and treaties. Despite attempts by some publicists to assert the supremacy of international agreements in the process of international lawmaking,[45] custom and treaties at least remain coequal. While general principles are typically invoked to provide essential first principles to new areas of international legal activity or to fill gaps in established legal doctrines, their importance should not be subordinated to a tyranny of treaties.

It is important to realize that there is a strong synergy between the various sources of international legal obligation. Understanding how these sources interact is vital to seeing how rules and doctrines evolve over time and thus how decisions and outcomes are achieved in international relations. The best illustration of this dynamic is the formation of rules for a relatively new field of transnational regulation—international environmental law. Before the 1920s or 1930s there was simply no law on this subject. One would have looked in vain for state practice, treaties, case law, or even academic writings on this subject.

Necessity is the mother of invention, and the exigency of creating law on this subject was impelled by a single dispute: the 1941 *Trail Smelter* arbitration between the United States and Canada.[46] This case featured a U.S. claim that an ore smelter in Trail, British Columbia, was generating such quantities of air pollution as to be causing substantial damage in Washington state. In the absence of any international law, the arbitrators were obliged to derive a rule from the domestic jurisprudence of states with federal systems (like the United States and Switzerland) that one entity should not use its territory in such a way as to injure the rights of another jurisdiction's territory. From this insight—a general principle of law recognized by a sufficient number of civilized nations—the arbitration concluded that Canada owed the United States a duty to prevent and minimize air pollution emanating from the smelter and to compensate for past damages.

From this kernel of a general principle grew the shoots of state practice, slowly at first but later with growing rapidity. Nations began to adjust more and more disputes regarding shared resources (including boundary lakes and rivers) or environmental concerns. In the 1950s, 1960s, and 1970s, customary international law began to crystallize around a small group of rules of international environmental law: avoidance of transboundary pollution, liability and compensation for environmental damage, and substantive standards to protect wildlife and prevent harmful emissions. This process was almost exclusively customary—there were exceedingly few treaties (either bilateral or multilateral) on this subject. At some point in this process there was a sufficient critical mass of state practice, combined with a realization that these norms had a binding and legal character (*opinio juris*), that they were confirmed as customary international law.

Beginning in 1972, with the Stockholm Declaration on the Human Environment,[47] treaty making began slowly to occupy this field of international law. Again, the process commenced as exclusively a manifestation of codification—organizing and rationalizing the body of customary norms. Codification, however, did not end the role of customary international law. Just as a tree that has been pruned continues to grow, a codified rule of custom will continue to be affected by subsequent state conduct. Indeed, customary practices might continue to exert an influence and change the rule. That might occur through the development of new rules or, more typically, through the process of treaty interpretation, in which treaty provisions are gradually given certain well-established meanings.

Treaty making in international environmental law quickly advanced from a footing of codifying custom to one of affirmatively legislating new rules of international conduct, "progressive development." The 1980s and 1990s saw an explosion in the number, variety, and complexity of treaties on international environmental law. Conventions were concluded on atmospheric issues, including ozone depletion, acid rain, and global warming. Many treaties focused on habitat protection, rational management of common resources (like fisheries), preservation of wildlife and flora, and trade restrictions to promote these goals. These "legislative" treaties often began as "framework conventions," merely sketching out the course of future negotiations. Like much soft international law, vague guidelines hardened into explicit norms and then into detailed regulatory regimes, with rules regularly updated by the parties through expedited or tacit amendment procedures. Some commentators have complained that international environmental law has become too "congested" with convention regimes and treaty drafting, so that effective observance, compliance, and enforcement of existing rules have been ignored.[48]

In less than sixty years we have seen one very significant field in international law go from a vacuum (with no rules of international conduct at all) to incredibly sophisticated regimes featuring detailed rules of behavior and complex institutional machinery to enforce them. This would have been impossible without general principles jumpstarting the process of international law formation (by effective borrowing from domestic legal systems), the dynamic of customary international law (which allowed the quick accretion of state practice in response to pressing needs), and the processes of treaty making (which permitted both the codification and progressive development of these rules). This kind of synergy explains the unique sources of international law—and the inherent strength of the international legal system.

Despite some expected indeterminacy, sources discourse in international law is on a firmer intellectual footing than debates about the bases of international obligation. The critical problem that remains for consideration of the basic construct of international law sources is the high positivism reflected in the language and structure of what is now article 38 of the ICJ Statute. Although general principles serve as a gracious and useful counterweight to custom and treaties, they cannot properly be regarded as a naturalist antidote to strict positivism in international lawmaking. It is also fortunate that no rigid ranking has been imposed on these core sources.

Profound difficulties do remain with defining the character of that extra ingredient of *opinio juris* that makes a widely followed usage into a binding rule of custom in international affairs. Only with such a determination is it possible to understand international actors' ability to influence the creation of customary norms in the global marketplace of law and to opt out of such rules. This is no mere theoretic concern. Given the exponential expansion of issues that are the legitimate topics of international regulation (a matter considered in chapters 4 and 7), customary law will continue to be relevant particularly in the realm in which disputes are most contentious: the formation of new rules for emerging areas of interaction in international affairs.

Likewise, only by appreciating customary lawmaking processes can the growing (and, some would say, dominant) role of treaties and international agreements be discerned. In an international society that risks undue dependence on treaty making as the primary way to fashion international obligations, custom and general principles retain their relevance through a number of mechanisms. At a minimum, they operate at the interstices of treaty rules. But much more importantly, customary usages and general principles derived from other autonomous legal systems provide the crucial context and background rules by which specific treaties are interpreted in particular circumstances.

The primary ambition of sources discourse is to confer neutrality and predictability on the selection of legal rules for the content of international law concepts and the practical settlement of disputes between international actors. In this sense, international law sources are what mediate between the theoretical world of the bases of international obligation and the functional arena of doctrines and outcomes. As a legal system, international law needs an objective set of sources of international law rules more than it necessarily needs a coherent theory of international obligation or authority. Whether international law sources can really satisfy the criteria of neutrality, objectiveness, and predictability that are essential to their function in a legal system for the international community can only be seen in context with other aspects of international lawmaking.

3 Methods and Approaches

As has already been indicated, the "classic" sources of international law only imperfectly describe the actual dynamic of international lawmaking. Focusing on general principles, custom, and treaties—even with their abstruse contours and interrelationships—can sometimes convey the false sense that that is all one needs to understand the formation and application of rules for international conduct. Sources appear to be neutral and objective, and that is intended as part of international law's claim to legitimacy. The reality of international life is, of course, rather more complex and enigmatic. To understand the essence of international law as a legal system, it is thus necessary to appreciate all available methods for divining the content of international legal rules as well as the various approaches to international lawmaking in contemporary international relations.

DEFINING AN INTERNATIONAL COMMUNITY

If anything can be derived from the discussion of the bases of international obligation and the formal sources of international legal rules, it is that international law is intended to serve the needs of a unique community: national and transnational entities. Essential to the construction of this legal system are clear rules for what are to be regarded as the "subjects" of international law (explored in detail in the next chapter), and it is worth considering now the nature of the international community and how its characteristics affect the process of international lawmaking. The exercise here is nothing less than defining the relevant community for international law.

This has been a traditional and favorite pastime for international law publicists. Treatises, particularly those from the nineteenth and early twentieth centuries,[1] devoted much attention to describing the limits of the legal system they were narrating. For writers of the high positivism period, there were only two eligible members of the international law community: states and polities that desired to be states.

The metaphor invariably used by these writers was to regard the international community as a "family of nations." Seen in this way, international law can probably be considered the tiniest articulated legal system in human history, affecting only a handful of state participants. The family idiom was meant to convey a small community of like-minded legal actors. Until the twentieth century, the number of constituents of the international legal system never numbered more than fifty (the number that signed the UN Charter in 1945) and was often substantially fewer. Today, with the advent of decolonization and the breakup of larger nations (such as the former Soviet Union and Yugoslavia), the number of independent states has topped out at about 195. While this growth has transformed the intimate family of nations into an unruly global village (with many significant structural and doctrinal consequences), one can hardly say that this is a large legal system, at least in terms of the number of state subjects.

The "family of nations" trope also had significant resonances with the moral and ideological underpinnings of international order. What began strictly as a legal system for a community of Catholic nations in Europe (in the Middle Ages)[2] was quickly required to embrace ecumenical values in recognizing and including Protestant polities after the Reformation. The Age of Exploration (beginning in the fifteenth century) brought Europeans into contact with African, Asian, and American peoples of various levels of political organization. As a consequence, the principle of "civilization" was typically used by Europeans to exclude outside participants. This was the central dilemma of Spanish publicists of this period, particularly Francisco de Vitoria,[3] in agonizing over but ultimately justifying European conquests of indigenous peoples in the New World. When European countries began to conduct diplomacy with powerful nations in Asia (particularly the Mogul Empire in India, Ming Dynasty China, and the Tokugawa Shogunate in Japan) attitudes did begin to change.[4] The ultimate catalyst for breaking the Christian monopoly on the standard of civilization for membership in the family of nations was the presence of a powerful, "alien" polity on the periphery of Europe itself: the Ottoman Empire. Hundreds of years of active diplomacy and adoption of legal norms by Turkey culminated in 1856 in an express recognition, by treaty, of its "participation in the advantages of the public law and Concert of Europe."[5]

By the beginning of the twentieth century, the archetype of civilization was on the wane in defining the international law community.[6] One might not have realized that in reading the Statute of the PCIJ (drafted in 1920), which referred to general principles "recognized by civilised nations" and required that judges on the Court be representative of "the main forms of civilisation and the principal legal systems of the world."[7] Rejecting the Western ethnocentrism of civilization as a standard, the international community embraced universalism, starting with the establishment in 1919 of the world's first truly global collective of countries, the League of Nations. The criterion of admission to the league, as with the later UN, was that a nation be "peace loving" and otherwise accept the obligations imposed upon it by the League Covenant and UN Charter and be "able and willing to carry out [those] obligations."[8]

It would appear, then, that in the course of five hundred years, universalism, rationality, and functionalism have replaced particularism and the false essentialism of civilization as the standard of membership in the international community. But this grossly simplifies international history and distorts the narrative of how the international community has organized itself to make international law.

As mentioned in chapter 1, modern international society began with the "Westphalian" nation-state. These beginnings of national self-consciousness (prevalent until the late eighteenth century) were essential to the identity of states and their participation in international life. These early-modern nation-states were all designed on monarchical models, and government administrations and bureaucracies were shallow and imperfect, even for the conduct of foreign relations. Diplomatic relations between princes and sovereigns were often personal, with little infrastructure for the sustained development of rules for international conduct. Peace treaties, ending lengthy and bitter conflicts, were often the only means of prescribing an international public law for disputed territories and claims (the chief staple of legal disputes at that time).

The advent of revolutionary, popular governments (first in the United States and then in France) marked the first transformation of the international community's organization of international lawmaking processes. Government administration, led by English cabinet-style government and French bureaucratic examples, became more sophisticated, with standing diplomatic establishments and instrumentalities. More significantly, balance-of-power international relations (what later became known as the Concert of Europe) regularized conference diplomacy, which, in turn, offered increasing opportunities for the creation of international rules. The Congress of Vienna, which concluded the two-decade-long period of conflict generated by the French Revolution and Napoleonic Wars, essentially created a protozoan international organization to keep European peace, if only through the maintenance of a situational balance of power.

The period of colonialism and imperialism, ushered in with the failed popular revolutions of 1848, channeled European aggression onto the periphery. As just discussed, this period (which coincided with the high positivism of thinking about international obligation) most immediately confronted the problem of the membership and institutions of what had previously been a Eurocentric law of nations. Former European colonies in the Americas played a crucial role in this transformation, although often through a gambit of challenging European international law with the creation of antagonistic regional norms.[9] This began a phenomenon of discrete regional or ideological competition with what was inevitably perceived as Western-dominated rule making. The period of high positivism also lent credence to the notion that international law sovereignty was an inherent aspect of overweening state power. The same rules of international law that justified colonial empire were certainly capable of granting legitimacy to militaristic, then authoritarian, and ultimately totalitarian regimes. Because international law was indifferent as to the forms of government that states as members of the international "club" adopted, neither civilization nor universalism was able to exclude or contain the polities most threatening to a peaceful world order.

The "Twenty Years Peace" between World Wars I and II thus ironically saw growing sophistication in international lawmaking institutions (particularly the League of Nations and related specialized agencies) coincide with atavistic and unlawful international behavior that had not been witnessed since the worst excesses of the Thirty Years War. The interwar period was significant in establishing international law's growing interest and competence in the vindication of values that were not necessarily state centered. Protection of minority groups was seen, particularly in Europe, as crucial for keeping the peace. Growing economic interdependence, accelerating even after the global economic depression commenced in 1929, introduced a critical new commercial aspect to many aspects of international relations. After World War II, Allied reaction to German and Japanese atrocities found voice in the provisions of the UN Charter that established protection of human dignity as a fundamental tenet of world order, side by side with preservation of international peace and security.

In contemporary international history, the Cold War was widely perceived as a period in which many processes of international lawmaking were stifled and many international law values went unvindicated. It was certainly true that the defining schisms of Cold War international relations—the East-West and North-South divides—did much to frustrate consensus on two intractable problems. UN organs, particularly the Security Council, were impotent in the face of proxy wars fought between surrogates of the Soviet Union and United States. At the same time, progress in addressing vast disparities of wealth and economic power between various regions of the world was exceedingly slow. The Cold War managed to merge a political struggle for power (ultimately won by the West) with an economic manifesto for a fairer distribution of global resources. These battles were waged in virtually every venue of international legal life: conference diplomacy, bilateral negotiations, official efforts to codify or progressively develop international law, international tribunal proceedings, and nongovernmental interactions.

The post–Cold War world order may have changed the power politics of international relations, but it did not alter the character of international lawmaking. Power struggles remain, although they have shifted to the challenges of terrorism, low-intensity conflict, ethnic strife, and national separatism in many parts of the globe. Economic disparities are as extreme as before despite the emergence of an international service economy and information society as well as all the things we now associate with globalism. Finally, the circle of elites that once exercised an exclusive monopoly over international law formation in most states has widened substantially.

The post–Cold War legal order is thus as perplexed about the identity of its constituents as were previous historic periods. When it comes to states as members of the international community, universalism may seem a neutral and dispassionate way to admit polities to the international system, but it may also be as irrelevant as the old standard of Western civilization. The reason is that international law is moving away from the posture of moral disinterest it previously exhibited with the form of government that states adopted. Democracy—meaning popular, accountable, and transparent government subject to a rule of law—may be emerging as a substantive standard of admission to the rights and privileges of international society. A new paradigm for "civilized" nations is the representative democracy. Such a form of government has been assumed, in both scholarly and policy circles, to be less prone to engage in aggressive war than its authoritarian brethren, more committed to respecting the human rights of its citizens, and generally more gracious in following rules of international conduct.

FUNCTIONAL ACTORS
IN INTERNATIONAL LAWMAKING

The near monopoly that states once exercised over the constitution of international society may also finally be broken. Very few publicists and commentators today speak of an international community in which nation-states (or pretenders to that status) are the only participants in the international lawmaking process. Substantial and spirited debate (which will be rehearsed throughout this volume, especially in chapters 4 and 6) has been waged over the extent of the role of such actors as international institutions, transnational businesses, nongovernmental organizations, and individuals in making international law rules. Although only a handful of commentators opine that these actors can make binding rules over the states' objection, no one seriously suggests that states make rules for international conduct without regard to these other transnational entities and constituencies.

States and Successive Paradigms of International Lawmaking

The diversification of functional actors for international lawmaking has had profound consequences on the sources and evidences of international law, along with the methods and approaches for handling those materials. Surprisingly, states themselves—and the way in which they conflict and collaborate in making international legal rules—have been most affected by this development. Indeed, the international community has experienced a significant, maybe even decisive, change in thinking as to the manner in which new international law rules are created.

Prior to the twentieth century, the prevailing metaphor for international lawmaking by states was struggle. Under this idiom, states were engaged in a constant battle to develop, refine, and repudiate rules of conduct for the international community. In a system where custom was the chief mechanism by which rules were added and modified, it made sense to regard this as not merely a competitive process, but—in a very Darwinian trope—a battle for very national survival and success. Lacking a supreme international lawmaker, individual members of the international community were obliged to resort to unfriendly means of asserting the rules by which they were prepared to abide in their conduct and of disclaiming those they did not wish to follow.

An excellent example of this dynamic of a "struggle for law" at work is in the doctrinal evolution of the law of the sea. The nearly five hundred–year history of the subject reduced to a fairly simple dynamic: the conflict between nations with predominant maritime interests and those states that desire to secure access to maritime resources close to their shores. There has been a cyclical process in which the competing interests of maritime powers and of coastal states have manifested themselves in significant legal changes. One such period was from 1500 to 1650, when emerging colonial powers Spain and Portugal were literally attempting to enclose vast areas of ocean spaces and to exclude such rival trading nations as Holland and England. In a pivotal case litigated in Amsterdam in the early 1600s, a young Dutch lawyer, Hugo de Groot (Grotius), wrote an impressive brief on the legal question of whether Portugal could legally exclude Dutch merchants from the East Indies and, as a consequence, whether the Dutch capture of a Portuguese carrack, the *Santa Catarina*, was lawful. De Groot won his case, and his brief was later the basis for his tract *Mare Liberum* (Freedom of the Seas).[10] Out of actual national conflict was birthed a central postulate of international law.[11]

By 1750, Grotius's position—that the seas were open to all and that coastal states could exercise only a narrow band of jurisdiction offshore—had completely won the day. In fact, this position held sway until after World War II. But in the nineteenth and early twentieth centuries, coastal states periodically claimed competence or jurisdiction over ocean areas beyond their territorial seas. In one instance, Brazil sought to enforce its revenue and antismuggling laws against foreign vessels "hovering" just beyond its territorial waters. The legality of such measures was reviewed by the U.S. Supreme Court in 1804, and Chief Justice John Marshall observed, "Any attempt to violate the [coastal state's] laws made to protect this right [of preventing smuggling], is an injury to itself which it may prevent, and it has a right to use the means necessary for its prevention. These means do not appear to be limited within any certain marked boundaries, which remain the same at all times and in all situations. If they are such as unnecessarily to vex and harass foreign lawful commerce, foreign nations will resist their exercise. If they are such as are reasonable and necessary to secure their laws from violation, they will be submitted to."[12] Marshall's dynamic of international law formation had nations "resist[ing]" unilateral or aggressive moves that are "vex[ing]" and "harass[ing]," or, alternatively, "submitt[ing]" to acts that are merely "protect[ive]" and "necessary."

These metaphors of struggle and resistance in the creation of customary international law rules were bound to change as explicitly negotiated agreements between states assumed greater importance in the late nineteenth and early twentieth centuries. For much of the past hundred years, the prevailing idiom for describing the evolution of international law doctrines has been a "marketplace" in which states affirmatively (and self-consciously) "bid" and "barter" and "trade" in new rules of conduct. Unlike a Hobbesian world of struggle, the marketplace mechanisms of international law creation are at once controlled and dynamic. Nowhere is this transformation from a paradigm of struggle to one of marketplace better seen than in the fundamental inquiry of whether to object effectively to the formation of a new rule of custom, it is sufficient for countries merely to protest diplomatically. That leads to the question of whether the actions of states should count more than their words.

The international community may well be moving beyond a market dynamic for the creation of new rights and duties. States are affirmatively being restrained from taking steps (often called countermeasures) to peaceably—but firmly—oppose another country's bidding of a rule of international law. Trade sanctions and diplomatic isolation, traditional tools states use to express their displeasure with other nations (short of going to war), are being limited. Likewise, in recognition that many international law principles benefit nonstate actors (such as individuals or transnational businesses), decision makers are more likely to accept a rule of conduct as binding on states even when the evidence of supporting state practice is equivocal or hostile. For example, in the *Reservations to the Genocide Convention* opinion, the World Court indicated that in many of the new international human rights agreements "one cannot speak of individual advantages or disadvantages to States, or of the maintenance of a perfect contractual balance between rights and duties."[13] Therefore, the Court concluded, states had a greater ambit to lodge reservations to such instruments and still be considered parties, provided the reservations did not frustrate the "object and purpose" of the treaty.

As a last instance of the disconnect between what states profess as their positions and their actual practice, some tribunals have indicated that certain human rights norms (such as the prohibition of state-sponsored torture) are binding on states, based on a lack of diplomatic objection, even while it is manifest that such practices continue in many nations around the world. It is not entirely satisfactory to observe the "fact that the prohibition of torture is often honored in the breach does not diminish its binding effect as a norm of international law."[14]

The cognitive dissonance in international law's preference for what states say over what they do has not gone unremarked or uncriticized. There is a substantial risk, as Martti Koskenniemi has prophesied, that international law will become too utopian—too divorced from the actual behavior of nation-states and, as a consequence, less and less relevant.[15] Adopting such a position can call into question the legitimacy of the essential sources of international law. If custom, according to some commentators,[16] can be created without reference to actual state behavior and expectations (the *opinio juris* requirement), then it will cease as an intelligible source of international legal obligation. Likewise, if treaties can be interpreted and applied without regard to state practice, even concrete forms of "bidding" and "trading" under a market model of international law will lack integrity.

Attempts have failed to cure this methodological muddle about states' true role in making international law. Some scholars have sought to examine episodes of conflict, authentic "international incidents," as the appropriate epistemological unit of international law.[17] This has been attacked as an antiquarian desire to return international lawmaking to a Hobbesian "state of nature" and struggle.[18] This critique may itself go too far. One can quite properly insist on evidence of actual state practice—some expression of concrete state authority—before attributing binding effect to some rule of international law, without necessarily requiring that every such evidence and expression be accompanied by "muscular" uses of national compulsion. At the same time, one may well be alarmed that in making a "kinder, gentler" world order, we actually deny the legitimacy of experience to some (if not many) international law rules. By proscribing struggle and fully regulating the vibrant market in rules, we may be coddling weaker doctrines in international law or allowing the crystallization of rules that would have otherwise been dissolved by the caustic process of state objection.

The "Domestication" of International Law Methods

To make the sources of international law more familiar to lawyers in both the Anglo-American common law and European civil law traditions, there has always been a tendency to conflate the role of such materials as legislative enactments and court decisions. Yet while these are recognized in ICJ Statute article 38, it is only as a "subsidiary" means of establishing *evidence* of the content of international law norms. It is important to explain why this is so.

There is obviously no central legislator in international law, no world parliament. It is true that some multilateral treaties, on certain subjects and with universal adherence, approach such a model. While there is a growing network of international institutions producing a body of international regulatory schemes, these are all in the form of treaty regimes. Suggestions, therefore, that the resolutions of UN bodies (particularly the General Assembly, where each nation has one vote) constitute a binding source of international law remain extravagant and have been attacked in the scholarly literature.[19]

These intimations have been construed as an attempt to provide an easy way to make international law rules, apart from custom and treaty and without an individual state's consent to be bound. This is not to say, though, that the UN is powerless to make binding rules for its own operations. In certain key respects, one UN organ (the Security Council) is the ultimate lawmaker in international relations. Acceptance of this idea raises serious—if not insuperable—problems with the constitution and role of international institutions that seek to be both representative and authoritative.

While international organizations were, in a momentous decision made by the ICJ,[20] recognized as international legal actors, this conclusion could not resolve the wider problem of institutions' capacity to be the locus of international lawmaking. Interestingly, the *Reparations* opinion was not unanimous, and there was a significant dissent to key portions of its reasoning by none other than the U.S. judge on the Court, Green Hackworth. Judge Hackworth was concerned that the *Reparations* opinion set a dangerous precedent by permitting an international organization to assert powers that were neither textually granted by its members in its charter or constituent instrument nor fairly implied from other provisions. Hackworth doubted that an international institution should be granted "inherent" powers and worried that an organization would quickly acquire a life of its own and depart from its intended "delegated and enumerated powers." Drawing on the idiom of American constitutionalism and the language of such landmark cases as *McCulloch v. Maryland*,[21] Hackworth feared giving international institutions potentially unlimited powers. An institution, driven by a majority of its members, could subvert its original purposes.

Not surprisingly, one of the major themes of the "constitutional law" of the UN and other organizations has been the issue of adjudicating charges that the organization has exceeded its intended role and has engaged in ultra vires acts. In a later case, the *Certain Expenses of the United Nations* opinion,[22] the problem was framed starkly. In the 1960s, both France and the Soviet Union objected to the deployment of UN peacekeeping forces in Africa and the Middle East. Both refused to pay their share of the costs of these forces and were thus in arrears on their dues to the organization. The question for the court was whether the cost of these forces, deployed by the UN General Assembly (rather than by the Security Council, as argued by the French and Soviets) was a proper UN expense within the meaning of the Charter.

The World Court decided that the costs of peacekeeping ordered by the General Assembly were a legitimate UN expense, and thus France and the Soviet Union were obliged to pay their fair share. The Court rejected the "separation of powers" argument made by the two countries and ruled that peacekeeping was within the scope of the powers of the General Assembly and was not exclusively within the authority of the Security Council. More importantly, the Court ruled, if organizational "dissenters" were unhappy with a decision made by the institution, their only recourse was to argue that the ultra vires act was contrary to the entire object and purpose of the organization, not that a certain decision should have been made by another organ within the institution. Thus, a minority's ability to object to the conduct of an international institution was severely circumscribed. The Court has flirted with but ultimately declined to exercise some form of review of Security Council decisions on the maintenance of international peace and security (under chapter VII of the Charter).[23] The World Court has thus expanded the legal personality of international institutions to permit them to take on a life of their own, even in defiance of the will of a substantial number of members.

A related—but analytically distinct—question is whether General Assembly resolutions, which are only "recommendations" under article 10 of the UN Charter, can make international law. One point that has often been made by commentators is that General Assembly resolutions, precisely because they are recommendations, lack the necessary *opinio juris* for custom. This is so even though states may repeatedly vote for a resolution and profess their support for the legal rule for which it stands. Such resolutions may nevertheless be evidence either of a rule of customary international law or of an authentic interpretation of a binding treaty. In certain situations, the ICJ has ruled that General Assembly resolutions may carry definitive legal consequences,[24] although that is not the same as saying they are themselves legally binding.

In a very different context, an international tribunal was obliged to deeply discount the legal effect of General Assembly resolutions. In the *TOPCO* (Texas Overseas Petroleum Company) arbitration,[25] Libya had expropriated the oil concession of a U.S. company. When the company initiated binding arbitration under the concession contract, Libya countered that under customary international law, it was not obliged to participate and that the tribunal had no jurisdiction. For this argument, Libya relied on three General Assembly resolutions. The sole arbitrator, Renee-Jean Dupuy, concluded, however, that none of these had been supported by a sufficiently wide cross-section of states. In fact, all economically developed and capital-exporting countries (like the United States) had either abstained or voted no. In essence, the arbitrator examined the *travaux prépara-toires* of the resolutions to ascertain whether they could even qualify as evidence of a potential custom.

Publicists' and international decision makers' traditional skepti-cism—if not downright hostility—toward international organiza-tions' lawmaking capacity may simply now be an irrelevancy. The truth is that international institutions, particularly the organs of UN specialized agencies and bodies of regional and functional institu-tions, have come to exercise a progressively strong ability to regulate many forms of international conduct. My choice of the word *regulate* is intentional, because states have appeared to delegate substantial regulatory competences to international institutions, typically (al-though not always) acting through broadly framed treaty regimes. Be-ginning with UN specialized agencies that had authority over aspects of international commerce and transport (such as the International Civil Aviation and International Maritime Organizations), "frame-work" conventions were negotiated that, in turn, led to elaborate bodies of regulation, often adopted using nonconsensual or tacit pro-cedures.[26] This paradigm has been repeated for a host of international environmental initiatives as well as for aspects of the management of global resources and the international economy.

So while international law doctrine appears to cleave to a rejection of international institutions as affirmative international lawmakers, the reality is that institutions are lawmakers. The manner in which they do make rules in a new international regulatory order is subtle. Such processes certainly defy characterization as some sort of proto–world parliament at work. Rather, they are regime specific and sensi-tive to changes in state priorities.

If international law has been ambivalent about the role of "legisla-tive" enactments, like the resolutions of international organizations, how has it treated the decisions of international and domestic judicial tribunals? Citing such decisions is the stock-in-trade of international lawyers, and, happily, there is a wide body of case law from inter-national tribunals (as well as domestic courts' decisions on international matters).[27] Aside from the World Court (PCIJ and ICJ), which has decided a broad range of cases and issues, there have also been many specialized tribunals. Examples would include international claims tribunals, which for more than two hundred years have settled financial and property disputes between countries. There have also been decisions by international criminal courts (including the Nuremberg tribunal after World War II and more recent institutions for Yugoslavia and Rwanda). After World War II there also developed human rights commissions and courts, the jurisprudence for which has become extensive. Finally, there are economic and trade institutions (including the European Union, NAFTA, and the WTO) that have adjunct judicial bodies resolving disputes.

This plethora of international tribunals—and international case law—is immensely gratifying for international lawyers. There is just one problem. The decisions of these tribunals are not, strictly speaking, binding precedent (or stare decisis), not even for the institution that issued the decision. This may come as a shock to a lawyer trained in the common law tradition, but in this respect international tribunals resemble more closely civil law jurisdictions (as in continental Europe) where the doctrine of stare decisis does not exist or is substantially impaired. In fact, article 59 of the ICJ Statute says emphatically that except between the parties to a dispute, a decision of the World Court has no binding effect.

Happily, the reality of judicial precedent does not coincide with the theory. The truth is that international tribunals almost invariably follow their precedents, especially on procedural issues, and it is very routine for international lawyers to rely heavily on judicial decisions to support their arguments and for a tribunal to cite its own judgments.[28] Yet it would be a grievous mistake to assume that an international tribunal (just like a domestic court) is obliged slavishly to follow its precedents.

Nevertheless, the use of judicial decisions as even mere "evidence" of international law exerts an important—and perhaps even subversive—effect on international law formation. The classic declaratory view was that as "judges do not in principle make law but apply existing law, their role is inevitably secondary since the law they propound has some antecedent source."[29] This philosophy of international judging can no longer seriously be sustained. It just cannot be doubted that judicial caution or creativity can exercise extraordinary influence over the outcome of disputes, the creation of doctrines, and even the entire direction and thrust of international legal regimes. Ironically, this phenomenon is best seen in the context of domestic tribunals' grappling with the application of international law rules in a municipal context that may be quite hostile to their acceptance (a point considered further in chapter 7). Whether it was prize courts' application of the common international law of maritime captures[30] or current tribunals' seeking to incorporate regional human rights regimes,[31] these tensions and opportunities are manifest.

In any event, the superimposition of a common law system of stare decisis fundamentally changes a key dynamic of international lawmaking. Discourse and argument about international law rules become progressively more inductive. Specific examples drawn from particular case decisions inform general propositions. In this sense, the use of judicial decisions seems merely to parallel the handling of evidence of state practice for purposes of establishing a custom. This may be misleading because customary international law processes do not replicate the essential lawyerly activities of analogizing and distinguishing decisions in earlier legal disputes. Since the overall flavor of international law reasoning has been deductive—a residuum either of a natural law tradition that established precepts from "right reason" or positivism's concern for uniform rule making by states— the injection of avowedly inductive approaches to the determination of legal rules is bound to have significant consequences.

Approaching the Fringes of International Lawmaking

So far in this discussion, it seems that states have retained their central position in the dynamic of international lawmaking under some slightly recalibrated market model, even as approaches emphasizing the regulatory role of international institutions and the inductive power of judicial precedents have gained favor. Taken together, these actors—states, international regulatory institutions, and tribunals—

form the core of participants in the international community's effort to make law. There is also an epistemic periphery, groups that have exerted growing influence over the course of international law's development.

Prominent among the denizens of that fringe are what Oscar Schachter presciently referred to as "the invisible college of international lawyers."[32] The ICJ Statute specifically recognizes the "teachings of the most highly qualified publicists of the various nations" as evidence of rules of law. In short, the writings of international law academics and practitioners—"publicists" in the language of the Statute—can notionally constitute evidence of international law. As Henry Wheaton observed in his famous treatise, "Without wishing to exaggerate the importance of these writers, or to substitute, in any case, their authority for the principles of reason, it may be affirmed that they are generally impartial in their judgment. They are witnesses of the sentiments and usages of civilized nations, and the weight of their testimony increases every time that their authority is invoked by statesmen, and every year that passes without the rules laid down in their works being impugned by the avowal of contrary principles."[33] International law commentators are thus cloaked in the mantel of "impartiality" (or at least a presumption thereof) and a common purpose and mission, an almost scientific pursuit of truth on behalf of the international community.

This curious aggrandizement of authority in the hands of individual scholars is purely illusory. Before the 1900s, the preference was for the "classic" writers of international law, and advocates and judges, foreign ministries, and executives routinely relied on such figures as Grotius (Hugo de Groot), Samuel Pufendorf, Cornelius van Bynkershoek, and Emmerich de Vattel. Such gratuitous citations became tedious even for judges in the 1700s. One English judge remarked that "there was something ridiculous in the decisive way each lawyer, as quoted, had given his opinion. . . . A pedantic man in the closet dictates the law of nations; everybody quotes, nobody minds him. . . . [A]nd who shall decide, when doctors [publicists] disagree?"[34] Even the U.S. Supreme Court, which permitted the use of commentators' writings in the 1900 case of *The Paquete Habana,* was quick to qualify that "Such works are resorted to by judicial tribunals, not for the speculations of their authors concerning what the law ought to be, but for trustworthy evidence of what the law really is."[35]

Today, there is hardly any pretense of reliance on publicists as actual authority for international law rules. Indeed, the World Court's custom is never to cite any publicist, and, in fact, domestic judicial regard for the writings of international law academics has turned neutral or downright malevolent. For example, one U.S. judge opined,

> I agree with the sentiment expressed by Chief Justice Fuller in his dissent to *The Paquete Habana,* where he wrote that it was "needless to review the speculations and repetitions of writers on international law. . . . Their lucubrations may be persuasive, but are not authoritative." Courts ought not to serve as debating clubs for professors willing to argue over what is or what is not an accepted violation of the law of nations. . . . The typical judge or jury would be swamped in citations to various distinguished journals of international legal studies, but would be left with little more than a numbing sense of how varied is the world of public international "law."[36]

Aside from the gratuitous qualification of international law as "law," Judge Robb's critique is emblematic of a wider concern about publicists and commentators: the lack of coherence and consistency in their characterization of state practices. Much more than that, international law commentary has been attacked for its lack of objectivity. As one critical scholar has noted, "In a discipline that views its scholarship as a source of law, it is no surprise that this scholarship is characterized by policy prescriptions that reflect author preferences, or criticisms of practices deemed to violate international law. These tendencies are exacerbated by a powerful idealism."[37] The irony of all of these critiques is that international law scholars have had the misfortune of being victimized by their success.[38] International law commentary has proliferated and diversified. It is no longer concentrated in the hands of European and American writers who generated "canonical texts" that purported to distill the essence of state practice while adding measured doses of right reason. The dissonance of the many voices in international law makes it unlikely that international lawyers will exercise much influence over the course of the discipline, at least through their academic writing.

Where international law academics and practitioners have achieved extraordinary prominence is in the subtler venues of persuasion, among them the public square and councils of power. International lawyers tend to be opinion leaders and, on occasion, even occupy positions of authority in national governments and international institutions. In a more immediate manner, international lawyers tend to dominate the crucial processes of codification and issue advocacy. Beginning with the Hague Peace Conferences of 1899 and 1907 and continuing with the 1930 Codification Conference and the modern work of the UN International Law Commission (ILC), a small cohort of international lawyers has tended to direct global efforts to rationalize certain doctrinal pockets of international law.[39] On occasion, these efforts have been strikingly successful, as with the early-twentieth-century initiatives culminating in the "Hague Law" of war and the ILC's later work in codifying the law of treaties, diplomatic relations, and the law of the sea. As for other doctrinal areas—including work on state recognition, succession, immunities, and responsibility as well as efforts to chart aspects of international environmental law and use of force—the results have been disappointing (as measured by the small number of states that ratify some ILC projects), destructive (because the codification fails to properly describe the experience of the international community), or embarrassing (owing to the amount of time taken in the effort). Alas, it appears that rules at the doctrinal core of state identity and sovereignty—state recognition, succession, immunities, and responsibility—may simply be impervious to effective and authoritative codification.

Processes for the codification and progressive development of public international law have also been gradually devoluted over the past thirty years. The ILC no longer occupies a central position in these efforts, although it remains the only forum where a systematic attempt is made to plan future projects.[40] Institutions such as the Hague Conference on Private International Law, the UN Commission on International Trade Law, and the Rome International Institute for the Unification of Private International Law have come to dominate the "private" side of international lawmaking, creating a peculiar schizophrenia between the two branches of the discipline (something that will be considered further in chapter 7). The advent of conference diplomacy—international lawmaking efforts typically convened under the auspices of the UN and its specialized agencies—has meant that very specific treaty-drafting projects are undertaken by bodies that meet solely for that purpose. The best example of this was the Third UN Conference on the Law of the Sea (1973–82), the longest-running international law negotiation ever. Thousands of delegates, hundreds of meetings, dozens of coalitions and interest groups, and a bewildering array of discrete issues vastly complicated the ultimate goal of drafting a literal constitution for the oceans. Conference-style efforts to advance international law objectives have also been undertaken on a much smaller scale, and whenever diplomats and technical experts meet to discuss such initiatives, international lawyers also are there.

With the plethora of nongovernmental organizations (NGOs) actively engaged in international law advocacy efforts, the hitherto invisible college of international lawyers has become loud, populist, and fractious. Interest-group politics has invaded the ethereal and elitist realm of academic international pursuits and the close-knit community of foreign ministry advisors. Powerful business interests, which had previously abstained from direct involvement in international lawmaking processes (preferring to merely influence domestic decision makers), are actively lobbying in diplomatic settings. These groups' interests periodically collide spectacularly (such as at meetings on environmental protection, international labor standards, or trade disciplines), leaving the participating lawyers and negotiators aghast and appalled.

NGOs as issue advocates have attempted to harness the power of domestic and local grassroots organizing and to convert that influence into definitive changes in the content of international law. This represents a frontal assault on the traditional monopoly enjoyed by national foreign policy elites. Nowhere can this better be seen than in international human rights litigation and in the setting of international environmental law standards. As for the first topic, international lawyers have been active before both human rights institutions and domestic courts. Petitions to the Human Rights Committee have profoundly affected the interpretation of the International Covenant on Civil and Political Rights.[41] Careful advocacy before the European and American Courts of Human Rights has expanded the scope of freedoms exercised under those regional human rights instruments.[42] The activities of international prosecutors and defense counsel (with their amici) in war crimes trials have clarified aspects of the emerging area of international criminal law. The well-publicized proceedings of domestic courts' adjudicating civil liability for "violations of the law of nations" (as under the Alien Tort Statute in the United States),[43] the activities of "truth commissions" seeking reconciliation in the process of nation building after internal strife, and attempts to extradite offenders to countries where they will be prosecuted have all been affected by the submissions of international lawyers as issue advocates.

International environmental campaigners have pursued a broad agenda including participation in negotiating forums as well as specific submissions before regulatory institutions. Nongovernmental participants have been active as either members of national delegations or accredited observers at a variety of treaty-drafting functions. In a few notorious instances—including talks to protect the Antarctic environment and to control global warming—environmental advocates played the dispositive role in leveraging changes in the ultimate treaty text adopted.[44] In addition, individual international lawyers were critical in developing trade restrictions as a way to promote protection of endangered species and habitats, an insight that has had substantial impact on globalization efforts for various aspects of the international economy.[45]

Traditional publicists of international law have thus transformed themselves into progressive codifiers, reformers, and advocates. The "invisible college"—objective, monolithic, and solicitous of state sovereignty and prerogatives—has given way to diverse "epistemic communities" of legal and technical experts involved in all aspects of international relations.[46] Coupled with the domesticated use of judicial decisions and the resolutions of representative institutions, this movement has virtually reconstructed the way that the sources of international legal obligation are considered in scholarly discourse and practical argument. Even more importantly, interest groups, transnational businesses, and cultural forces have come to compete directly with states over access to the machinery of international lawmaking.

TECHNIQUE

"Legal technique" can best be thought of as the modes and styles of legal argumentation and decision making. In the sense I use the term here, *technique* describes the way that international lawyers use the sources, methods, and approaches of international legal obligation to determine the relevant community of expectation in international affairs. International legal technique is, therefore, the style of reasoning used by advocates and decision makers in making arguments and reaching conclusions about the content of international legal norms. While few international lawyers self-consciously think about the technique they use in various settings, advocates, judges, and scholars have embraced some general assumptions. It is important to reflect on these.

An example of international legal technique at work is the manner in which treaty texts are interpreted. Treaty interpretation is supposed to be neutral and objective, and modes of argument about treaty construction are (to a surprising degree) divorced from the type of international agreement involved, the interpretive position being advanced, and the identity of the disputants. Treaty interpretation should be no different from the construction of other legal writings, and the "schools" or techniques of treaty interpretation largely replicate those for statutes, contracts, wills, and constitutions.[47] If anything, treaties may be more vague, ambiguous, and otherwise difficult to interpret than other kinds of legal writings. The nature of many treaty texts as political or diplomatic compromises often means that contentious issues of application are deferred to a later day to win agreement in the here and now. Some established principles of treaty interpretation are essential for the smooth running of the international legal system.

Virtually any attempt at treaty interpretation begins with the text of the relevant provision itself. The Vienna Convention on the Law of Treaties (VCLT) makes an unexceptional call for an examination of a text's "ordinary meaning."[48] Textualism can also be a form of cross-reading of different provisions in a treaty text to reach a sensible result. Sometimes it is not that easy. Consider article 3 of the 1919 International Labor Organization Convention on the Employment of Women during the Night: "Women without distinction of age shall not be employed during the night in any public or private undertaking, or in any branch thereof, other than an undertaking in which only members of the same family are employed." The proper meaning of this provision was challenged when a group of employers wanted the ability to employ women at night in managerial or supervisory posts. The PCIJ gave an advisory opinion,[49] concluding that although the treaty had never been intended to bar women managers from working at night, the text of article 3 clearly extended beyond women working as manual laborers. The provision carved out just one exception: women who work in a business solely with other family members. The World Court reluctantly agreed that although its interpretation of article 3 might lead to a strange and counterprogressive result, the Court was obliged to follow the text.

One can see an obvious tension between the text of a treaty provision and the intent of the drafters. An intentionalist approach to treaty interpretation has never been popular in international law. The VCLT relegates sources shedding light on the intent of the drafters— including the negotiating history (or *travaux préparatoires*) of a provision—to a secondary role. *Travaux préparatoires* can be used only where the text is "ambiguous or obscure" or where the plain meaning of the text leads to a "manifestly absurd or unreasonable" result.[50]

One reason that *travaux* may be somewhat disfavored in international law is the concern that some countries might sign a treaty long after it was negotiated and signed. Should these newcomers be bound not only to the text but also the informal understandings of the drafters? This would unduly privilege the interpretive positions of the original signatories. Likewise, use of negotiating history—including earlier drafts of a treaty, reports and commentaries, and diplomatic statements—can be selective and manipulable. Despite these cautions, use of *travaux* has become a constant feature of interpretive disputes over treaties. It can be a two-edged sword. Tribunals, especially in situations where one side or another has a negotiating advantage, will often insist that in case of ambiguity, a treaty will be interpreted contrary to the interests of the drafting state (the *contra proferentem* canon).[51] Maxims of construction are thus dragooned as a sort of tiebreaker in cases of interpretive doubt.

That leaves the third school of interpretation: seeking to effectuate the purpose of a treaty rather than slavishly following the text or attempting to divine the intent of the drafters. Known in international law as a teleological approach, we might also call it purposivism. It is captured in the VCLT's requirement that treaties be construed in light of their "object and purpose" and in view of "relevant rules of international law."[52] The idea here is to interpret a treaty in a way that gives scope to the fundamental reason or problem that the international agreement was supposed to address. This approach is especially common with more "organic" or "constitutional" treaties, including those that establish international institutions (like the UN Charter of 1945) or that fashion a framework for further international legislation. There are limits to teleology in treaty construction, and interpreters cannot take the purpose of a treaty too far. For example, the ICJ has flatly rejected the notion of "maximum effectiveness," construing a treaty to give it the fullest effect. In a 1950 advisory opinion,[53] the Court ruled that peace treaties concluded by Eastern European states containing arbitration clauses could not be construed to give the UN Secretary General the power to appoint arbitrators if the states themselves had refused to do so.

One style of international law argumentation and decision making is to use combinations of textual, intentionalist, and teleological methods in interpreting a treaty text. The starting point of any construction is the words of the agreement, but that must necessarily mean understanding the entire treaty, its structure, and its form. Where there is a background to the treaty—the diplomatic circumstances giving rise to the deliberations and the negotiating history—that should also be studied. Finally, a skilled interpreter of a treaty recognizes that there is usually some fundamental object and purpose for an agreement and even for its particular provisions.

If treaty interpretation reveals an eclecticism in technique, other problems involving sources and approaches show greater tensions. The ICJ has, for example, developed some definitive methods for identifying an emerging custom under conditions of conflict and competition. It is important to appreciate these approaches because they not only illustrate the practical reality of custom as a source of international law but also show how the ICJ and international advocates can use custom to achieve different sorts of client objectives and decisional outcomes. The best way to understand these approaches to custom is by comparing two cases decided by the World Court.

The first of these, the *Asylum* case,[54] implicated a most peculiar custom. The case arose when a Peruvian military leader, Víctor Raúl Haya de la Torre, took refuge in the Colombian embassy in Lima after leading an unsuccessful coup attempt. Elsewhere in the world, this would have resulted in a very long stay for Haya de la Torre, for while all nations respect the inviolability of foreign embassy premises, there is certainly no rule requiring a host state to allow a political refugee safe passage out of the embassy, out of the country, and to the asylum state. In Latin America, however, there has evolved a regional custom of diplomatic asylum.

The most significant aspect of this case was the ICJ's treatment of a state's reaction as proof of its opposition to the formation of a custom and its discounting of regional custom as a source of international law. The Court ruled that where a regional (as distinct from a global) custom was concerned, silence on the part of the state in the face of an emerging practice meant that that state objected to or protested the rule. In short, a silent or ambiguous response meant rejection. This was contrary to the general presumption that states are obliged to protest loud and often if they wish to avoid being bound by a rule of emerging global custom.

Why, then, did the World Court change the calculus of consent for regional custom in the *Asylum* case? One can only conclude that the

Court wished to suppress regional custom, and there is no more effective way to do so than to declare a presumption that fundamentally disrupts the formation of such regional practices. While the ICJ has no qualms about applying rules derived from regional (or at least non-global) treaties, it was concerned that development of distinctive bodies of regional rules—not just for Latin America but perhaps also for Europe, Africa, and Asia—might unduly interfere with the universal aspirations of international law. More pertinently, the allowance of easy-to-make regional customs might also challenge the institutional role of the World Court as a place for authoritative pronouncements on international legal rules. I speculate this because in an analytically similar case, *Right of Passage over Indian Territory*, decided in 1960,[55] the ICJ reached a very different conclusion.

The problem raised in that dispute was Portugal's asserted right to be able to transit both civil administrators and troops and munitions from the Portuguese colony of Goa (on the coast of India) to little Portuguese-controlled enclaves in the Indian interior. During the late 1950s—a critical time for the process of decolonization around the world—India made no pretense of its desire to drive the last vestiges of colonialism from the subcontinent, and Indian authorities denied Portugal's right of passage, assuming (correctly) that if the enclaves could not be resupplied, they would be ripe for the picking.

The ICJ could have decided the dispute as a matter of global custom: whether there was some inherent right of passage by one nation over the territory of another, especially in situations where part of one nation's territory was completely surrounded by another. The judges on the Court declined to undertake this analysis, and one can hardly blame them. It would have been a daunting and difficult task of collecting many centuries of state practice over many continents to derive a set of customary rules for all these situations.

Instead, the World Court chose to limit the scope of the analysis to an exceedingly narrow shutter. The question became whether Portugal and India (and its predecessors, the British and Maratha rulers) had developed a special or local custom allowing the Portuguese right of passage. The Court sifted through evidence of the dealings between the two sides over the course of many centuries. The ICJ ultimately concluded that Portugal's right of passage for civil administrators was binding custom on India, although India retained the right to suspend such passage in exceptional circumstances. As for a right to move troops and weapons over Indian territory, previous permissions to do so had been "mere" comity or courtesy, and, in so lacking *opinio juris,* it failed as a custom.

The Court essentially decided that it was futile to declare a global custom in a case where it was easier to describe and characterize a "course of dealing" between the two parties to the dispute. And in using a local or special custom, the Court resorted to the typical presumption that silence in the face of an emerging practice means acquiescence or acceptance.[56] In these bilateral situations, it appears especially incumbent on states to protest if they are unhappy with the legal positions taken by their neighbors.

In the Court's divergent treatment of regional custom and local (or special) custom, one also has two very different models of the role of international dispute-settlement machinery.[57] In the *Asylum* case, the ICJ emphatically asserted its prerogative to declare the content of customary international law, not only for the benefit of the parties to the case but, more importantly, to the global community at large. Whenever the ICJ takes on the difficult task of defining principles of global custom, it is as much to declare what the law is as to settle a dispute. In *Right of Passage,* one observes a far more modest (and typical) role for the Court: simply settling the dispute without making great pronouncements. As a result, in such situations, recourse to special custom and to the very particular course of dealing between two nations is very attractive for the ICJ. Essential to either approach is the Court's understanding of the role of consent in making customary rules.

If international legal technique can reflect on styles of judicial rectitude and ambition (a matter that will be considered further in chapter 10), it can also profoundly influence the actual process of international lawyering. Consider for example another pairing of cases. Those lawyers who think it easy to prove a rule as a general practice might learn a lesson from the French counsel in *The SS Lotus* case decided by the PCIJ in 1927.[58] The underlying facts involved a French vessel, the *Lotus*, that negligently collided with a Turkish vessel on the high seas (beyond any nation's control), killing eight Turkish nationals. The *Lotus* foolishly sailed into Istanbul, whereupon Turkish authorities arrested the French officer on whose watch the accident occurred and charged him with negligent homicide. France protested Turkey's assertion of criminal jurisdiction over a French national for an act that occurred on a French vessel outside of Turkey's territory.

To France's dismay, the Court ruled at the outset that since France was challenging Turkey's exercise of jurisdiction, it was incumbent on France to show that Turkey violated customary international law. The Court thus assigned France the burden of proving that Turkey breached international law. That pretty much sunk France's chances of winning the case, because it meant that the French counsel was obliged to collect sufficient evidence of state practice indicating that Turkey's prosecution was improper. Unfortunately for France, its advocates were given the task of showing evidence of state practice indicating that exercise of criminal jurisdiction over a foreign national on a foreign-flagged vessel on the high seas was improper.

That proved impossible. The PCIJ was able to distinguish every earlier case or incident on which France relied for the proposition that the state of nationality, or "flag-state," had exclusive jurisdiction in such circumstances. Not only was there a lack of objective evidence supporting France's supposed general practice, but even if there had been (the Court intimated), it would merely show that states had often abstained from instituting criminal proceedings but had not necessarily felt obligated to do so. Even if the French lawyers had shown (which they could not) a "smoking gun" of an earlier incident where Turkey had declined to prosecute a foreign national, doing so would not have been conclusive. The only possible way that France could have carried its burden was to have documented a case where a Turkish vessel had collided with a foreign ship, that foreign country had prosecuted a Turkish mariner, and Turkey had protested and prevailed. Only in this classic "shoe on the other foot" scenario could France have proven a contrary general practice accepted as law by Turkey.

By contrast, in the 1951 *Anglo-Norwegian Fisheries* case,[59] the United Kingdom and Norway contested access to fisheries off the

Norwegian coast. Norway had attempted to claim ocean areas through some creative cartography: by drawing "straight baselines" from points along its rugged coastline and asserting that the enclosed areas were exclusive Norwegian fisheries. Norway's zealous "bidding" of a straight-baseline rule, combined with Britain's lack of effective (and well-documented) protest in the early 1900s, meant that Britain had waived its subsequent objection. The Court indicated that Norway's straight baselines were thus not "opposable" by the United Kingdom.

The *Lotus* case manifestly shows the limits to analogical reasoning in international legal technique. The French lawyers were essentially given the task of explaining why the Sherlockian dog did not bark—why there was no apposite case law, diplomatic exchanges, or state practice for their position. Lawyers from common law traditions tend to hope for custom on point to prove their submissions, but the strong casuistic predilections of many international tribunals leave lawyers disappointed. Induction has its limits, but the World Court's handling of the *Anglo-Norwegian Fisheries* dispute shows that it is periodically prepared to derive a rule of international behavior from evidence of a very specific transaction between international actors.[60]

More importantly, international lawyers—like their domestic counterparts—instinctively understand the burdens of proof and persuasion that are allocated among the parties in a dispute. Lawyers, like judges, cannot tolerate equipoise. So one important technique to avoid deadlock in the resolution of controversies is to assign burdens that accord with general preferences for ideal outcomes. The *Lotus* presumption, as it has come to be called, is solicitous of state sovereignty and assertions of jurisdiction. It is reflective of a deep conservatism, verging on skepticism, about the proper role of law in the international community. It is today intensely controversial. In contrast, the principle of opposability in *Anglo-Norwegian Fisheries* is actually a nonrule. Like the holding in *Right of Passage,* a norm is prescribed for the parties' exclusive benefit, without any desire to have this norm enjoy wider or deeper application.

International legal technique appears to operate on many discrete levels. It mediates the classic sources of international legal obligation and the actual modes of international lawmaking. It serves as a vital set of tools that advocates, decision makers, and scholars employ to arrive at arguments and conclusions about the substantive content of international law rules. Some techniques (like those for treaty interpretation) are multivalent, "open textured," and capable of nuanced appreciation. Other techniques demand important value choices on the part of the user and come with significant assumptions about the nature and operation of the international community. Technique matters not only for the proper appreciation of international lawmaking processes but also for understanding the identity of international legal actors and the legitimate topics of international legal regulation. In addition, technique is largely what gives international law the coherence and sophistication it has or to which it aspires. These matters will be taken up in the next two chapters.

4 Subjects and Objects

Just as with the bases of obligation, international lawyers historically have had a peculiar preoccupation and fetish with the subjects and objects of the discipline. Many international law treatises (including current ones) are structured around this division between subjects and objects.[1] Yet these two terms have caused substantial confusion among students and practitioners of international law (and even among scholars and judges), so careful definition is necessary. By a *subject* of international law, I mean an entity that bears international legal rights or duties. Subjects of international law are also known as international legal persons, a phrase that is meant to convey the idea of full-fledged participation in the international legal system by entities that are capable of exercising rights and observing duties under international law.[2] The subjects of international law are the actors, or players, on the international scene. In contrast, the *objects* of international law are the who, what, and where that are being acted on. The objects of international law are the legitimate topics of international legal regulation.

The distinction between subjects and objects of international legal regulation has been discussed and debated for centuries and can be traced back to the writings of Grotius and Pufendorf. Such distinctions are probably a bit anachronistic today because the subjects and objects of international law have been radically transformed in the twentieth century. During the course of the past hundred years, international law became concerned with new issues that demanded international cooperation. The management of existing and emerging global commons and resources moved to the top of the global agenda. Likewise, the demands of an increasingly integrated and interdependent global economy required the creation of financial and trading strictures that were regarded as a legitimate topic of international legal regulation. International law has come to involve virtually every aspect of human conduct, every kind of business transaction, and every type of social and cultural relationship that crosses national frontiers. International law has permeated every facet of international life.

At the same time, we have had a revolution in the subjects of international law. One of the most notable trends in modern international law has been the change in attitude toward the identity of international legal actors. States used to be the only recognized subjects of international law, the only real players on the international scene. But the subjects of international law have been broadened to include other kinds of actors, including international organizations or institutions as collectivities of nations and, perhaps even more importantly, individuals as holders of international rights and duties.

As international legal actors have diversified and the legitimate topics of international legal regulation have expanded, the dividing line between subjects and objects has blurred, and that is probably for the best. It remains essential to fully understand both the roster of international legal players and the playing field that is the permissible range of international legal regulation.

Discourse about international law subjects and objects has reflected and reinforced conclusions about the relevant sources of international legal obligation and the actual processes of international lawmaking. Just as the mechanisms for forming new rules of international conduct have become more open and transparent, so too have ways of regarding those actors that can be said to be stakeholders in the international legal order. As with approaches to international lawmaking, the revolution in thinking about international legal personality has most affected states. Indeed, the notion of personality in international law was originally dominated by states and sovereignty, a clear expression of the idea that sovereign states were like autonomous individuals in a civil society.

The concept of states as functional actors in international law has already been considered in chapter 3. The purpose here is to discuss their juridical status as subjects of international law. International law doctrine has no fewer than three primary ways of defining that status. One is through rules of identity, defining statehood and the concomitant role of diplomatic acceptance in state relations. Another means is through principles of conduct, describing how a state acts through various organs and the legal consequences of those actions. The last way is through expectations about the legitimacy of states, norms bearing on the relevance of states for international relations. This cluster of doctrines is drawn from a variety of fields of international legal regulation (including recognition of states and governments, state succession, self-determination, and state responsibility), and each reflects deep uncertainties and confusion.

States remain the preeminent actors in international law. Barring a move toward world government, nations will always be at the center of international law and lawmaking. The positivist essence of statehood is sovereignty, the principle that each nation answers only to its own domestic order and is not accountable to a larger international community, save only to the extent it has consented to do so.[3] Sovereign states are thus conceived as hermetically sealed units, atoms that spin around an international orbit, sometimes colliding, sometimes cooperating, but always separate and apart.

If statehood is considered a definite status, membership in the family or community of nations is highly desired. Even if the notion of fundamental rights of states has been rejected,[4] nations are unqualifiedly entitled to the full panoply of rights and duties under international law. Among these is the capacity to enter into treaties, which is essential to the formation of consensual rules of international behavior. (States are also critical to the process of forming customary international law, although other types of international actors may also be involved in developing new rules of conduct.) Likewise, only states are eligible to become full members of international organizations. Nations are also able to claim breaches of international law obligations and to seek redress. States alone usually enjoy the full range of privileges and immunities from other nations' exercises of jurisdiction (including the significant right to claim sovereign immunity). Finally, and most importantly, only nations (or insurgent groups aspiring to statehood) have the right under international law to engage in war or armed conflict as an instrument of policy, and even then under prescribed circumstances.

International lawyers regard this bundle of rights as the core of sovereignty. Of course, international law imposes concomitant duties on states, not the least of which is the responsibility not to violate other nations' rights. All of this leads to the not-so-surprising conclusions that political entities aspire to statehood and that such assertions of state identity can often lead to intractable legal disputes.

The classic statement of the elements of statehood under international law can be found in the 1933 Montevideo Convention. Article I of this treaty declared, "The state as a person of international law should possess the following qualifications: (a) a permanent population; (b) a defined territory; (c) government; and (d) capacity to enter into relations with other states."[5] And although this formulation has been criticized,[6] the dominant view is that this remains the customary international law standard of statehood.[7]

There is, of course, an unspoken assumption in the criteria for statehood enunciated in the Montevideo Convention—that other nations are prepared to treat a particular entity as a member of the family of nations. Issues revolving around the recognition of states and the governments of states have proven to be some of the most contentious in international relations. Unfortunately, the international law on these topics has been unsatisfactory, to say the least. The doctrines surrounding recognition of political entities as states are distinct from the question of whether the government or particular leadership of a state should be dealt with diplomatically.

Recognition of states has been bedeviled by a theoretical construct that can fairly be described as arcane.[8] At one extreme are those who believe recognition by other states is a requisite, or constitutive, of statehood. In other words, recognition should be added to the four Montevideo elements. But just because other nations will not work and play with a new political entity does not necessarily make it any less a state or its government any less effective. At the other extreme is a declaratory theory of state recognition that argues that statehood is purely objective—an entity has the attributes of being a state, or it does not. In any event, for statehood to mean anything—to have international legal consequences—there must be some form of recognition.

This sounds like the international law equivalent of a philosophical disquisition of whether a tree falling in the forest makes a sound if no one is around to hear it. The arid debate between constitutive and declaratory theories will never be resolved because, ultimately, the problem is one of politics. The political reality is that entities that can effectively act like states are treated as states. With breakaway or separatist entities, although most nations are skeptical about the chances of autonomy, when the new entities achieve some measure of independence and are safely and permanently established, recognition should follow. This occurred for the revolutionary government in the United States, the former Spanish colonies in Latin America, and so forth in the history of the past two centuries. If one doubts the power and effect that recognizing new states has, just recall the breakup of the former Soviet Union and Yugoslavia and the subsequent conflicts that arose in those parts of the world.

Recognition of governments does, however, carry with it tricky legal consequences. On the international plane, changes in governments should not—and typically do not—matter. As long as the identity of the state has remained unchanged and there has been no state succession, whether a state has elected a new president or the government has been forcibly overthrown by a coup d'état or the entire regime has been replaced by revolutionary means should not matter for the state's international obligations.[9] A state succession occurs only when there has been a fundamental transformation in the identity of the state itself, not its government.[10] Such a change of identity can occur in a broad range of circumstances. States can break apart or merge into a union. Former colonies can achieve independence. Parts of one state's territory can be sold or otherwise transferred to another nation.

The legal consequences of international identity thus seemingly turn on semantics. Changes in states may result in such effects, according to the very formalistic law of state succession (considered further in chapter 8). When governments come and go, that is a matter for politicians and diplomats, and any impacts tend to be confined to the domestic law of the disputing countries (see chapter 7). Recognition as a means of mediating the identity of states as subjects of international law appears to lack coherence.

By way of contrast, legally defining the nature and extent of state conduct is a far more certain exercise. The question has arisen consistently in many contexts involving state responsibility and diplomatic protection.[11] The question usually becomes one of demonstrating that a respondent state is responsible for the acts that gave rise to the international claim. Such acts might include expropriations of foreign property or investments, regulatory interferences with foreign contracts, or denials of justice. (States are also liable for their omissions, such as the failure to protect an alien's property from depredation.) Whatever the underlying wrongful act or violation of a duty owed under international law, the legal inquiry is whether that conduct is attributable, or imputable, to the respondent government.[12]

The reason for the attribution requirement is that, under international law, host states cannot be the absolute guarantors of the safety of foreign visitors or the profitability of foreign business concerns. A tourist is mugged on the street by a bunch of thugs. While regrettable, that does not normally engage the state's responsibility because the robbers' act cannot be properly attributable to the host government. A commercial competitor engages in "opposition research" (read industrial espionage) to acquire a foreign company's valuable trade secrets. That act also is not imputable to the state.

But if a low-level government official extorts a gold watch or other valuables from a foreign visitor or colludes with a business rival to acquire valuable intellectual property, his conduct is attributable to a respondent state. International tribunals consistently have ruled that when any government official or agent engages in an act affecting the rights of aliens, even if that conduct is illegal or ultra vires under the laws of the host state, it is still attributable to that government.[13] Likewise, even though the acts of mobs or rioters may not normally be imputable to a government, if it is manifest that police authorities failed to take reasonable measures to protect the lives and property of foreigners, then state responsibility is engaged.[14]

Indeed, when any person purports to act on behalf of the state, that individual's conduct is imputable for purposes of state responsibility. When Iranian militants stormed the U.S. Embassy in Tehran in 1979 and took hostage the American diplomats inside, despite the revolutionary government's attempt to disavow that activity, the World Court nevertheless attributed that conduct to the new Iranian government.[15] Revolutionary movements or insurrections that later come to power may also be held responsible for their earlier conduct.[16]

Attribution under the international law of state responsibility is thus analytically similar to the "state action" problem under domestic constitutional regimes. International law, like municipal law, is compelled to circumscribe the outer limits of state authority, if for no other reason than to detail when governments will be liable for breaches of duty.[17] State practice, as largely reflected in the decisions of international claims institutions and ad hoc arbitral tribunals, offers rich detail as to what activities by which organs of government will be imputed to the state.[18] The reasoning of these authorities tends to be casuistic and, unlike the diverse precedents on state recognition (which are infected with political and diplomatic considerations), follow coherent patterns. As already noted, rules of attribution in state responsibility have hitherto been indifferent to codification attempts.[19]

Identity and conduct define states as international legal persons, but rules of recognition and attribution do not, of themselves, lend legitimacy to states as subjects of international law.[20] Without that missing element of legitimacy, states have come to be regarded with suspicion as international actors. In this discussion of statehood, one thing to keep in mind is that the legitimacy of a state system based on sovereignty is the principle of self-determination.[21] For nation-states to have any meaning and validity, they must truly represent peoples and national aspirations. If international law is going to privilege states as the critical actor in international relations, then statehood had better mean that each state and its institutions are supported by some form of national consensus.

This does not currently mean that the government of each state must be supported by popular sovereignty or democratic principles to be legitimate under international law, although there may well be an emerging norm to that effect (discussed further in chapter 6).[22] Rather, self-determination is a principle related to the rights of peoples and distinct nationalities to have a state that represents their national aspirations. As principles go, this has developed only since the early 1900s,[23] accelerating in the aftermath of the two world wars and the process of decolonization in the 1960s and 1970s.

Self-determination has proven a most troublesome and paradoxical concept. While it lends legitimacy to states that would otherwise be lacking it (especially accounting for a "democratic deficit"), it is also caustic of international order. Self-determination in the service of decolonization is laudable, but it is neither as useful nor as predictable a doctrine when it comes to the "rights of peoples," separatist or irredentist movements, or distinct ethnic or linguistic groups (including indigenous peoples).[24] Even though states, as the prime subjects of international law, have developed significant rules of recognition, change, and adjudication—in the sense H. L. A. Hart used these terms[25]—there is still no legal doctrine conferring legitimacy on nations as international actors.

The current perplexity surrounding the international legal personality of states can be neatly contrasted with that for international institutions and individuals. Collectivities of nations have become a notable feature on the landscape of international relations.[26] Even so, international law was rather slow in recognizing the international legal personality of these entities.[27] The story of this transformation in international law—recognizing an international actor other than states—not only presaged the revolutionary idea that individuals could carry international legal rights and duties but also represented a significant advance for functional cooperation among countries.[28]

What does it mean for an international organization to be a subject of international law, to have international legal personality? International public institutions and multinational public enterprises are the creation of states, and the formation of such institutions is usually accomplished by treaty or some other form of constituent instrument. The charters of international organizations are unique texts in international law, combining elements of public constitutions and articles of incorporation. Whether the charters are short or lengthy, magisterial in tone or pedestrian in detail, they provide for organs through which the institution does its work. Finally, and most importantly, the constituent text typically ensures that the organization will be governed by international law, not the domestic law of one of the members. This combination of constituent texts, organs, and international law governance is at the core of a status for international institutions separate and distinct from their state members.

The seminal case recognizing the international legal personality of an international organization was the ICJ's 1949 decision in the *Reparations for Injuries Suffered in the Service of the United Nations* advisory opinion.[29] The "injuries" alluded to in the title of the opinion referred to an extraordinary incident in modern diplomatic history and represented one of the gravest challenges to the fledgling UN (created in 1945). Just after World War II, Jewish settlers in Palestine began a revolt against Great Britain's mandate government. Jewish army units formed to fight the British as well as to displace Arab populations. The British began a process of withdrawal, and into that political vacuum the new UN organization dispatched a well-respected Swedish diplomat, Count Folke Bernadotte, to mediate between the Jewish and Arab groups. But radicals among both sides did not want a negotiated settlement, and Jewish extremists assassinated Bernadotte as he was leaving a Jerusalem hotel in 1948.

The international community was understandably outraged, and UN officials were particularly upset. (Recruitment of qualified international mediators, never an easy task, is certainly complicated if they are routinely murdered.) Calls began to emerge for the organization to bring an international claim against the parties responsible. The Jewish settlers had, after all, guaranteed Bernadotte's safety while he was in Jerusalem and had manifestly failed in that promise, and they seemed the obvious choice to receive an international claim. There was just one problem. At the time of the killing, the Jewish settlers had not yet declared the new state of Israel, and it was not yet a UN member.

Another, far more serious, issue lurked here: did the UN even have legal standing to bring a claim for the assassination of one of its envoys? The ICJ was thus asked whether the UN had sufficient capacity to bring an international claim against Israel for Bernadotte's death. Or, in other words, did the UN have "international legal personality"—was it a subject of international law?

The Court's answer was a resounding yes. In a key passage, the Court addressed the question of whether states were the only subjects of international law: "The subjects of law in any legal system are not necessarily identical in their nature or in the extent of their rights, and their nature depends upon the needs of the community. Throughout its history, the development of international law has been influenced by the requirements of international life, and the progressive increase in the collective activities of States has already given rise to actions upon the international plane by certain entities which are not States."[30] With these words, the Court in 1949 declared an end to a conception of international law as merely a law of nations in which states were the only actors or players.

What followed in the Court's opinion was the conclusion that the UN had international legal personality, even though the UN Charter had not so provided. The ICJ relied on a teleological approach to interpreting the Charter to give it real effectiveness. Key to the organization's success, the Court reasoned, was an independent and loyal secretariat, and if the UN lacked the capacity to bring claims on behalf of employees injured in its service, it would not attract top candidates. The ICJ went on to rule in its opinion that the UN was free to bring an international claim for reparations (including money damages) for any employee injured in its service, even against the staff member's own nation.[31] (Thus, even if Bernadotte had been an Israeli citizen, the UN would have been entitled under this reasoning to claim against Israel.) Finally, and of great consequence, the Court held that it did not matter that at the time of incident, Israel was not a member of the UN and had not thus affirmatively recognized the organization's legal personality. By its nature, the UN had an "objective" character that was binding even on nonmembers.

The move to recognize the legal personality of international institutions today seems obvious and unexceptional. But it would not be extravagant to say that in the aftermath of World War II, this idea was revolutionary, and, as has already been intimated, the real revolution in the subjects of international law has been in the recognition of individuals as capable of both exercising international rights and respecting international obligations. This development, standing alone, has transformed a law of nations—the exclusive preserve of states, national interests, and sovereignty—into today's dynamic international law. Persons are no longer the passive objects of international legal action, things on which states act at their whim.

Before individuals could acquire affirmative rights under international law, they first had to be burdened with obligations. In fact, this process of requiring individuals to conform their behavior to international norms—and directly punishing such persons (quite apart from their state of nationality) for infractions—has been ongoing for nearly five hundred years. Even in the era of the law of nations, where only states and national conduct mattered, individuals were recognized as subjects of international law duties and could be punished accordingly for international crimes such as piracy and violations of the laws of war. Personal accountability for international crimes—a process begun at Nuremberg and Tokyo—has culminated in an elaborate regime establishing an International Criminal Court (ICC) with broad competence.[32] In a new twist, some international human rights regimes impose duties on individuals in relation to their own states or in the service of regional solidarity.[33]

The rights/duties paradigm, which is at the conceptual core of international legal personality, has ironically had greater force in application to individuals, relative newcomers as international law subjects. Even so, there has been substantial debate as to exactly how individuals acquire rights under international law.[34] Some commentators argue that to have any real meaning, the source of rights for persons on the international plane must be states.[35] This is a notion that people can only be given rights by the affirmative grant of sovereign states. This clearly conflicts with a view that individuals, because of their fundamental human dignity, are endowed with rights quite apart from the will of governments.[36] This debate—which pits natural and positive sources of international law—is today largely irrelevant. The fact is that persons do have rights under international law, so speculating about the philosophical source of those rights is, with a few exceptions, a theoretical distraction.

One thing is certainly clear: people do not have the same sets of rights as do states under a classic formulation of international law. Individuals cannot make treaties. Indeed, it is certainly doubtful in some situations whether certain kinds of contracts between persons (including business associations) and states are fully enforceable as a matter of international law. Individuals certainly cannot acquire territory. Finally, persons cannot wage war in a way that will be recognized under international law, unless in such large aggregates as to constitute an insurgency or national liberation movement. As the World Court recognized in the *Reparations* opinion, different subjects of international law possess various attributes and can claim only certain rights and duties.

One crucial qualification of the rights exercised by individuals in international affairs is that persons may not have available to them the full panoply of international law remedies that are open to states. It is usually assumed under the domestic law of most nations that when a right is granted, so too is a remedy. It would be a nonsense to say that the law gives a right but denies an effective remedy for that right. In international law, that kind of paradox is more readily accepted. Persons may, for example, be given rights under treaties. (And, of course, positivists cite such treaty-based rights in support of the assertion that all rights for people in international law must flow from states.) Only in exceptional cases are individuals (or corporations) given a direct right of access to international tribunals or institutions for the satisfaction and enforcement of those rights.[37] Nevertheless, the World Court ruled as early as the 1920s that treaties can give individuals rights that can be enforced in domestic courts.[38]

The really critical question is whether the rights of individuals can be vindicated in a structure of international law that still, to a great degree, emphasizes states and sovereignty. Two broad mechanisms have been developed over time, one emphasizing state responsibility principles (applicable where one country injures aliens living within its territory) and the other emphasizing human rights (allowing individuals to assert rights against their own country of nationality).

There is a dramatic tension between these approaches, one that reappears consistently in any examination of the enforcement mechanisms available for rights under international law (see chapter 9). These conflicts are especially apparent in the treatment of business entities (particularly corporations and partnerships) as international legal subjects, capable of enforcing contracts made with governments and of using particular claims processes.[39] The rights of individuals and businesses to enforce international law rights have become an important part of the polemic between protection of capital investment and promotion of sovereignty by nations in the developing world.[40] In addition, the role of corporations as agents or partners of government—particularly in the commission of human rights abuses—also has been contentious.[41] International law has not responded coherently to the blurring of the lines between business activities and governmental prerogatives.

That leaves for consideration what may be new subjects of international law, just over the intellectual horizon. One subfield of the discipline has, more than any other, engendered discussion about new potential rights holders on the international plane. International environmental law's rich brew of theory and practice has managed to raise substantial challenges to traditional notions of what can constitute the conceivable class of international legal persons.

Some writers on international environmental law have, for example, proposed that certain species of animals should be regarded as sentient and should thus be regarded as subjects of international law. At a bare minimum, these writers have argued, legal standing should be accorded to the animals' interests.[42] This assertion of personhood for such appealing species as whales and elephants represents a significant substantive shift in international environmental protection: preserving nature for nature's sake, not just for the utility the global ecosystem provides to human beings. Furthermore, a claim for animals to be affirmative rights holders under international law manages to blend what had previously been regarded as two separate inquiries: whether something (or someone) is capable of holding rights under international law (the personhood question) and whether an entity can vindicate a certain right in a particular situation (the standing problem). *Ius standi* has always been a tricky problem for international tribunals,[43] and it would become particularly troublesome if determinations had to be made of who would represent parties and interests that could quite literally not speak for themselves.

Another group of scholars has made an even more radical suggestion for a potential subject of international law: people not yet born. Under this notion, the international community owes an obligation to future generations,[44] a duty that might profoundly impact the making of rules for management of common resources and, indeed, of all public goods that are conceivably exhaustible. If such duties to future generations are somehow to be enforceable, there must be some way to render people yet to be born as subjects of international law. Aside from the obvious problem of identifying an inchoate and unknowable group,[45] there is again the issue of standing. Even more, the introduction of a temporal element into the determination of international legal persons adds a dimension that few could have anticipated with the explosion of international law subjects in the twentieth century.

Indeed, there has been broad speculation that as the international community enters the twenty-first century, it is taking on attributes that are more akin to political life of the Middle Ages in Europe.[46] Under this theory, sovereignty is becoming more fluid. States are increasingly required to share power and authority with subnational units (such as vassals of old), supranational political entities (likened to a Holy Roman Empire), and powerful nongovernmental forces (analogous to the Roman Catholic Church). Regional integration could serve as a counterweight to state particularism. Technology could be making state authority less and less relevant, even while private international violence is proliferating.

"Neomedievalism," as this trend has been called,[47] is simply the flip side of what has come to be regarded as globalism. Neomedievalism, at least in the way it is presented here, appears to predict a growing roster of international legal actors and an unequivocal break in states' authority to fashion international legal rules. Neomedievalism thus appears to describe a trend in the relevant subjects of international law. By way of contrast, discussion of globalizing patterns in international law have mostly concentrated on the explosion of new, legitimate topics of international legal regulation. The "new" international economy, environment, technology, and culture are all portrayed as correspondingly fresh venues for the development of international law rules, new objects for international law to command. If neomedievalism speaks to a diversity of international law actors, globalism summons images of new frontiers of functional cooperation and challenge.

Whichever of these newfangled metaphors is selected, one should not be too quick to believe that the patterns of authority that have controlled the identity of subjects and objects of international law for the past few centuries will be quickly or effortlessly dissolved. States may not wither away, neo-Marxist fantasy notwithstanding. Sovereignty may prevent certain issues from being placed on an international agenda. And the real irony of thinking in terms of neomedievalism and globalism is that in each trope, the other is ignored. Globalism imagines certain trends that have occurred beyond the volition of international actors. Neomedievalism is largely indifferent to exactly what niche these new actors will fill. The real move in international law discourse may be to see that the dividing line between potent international subjects and passive objects of legal regulation is illusory and unnecessary.

5 Coherence and Sophistication

In this volume, I have continually referred to international law as a primitive legal system. Before proceeding further, it is necessary to explain in more detail what this means. Far from being a pejorative labeling of my topic, characterizing international law in this fashion not only reveals some important features of its system and method but also indicates some of its signal strengths.

A number of characterizations have been attributed to primitive legal systems.[1] Some of these describe the contents of primitive legal doctrines, most notably the lack of certainty and security of expectation, the limited range of norms, and the use of retaliation (rather than social sanction) as the decisive element of enforcement. Other characterizations describe what might be called the process elements of primitive law. Legal fictions, which transformed doctrines by subtly changing their underlying assumptions as social demands required, competed with formalism, which exalted form (the integrity of ritual) over substance (the adaptability of rules).

Moreover, the sources of legal obligation can be called primitive. Two phenomena have been observed in this respect. First, there is the importance of custom in determining the content of norms. It is axiomatic that law begins everywhere with custom, and it seems especially so with international law. We take it as an article of faith that the modern law of nations derives its legitimacy from the consent of states. We have completely accepted the notion that custom is a form of positive law. To call international law primitive, because its sources of obligation are rooted in custom, is no insult. Indeed, we regard the customary character of international law as an important attribute.

In the sense I (and others)[2] use the term, *primitive* is meant to convey a sense that international law is a highly decentralized and institutionally undeveloped legal system, not that it is ineffective or unsophisticated. Describing international law as *primitive* is not a mere repetition of the Austinian critique introduced in chapter 1. Nor can one seriously entertain the idea that international law is primitive because it relies on either naturalist sources of obligation or customary practices of international actors. Rather, the point is that there are certain limiting conditions in the construction of international legal order that require that the system remain, to a large degree, inchoate and abstract.

International law is, of course, posited as a law governing independent, sovereign nations—polities that would otherwise recognize no superiors, no sanctions, and no rules. H. L. A. Hart has said that international law has a "doubtful" claim to being a legal system.[3] This is a corollary to Hart's assertion that in primitive legal cultures there are no "secondary" rules, by which Hart was referring to three types. The first is guidance in recognizing the legitimacy of legal standards, which is necessary to counter uncertainty in primitive cultures about legal expectations. The second are rules for change, to remedy the static nature of such systems. The third grouping of secondary norms are those for the allowance of adjudication, to handle the social inefficiencies in applying the "primary" rules of primitive societies.[4] These rules of recognition, change, and adjudication roughly correspond with the notion that the central features of any modern legal system are institutions and processes that make law, interpret and apply norms, and enforce sanctions.

International relations theorists also have observed these conditions in discussions of developing "regimes" governing aspects of international life.[5] International law academics have tended to seek some fundamental measure of a coherent legal system and to ascertain whether that standard obtains for international law. This discussion is not so much about particular substantive or doctrinal values espoused by international law (more on which in the next chapter). Rather, these jurists and commentators seek to ascribe certain organizing principles for the systemic process of identifying international law rules. The real question here is whether international law, as its own system, has sufficient mechanisms to produce rules that are objective, clear, consistent, efficient, and flexible.[6]

Thomas Franck has powerfully argued that the key to the international legal order's legitimacy is promoting the predictability of rules and legal outcomes while ensuring the adaptability of regimes.[7] This sentiment has been expressed by the World Court, which has referred to "the stability which it is the object of international law to establish in international relations."[8] International tribunals have also indicated a desire to achieve results that can fairly be regarded as efficient and nonformalistic.[9] It appears that both jurists and publicists are actively engaged in an intellectual project to confer on international law the predictability and stability of expectation that seem to be lacking in primitive legal systems.

It remains to identify the methods by which international law promotes coherence and sophistication in its doctrinal content. Five broad categories of "secondary rules" (to use Hart's idiom) can be discerned. Once again, these need to be seen as organizing principles for structuring international law rules, not as the substantive values embedded in many international law doctrines.

ANALOGY

The first, already mentioned in chapter 3 in the context of an emerging role of stare decisis for judicial decisions, is the concept of analogy in international law decision making. Whether seen as a series of transactions, incidents, or disputes, international law is constantly being called on in decisional processes. Many of the outcomes of these decisions are recorded and preserved in some fashion and not just in the decisions of tribunals (domestic and international). Precedent—the fundamental notion that like cases should be treated alike and unlike cases should be treated differently—has been embraced to a large degree in international law, even while formal doctrines of stare decisis have been eschewed.

Arguments by analogy have been employed in the specialized context of disputing parties asking international tribunals to clarify their decisions. Article 60 of the World Court's Statute permits it to "construe" the "meaning or scope of the judgment." The Court has indicated that its task in such situations is to "make quite clear the points which had been settled with binding force in a judgment."[10] This has opened the door for the Court, along with other international arbitral institutions,[11] to separate the essential holdings of their judgments (what common lawyers would call the *ratio decidendi*) from the rest (dicta). This idea advances an important principle of res judicata for international disputes and a procedural mechanism for ensuring repose among parties.

Analogy as a tool to ensure symmetry and reciprocity in the application of international law rules is not limited to the use of judicial precedents. It has been a powerful instrument for the identification of general principles of domestic law to be elevated to the international plane. For example, in the *Trail Smelter* arbitration (discussed in chapter 2), the tribunal observed, "it is reasonable to follow by analogy, in international cases, precedents established by the [U.S. Supreme Court] in dealing with controversies between States of the Union or with other controversies concerning the quasi-sovereign rights of such States, where no contrary rule prevails in international law and no reason for rejecting such precedents can be adduced from the limitations of sovereignty inherent [in U.S. constitutional order]."[12] From this authority, the tribunal inferred a general principle that one political entity should not use its territory in such a way as to harm that of another.

There are limits on the usefulness of analogizing from municipal legal doctrines, and these have been famously noticed in the academic literature.[13] As already observed, general principles drawn from internal law may be sufficiently abstract and widely observed yet devoid of the needed specificity to be truly useful to a decision maker. Alternatively, a rule may have the required level of "concreteness" to be effectual but may consequently lack the needed observance in a broad cross-section of legal cultures around the world. The irony of general principles is that the truly useful rules rarely pass the test of generality. As a consequence, international lawyers have tended to err on the side of a lowest-common-denominator kind of logic in which very abstract principles are derived from national legal systems and then shoehorned into appropriate legal submissions. Interestingly, this has most often been seen in "mixed" international arbitrations (involving commercial disputes between sovereigns and private parties) where a "new" *lex mercatoria* has been derived from general rules of domestic commercial practice.[14]

While judicial precedents and general principles would appear to be fruitful materials for analogical reasoning, probably the most favorable avenue for this method of promoting coherence is through custom. State practices in one doctrinal realm can be translated into others. This process is often slow, as with the development of the particular underlying customs themselves, but a kind of momentum can be observed when one idea makes the jump between doctrinal chasms in the discipline. When the World Court adopted a "real and effective nationality" test as a condition for diplomatic protection and vessel registration—something that hitherto had been confined to other purposes—it was an example of such an analogical transformation in custom.[15] Likewise, the court observed in the *Tunisia-Libya Continental Shelf* case, "When applying positive international law, a court may choose among several possible interpretations of the law the one which appears, in the light of the circumstances of the case, to be closest to the requirements of justice."[16]

Lawyers intuitively understand and use analogy as a tool of their trade, and international lawyers are no exception in this regard. The underlying appeal of claims by analogy is that a rule employed to govern the outcome in one transaction or dispute is appropriately embraced to determine the result in a similar situation. Such arguments tend to be intensely contextual because the weight of the argument by analogy is only as strong as the factual similarity between the circumstances. Analogy remains the most common methodology for structuring international law rules.

LACUNAE

By way of contrast, only a handful of international decision makers have confronted the true "case of first impression," a situation for which there is no legal rule. Unlike in domestic legal systems, this can be a real problem for the internal cohesion of international law.

Many publicists have rejected the notion of *non liquet:* absent a positive showing that applicable international law exists, a tribunal must conclude that no rule of law inheres and that, therefore, the court cannot render a decision.[17] Jennings and Watts's edition of Oppenheim flatly declares, "It is . . . impermissible for an international tribunal to pronounce a *non liquet.*"[18] Others have observed that when faced with a paucity of state practice, a decision maker should refuse to rule and instead announce that there are no applicable principles of international law and accept that a *non liquet* is inherent in the concept of customary law, which is not a complete legal system.[19]

International tribunals and authorities have suffered from a similar schizophrenia in reacting to real or perceived gaps in the content of international law. In a project on arbitral procedure, the International Law Commission noted that a "tribunal may not bring in a finding of *non liquet* on the ground of the silence or obscurity of the law to be applied."[20] The drafters of what later became article 38 of the ICJ Statute were clearly concerned about the presence of lacunae in treaty and customary law and saw general principles as a convenient gap filler, "necessary to meet the possibility of a *non liquet*" and to avoid "especially the blind alley of *non liquet.*"[21] Arbitrations have consequently declared their power to use judicial fiat unilaterally to fill gaps in international law rules, even without the consent of the parties.[22] Such rulings would still be considered as made with respect for rule of law, not merely *ex aequo et bono* (what is just and good).

The World Court has occasionally declared a *non liquet,*[23] sometimes spectacularly so. In response to the UN General Assembly's request for an advisory opinion on the *Legality of the Threat or Use of Nuclear Weapons,* the Court (evenly divided, with the president casting the deciding vote) pronounced, "It follows . . . that the threat or use of nuclear weapons would generally be contrary to the rules of international law applicable in armed conflict, and in particular the principles and rules of humanitarian law; [h]owever, in view of the current state of international law, and of the elements of fact at its disposal, the Court cannot conclude definitively whether the threat or use of nuclear weapons would be lawful or unlawful in an extreme circumstance of self-defence, in which the very survival of a State would be at stake."[24] Thus, on the ultimate issue of the legality of using nuclear weapons in situations of national self-defense, the Court could not bring itself to decide. Despite a suggestion that such self-abnegation was appropriate in rendering advisory opinions—as distinguished from contentious cases between disputing states—the real question turned, as Judge Vereshchetin observed, on the correctness of "the view that a court should be prohibited from declaring *non liquet* . . . as a corollary of the concept of the 'completeness' of the legal system. Those . . . who do not deny the existence of gaps in substantive international law consider that it is the obligation of the Court in a concrete case to fill the gap and thus, by reference to a general legal principle or by way of judicial law-creation, to provide for the 'completeness' of the legal system."[25]

Non liquets are thus the logical antidote to the use of analogy in extending international law rules. The availability of a *non liquet* doctrine can serve as a significant escape valve for relentless expectations of international law to grow beyond its logical or functional limits. International lawyers tend to abhor a juridical vacuum, and analogical reasoning assumes that the history of international law is a progress narrative in which the trend is toward a more complete, coherent, and comprehensive system. For those who recognize that international law remains primitive and incomplete, it is periodically necessary for decision makers to acknowledge such and cautiously decline to extend the law in a direction that has not been blazed by established sources and methods. Acknowledgment of lacunae can also serve the purpose of marking the outer boundaries of international law doctrine, not only in terms of substance but also when it comes into conflict with power politics and national sovereignty. In this sense, the result in the *Use of Nuclear Weapons* opinion was foregone, and perhaps the only surprise is that it took the casting vote of the Court's president to settle it.

RULES AND STANDARDS

If analogy reflects an aggressive tendency for international law to grow, while *non liquet*s are a prudential brake on that process, these are really extreme positions on the continuum of international lawmaking. International decision makers rarely engage in a self-conscious exercise of either pushing the envelope of legal doctrine for its own sake or recoiling in horror at the prospect. Instead, the process is more subtle and tends to be played out in exploring fine gradations between "hard" rules and "soft" standards.

The rules-standards distinction was raised in chapter 2 through a discussion of soft law. I previously observed that there was a tendency for softer standards to tend to harden over time into more concrete rules. Aspirations inevitably become expectations and then entitlements. Articulated in this fashion, this seems a retelling of the progressive story for international law to which I have already alluded. This is a significant modality for international law's practical operation, and it is necessary to explain how this works. Two examples might suffice.

An oft-told tale concerns the Universal Declaration of Human Rights, adopted in 1948.[26] This is one of the great documents of international law. Drafted by a blue-ribbon panel of intellectuals and advocates (led by Eleanor Roosevelt) with the input of national delegations, the Declaration is lucidly worded. Each provision rings with authority and certainty. Article 1 proclaims, "All human beings are born free and equal in dignity and rights. They are endowed with reason and conscience and should act towards one another in a spirit of brotherhood." Article 3 says simply and unqualifiedly, "Everyone has a right to life, liberty and security of person."

The thrust of the Universal Declaration was primarily the enunciation of civil and political rights—those freedoms necessary for individuals to operate within a polity. In addition to this "first generation" of rights, the Declaration also prescribes some "second generation" economic and social rights. Even though the Universal Declaration was adopted without dissent, it was not without controversy. Socialist countries were concerned about article 17's enshrinement of the right to property. The United States was concerned about the First Amendment implications of article 12's requirement that attacks on individual honor and reputation be barred.

The reason that the Declaration could be adopted by consensus, despite controversial provisions, was that it was understood by all that it was not a binding legal instrument. An early example of a multilateral soft law instrument, the Declaration specifically indicated in its preamble that it was "a common standard of achievement," something for which national governments should "strive" through "progressive measures." The United States issued a statement after the Declaration's adoption that noted, "It is not a treaty; it is not an international agreement. It does not purport to be a statement of law or legal obligation."[27]

Nevertheless, more than fifty years later, virtually all of the Universal Declaration's provisions concerning civil and political rights have come to be recognized as human rights norms in customary international law or in other multilateral instruments.[28] Perhaps just as importantly, the high tone and moral authority of the Universal Declaration set an important benchmark in subsequent international discussions and negotiations about human rights. The Universal Declaration's hardening into customary and conventional law appears to be a vindication of a linear model for standards becoming rules.

An alternative approach is reflected in a very different area of law, that of marine delimitation for offshore areas under claim by competing states. These disputes have triggered difficult issues of customary and treaty law. The *North Sea Continental Shelf* case[29] rejected the uncritical use of a hard rule: equidistance, the practice of drawing a delimitation line every point of which is an equal distance from each coastal state's shore. Article 83 of the 1982 UN Convention on the Law of the Sea stipulated an "equitable solution" for maritime delimitations of continental shelves and exclusive economic zones (EEZs). This has meant in practice that an equidistance line might be the start of the process, but that line can be altered by "relevant circumstances."

What the appropriate relevant circumstances are has been decided by international tribunals on a very particularistic case-by-case basis.[30] Historic rights to fish or to exploit resources in a particular area may be significant, as might be one nation's acquiescence in letting another state do so.[31] The legal import of particular geological formations has been rejected, as have economic disparities between the two states.[32] Finally, a principle of proportionality has been employed in which the length of a state's coastline is compared with the amount of ocean real estate it has acquired under a delimitation. Together, these special circumstances have been used by tribunals to produce equitable delimitations for coastal states (a matter to which I will return in chapter 8 in the context of pragmatic adjudication).

Standards, therefore, can be aspirational and harden into eternal truths, or they can be functional and subsequently applied situationally and casuistically. Standards can be an expression of rights formalism or practical equity. The significant point here is that international law decision makers can employ the rules-standards distinction in a variety of ways to achieve either certainty or flexibility, consistency or sophistication.

INTERTEMPORALITY

This insight leads to a question of timing. If the expectation is that international law rules are evolving—sometimes hardening from standards into rules, occasionally being extended by analogy until reaching a wall of *non liquet*—how does that affect international actors, whose conduct must conform with the changing law? Publicists give this *problematique* the formidable but descriptive label *intertemporal law*. The question implicated here is nothing less than the role that time plays in international decision making.[33]

Questions, for example, arise in interpreting treaties concluded some years ago. The Vienna Convention on the Law of Treaties (VCLT) requires that an interpreter construe the text in light of "any relevant rules of international law applicable in the relations between the parties."[34] But what if the background customary law has changed? Somewhat contradictorily, the World Court, in its 1971 *Namibia* opinion, indicated that "the primary necessity of interpreting the instrument in accordance with the intention of the parties at the time of its conclusion" must be balanced with the realization that the concepts embodied in a treaty are "by definition, evolutionary" and "cannot remain unaffected by the subsequent development of law."[35] The "subsequent development" referred to in that case was the emergence of a right of self-determination of peoples and an expectation of decolonization, which required that the Court give a different interpretation to a League of Nations mandate than its drafters might have expected. The Court emphasized that "an international instrument has to be interpreted and applied within the framework of the entire legal system prevailing at the time of the interpretation."[36]

One important principle of intertemporality is that established rules might later be changed and trumped by higher-order principles. An emerging rule of *jus cogens* (nonderogable "supercustom") will prevail over an earlier treaty.[37] While certain terms of a treaty can be sensibly understood only in the context of the time they were drafted, for others the construction of generic terms is "intended to follow the evolution of the law and to correspond with the meaning attached to the expression by the law in force at any given time."[38] The distinction being made here is an important one for lawyers of all stripes. Technical terms carrying particular legal meaning ("terms of art") have a fixed connotation in time, while generic terms or politico-diplomatic formulations are free to evolve in definition.[39]

The most spectacular difficulties with intertemporal law have occurred not in relation to treaty interpretation but in the context of territorial acquisition. The cause célèbre of this subject remains the *Isle of Palmas* case, an international arbitration decided in 1928.[40] At issue was sovereignty over an isolated island less than two square miles in size. The United States claimed title under an 1898 treaty in which Spain ceded the Philippines after the Spanish-American War. The United States argued that through Spain, title could be traced back to the islands' original discovery in the early 1600s. The Netherlands claimed title by virtue of a series of contacts, beginning in 1648 and 1677 and culminating in a (more or less) intermittent trading presence in the late 1800s.

The arbitrator for this case (Swiss publicist Max Huber) was thus faced with a dilemma. Should he recognize Spanish (and thus American) title based on the discovery doctrine—the old rule of international law, in force in the early 1600s—or should he apply what was universally recognized as the new rule, the principle of effective occupation? Under this new rule, states must exercise effective control of a land territory to maintain a claim of title: symbolic discovery, without more, was insufficient.

Huber's solution was elegant, although controversial. He applied the international law in force at the moment of what he regarded as the "critical date." For Huber that date was 1898, the year in which the United States acquired title and thus metaphorically stepped into the shoes of the former claimant, Spain. By 1898 the new customary international law of effective occupation was recognized, so that was the rule to be applied. By that year, the Netherlands—not Spain—had taken more steps to effectively occupy the island. Holland, not the United States, was the owner.

Huber's decision raised a host of concerns. One relatively minor issue was how exactly a state effectively occupies a small island? The more serious problem—and the one of wider relevance to international lawyers—is the choice of law implicit in Huber's decision. Does a decision maker apply the law in force when a legally significant act took place or instead require that additional acts be taken, conformable with the law as it evolves? The first option would lock into place the legal consequences of acts that would today be regarded as invalid. The second option means that no international law claim is ever safe from challenge because some party or other can assert that there has been a change in the law favorable to its position. Huber tried to soften the effect of this paradox by his selection of a "critical date" that made sense in the context of the arbitration.

Obviously, the selection of a "critical date" is decisive for the solution of the intertemporal law problem. On that choice turns the application of the relevant body of international law. As Sir Gerald Fitzmaurice noted in pleading before the World Court, "the whole *raison d'être* of the critical date rule is, in effect, that time is supposed to stop at that date. Nothing that happens afterwards can operate to change the situation as it then existed."[41] Using this idiom, intertemporality is an end of history, the ultimate protection for the value of repose. Any attempt to precisely fix critical dates is doomed to failure. Attempts to codify such rules, either for general application or in relation to specific problems (such as timing issues in the international

law of state responsibility), have been at such an abstract level as to
be useless.[42]

Intertemporality nevertheless remains an important consideration
in international law method. This is certainly true at the intersection
lines between international and domestic legal systems. Incorporation doctrines and the relevant order of precedence among customs,
treaties, and statutes—formed at various times—can be difficult issues.[43] Problems of timing will remain central in the process of making international law a more complete and coherent legal system.

DOCTRINAL CONGRUITY

The last kind of methodological tool available to international lawyers is the structure of international law doctrine itself, the way that
the discipline organizes rules into various and discrete categories. The
inquiry here is what defines the boundaries between doctrinal areas
and how subdisciplines are created within international law. Just as
significant is the manner in which certain kinds of rules manage to
cut across intellectual boundaries. In this regard, it is worth reflecting
on Oscar Schachter's extended and gracious metaphor of the intellectual landscape of the discipline:

> We may envisage international law as a large terrain made up
> of towns and villages with interconnecting paths and highways.
> The specialized branches of the law form the separate towns and
> villages, each centered on its own affairs. Narrow paths run from
> one to another, used occasionally. Across the entire terrain are
> the superhighways, the connecting links, which in the metaphor
> convey the general principles and concepts. Those who travel on
> the highways are generally only dimly aware of the lively activi-
> ties in the towns and villages. Those who remain only in the local
> communities immersed in their specialities tend to lose sight of
> the interconnections and coherence of the larger whole.[44]

There is certainly a doctrinal core of international law that com-
prises rules that define the legal system's sources, subjects, and ob-

jects. Norms that touch on the identity, succession, jurisdiction, immunities, and responsibility of international legal actors occupy this central constellation. In addition to these "rules of recognition" (to use Hart's phraseology), certain crucial doctrines evince both substantive and transactional characteristics. Treaty law, diplomatic privileges, and the procedures of international institutions certainly fall into this category. The common characteristic of these core rules is that they transcend particular topics of international legal regulation.

Just outside the doctrinal core of international law are galaxies of "top level" domains of rules. Among the most prominent of these would be the international law of human rights. This subrealm of international law is fundamentally defined by its values, chiefly the goal of promoting individual dignity, autonomy, and freedom. Indeed, human rights law has regarded itself as a special aspect of international law: something more than a subdiscipline but not quite a complete body of law in its own right.

By contrast, private international law managed to escape the orbit of public international law's influence in the mid–nineteenth century, a development that will be considered in chapter 7. Private international law subsumes such topics as conflicts of law and some aspects of international economic relations as between purely "private" transnational agents. Of course, as public international law diversified its subjects and came to embrace individuals and businesses as legal actors, this distinction has blurred rapidly.

Two other top-level domains are significant. One is what I call the international law of common spaces and resources. Subsumed within this is the venerable law of the sea, management of the international environment, regulation of the "public" aspects of the international economy (including commerce, trade, finance, and investment), and control of other international public goods as diverse as polar regions, intellectual property, and cyberspace. This realm is characterized by its essentially functional nature—international actors are compelled to participate in this marketplace of rules because of global interdependence.

The last domain is conflict management. The ultimate test of international law is how well it manages conflict between states and other international actors. This cluster of issues includes the ways that states practically enforce or demand their rights under international law and the manner in which the international community has imposed controls on recourse to armed conflict and restraints on states in initiating hostilities. The role of international law does not end with a declaration of war between countries. Over centuries, international law has developed a definitive law of war, which today includes substantial protections of civilians, noncombatants, prisoners, and other individuals deserving protection. Finally, there are a number of mechanisms available for the peaceful settlement of disputes.

These domains—human rights, private international law, common resources, and conflict management—dictate thinking about the substantive "grammar" of international law. The more commonly known subdivisions are situated within these categories, although sometimes uncomfortably. While the law of the sea may be regarded as a paradigmatic topic of common resources, rules regarding the protection of foreigners and their property within the territory of another state (known as "diplomatic protection") can straddle human rights, private international law, and common resources concerns. Of course, any particular topic of international legal regulation can implicate conflict-management and dispute-settlement mechanisms. Nevertheless, to a degree perhaps not fully appreciated by participants in the international legal system, the top-level domains are often regarded as insular and doctrinally discrete. Thus arises Schachter's concern that in the process of becoming more sophisticated and specialized, international law runs the risk of becoming incoherent. To extend Schachter's urban metaphor, international law is at risk of becoming an intellectual sprawl.

Doctrinal coherence is best provided by the underlying values of the international system itself. Such discipline and intellectual rigor cannot be imposed by structure alone. While the essential values of international law will be considered in the next chapter, it cannot be forgotten that certain doctrinal clusters defy the inevitable process of specialization and alienation that Schachter feared.

Consider, for example, the set of connected concepts that have tended to liberate international law from the narrow confines of state consent. *Jus cogens* are customary norms that may not be derogated by treaties.[45] *Erga omnes* obligations are owed to the entire international community, while *actio popularis* are those violations for which any member of the international community can seek redress.[46] Objective regimes—such as the international legal personality of the UN—do not require affirmative consent through treaty membership and constitute an exception to the rule of *ius tertii*.[47] Universal jurisdiction extends the authority of international actors to punish a wide variety of offenses. Individually, these doctrines are regarded merely as aspects of discrete pockets of international law doctrines: criminal jurisdiction, state responsibility, treaty law, and the formation of custom. When aggregated, these doctrines have immense significance and application. Furthermore, they reflect an important insight about the nature of international law that cuts across formal doctrinal boundaries. Likewise, the concepts of acquiescence, estoppel, opposability, good faith, and abuse of rights—all fundamentally equitable principles[48]—exercise substantial influence on the evolution of rules (particularly for human rights, treaty compliance, and common resource questions) as well as the practical settlement of disputes.

International law has many methods for promoting coherence and sophistication. These offer rational approaches for overcoming the inherently primitive nature of the international community. More importantly, they serve as the connective tissue between primary norms of state conduct (including the key values of the international system) and the modes of enforcement for international rights and duties. These organizing principles ensure the integrity of the legal system. They guarantee its internal rationality and logic. They are not, however, without their drawbacks, and these limitations manifest themselves through problems of enforcement and compliance, the divergent conservative and progressive natures of some international law rules, and paradoxes afflicting the central values of the system itself.

6 Values and Paradoxes

Only recently have international law actors and commentators come to self-consciously reflect on the policy values and choices that undergird the international legal system. In many primitive legal systems, practices were adopted and maintained for reasons necessary to the community's coherence and legitimacy, but rarely was this the subject of much speculation or doubt. In a similar fashion, as Thomas Franck has observed,[1] the legitimacy of the primary rules of the international legal system depends on the determinacy of the norms, the symbolic validation they confer, the coherence of rules in commanding compliance, and the ability of actors to adhere to those rules through effective process. While that insight answers concerns about the character of international law rules that can be deemed legitimate for the international community, it does not necessarily address the values and paradoxes inherent in the selection of those rules. That is this chapter's task.

When international law was in its infancy as a legal system, few publicists tended to question that its primary value was the maintenance of the sovereignty—the internal legitimacy—of its primary actor and subject, states. When doubts were raised on this point, they tended to be couched in the idiom of the naturalist-positivist debate about the nature and sources of international legal obligation. When Grotius, Pufendorf, and Vattel speculated on whether states were subject to a higher law than the prince's own whim and raison d'état, the discourse rarely ventured beyond a fairly binary debate between sovereignty and justice.[2] Immanuel Kant, writing in the late eighteenth century, was among the first to challenge the state-centered values of the law of nations by placing international peace as an affirmative value alongside state power.[3]

The revolutions in America and France in the 1770s and 1780s certainly reflected a time of new ideologies. As a consequence, new fissures and stresses appeared in the international political order. These challenged accepted values of the international system and continued with the popular revolutions of 1848 and the accelerating pace of European colonialism in Africa and Asia. Likewise, the 1917 Bolshevik Revolution profoundly upset international expectations by placing one of the traditional Great Powers on an ideological collision course with the rest.

State sovereignty's monopoly over international law's value system was thus only seriously challenged at the beginning of the twentieth century. The Hague Peace Conferences of 1899 and 1907 (with their disarmament and conflict-control agendas), as well as the creation of the League of Nations in the aftermath of World War I (as the world's first universal organization devoted to collective security), elevated peace as a central value of international law. The irony of the timing of this accomplishment cannot be lost. The hostile behavior of states in the interwar periods, combined with the extraordinary human rights abuses before and during World War II, have caused later diplomats and commentators to regard it as a time of undoubted failure for international law.

In a similar way, 1945 is regarded as a watershed for international law's values. Captured in so many developments (some of which have already been narrated in this volume), the international community accepted that state sovereignty could not alone guide international affairs. While the UN Charter certainly embraced Great Power realpolitik in its structure (an important change from the League's fairly utopian vision), it also explicitly dissolved state sovereignty in its twin goals of preserving peace and protecting human rights. Of these two competing values, the human rights revolution of the postwar era was probably the more significant. By elevating respect for the dignity and rights of individuals, enforceable even against their own states of nationality, international law has come within the past fifty years to recognize a variety of essential values, just as it has embraced a diversity of subjects for its rules.

It would be a profound mistake to believe that the periodic cycles of challenge to "established" international law values are now no longer likely to occur. If anything, they seem to be accelerating in tempo.

The process of decolonization, starting in the 1950s and 1960s, has certainly raised profound questions about the Eurocentric character of many international law doctrines. The end of the Cold War and the (arguable) emergence of a single superpower has likewise put in doubt international law values that depended on bipolar, hegemonic assumptions. Multipolarity in international relations has been translated into multivalent objectives for a rule of law. Religious fundamentalism and virulent nationalism, long suppressed during the Cold War, have reemerged as major forces in shaping international law concerns. Finally, the combination of economic, technological, and cultural phenomena we call globalism has added new dimensions and demands for functional cooperation between international actors. At the same time, the legitimacy of international law is being challenged by those who fear its predilection for centralization and bureaucracy and the consequent lack of transparency and accountability that are required for democratic processes. In short, new social ideologies and forces are impacting international law to a degree not experienced for centuries.

This multiplicity of values has become an extraordinary topic of conversation for publicists of the last two generations. Beginning with the work of Myres McDougal and Harold Lasswell of the New Haven school, reflection on policy has become an expected part of international law discourse.[4] Of course, explicitly accepting that international law rules are influenced by underlying substantive objectives for the international community runs the risk of making international law too dependent on international politics and less autonomous of the whims of international actors. "Values talk" can make international law appear less legal, and for any legal discipline that at the outset appears to suffer from a deficit of "legality," this may seem like folly. Yet the overwhelming scholarly consensus is that international law must understand and embrace its core values if it is to thrive.[5]

There are, however, real concerns raised by the bewildering array of values that have been propounded for international law rules. One objection is that international law will cease to be an ostensibly neutral body of norms, equally applicable to all international actors, if certain values are advanced that embrace policies that discriminate (in reality or even appearance) against the political, economic, or social goals of particular international actors. This potential loss of neutrality in international lawmaking could be a crippling blow to the system's legitimacy. Apart from this "external" challenge, there is an even more powerful concern implicated for the "internal" integrity of the system. A conglomeration of values carries with it the risk of incoherence for international law doctrines or, even worse, outright conflicts between competing goals. An international legal system that serves too many central objectives, according to this view, can satisfy none. These internal and external critiques of international law's now-diverse value system will be considered in the balance of this chapter.

NEUTRALITY OF DIVERSE VALUES

As with the analytic structure of doctrines in the discipline, the values inherent in international legal rules can be mapped. As suggested in the historic narrative just sketched, international law began with a handful of central concerns and goals that have substantially diversified over time. Just as an inkblot spreads over a page, these objectives have widened but also (to some degree) become diluted and diffuse.

Core Values: Sovereignty and Peace

Participants in the system typically regard some of the central values of international law as self-evident. Characterizing particular doctrines as intended to advance sovereignty or peace or human dignity is viewed as an absurd exercise because all international law rules should be seen as pursuing those objectives. In addition, there is sometimes a false sense of conflict inserted into discussions of international law values. Sovereignty and peace are often articulated as state-centered objectives, while human dignity is posited as a naturalist counterweight.

The reality of the central objectives of international law rules is neither so manifest nor so dichotomous. For example, sovereignty and peace are rightly regarded as values that maintain both the external order of participants in the international system and the internal legitimacy of those actors. To the extent that international law expects that states will treat each other with the respect and dignity due independent, autonomous, and sovereign polities, this not only serves the ends of peace and harmony within the international system but, perhaps even more importantly, gives domestic regimes the authority they need to conduct their affairs. In a similar vein, promoting international peace and security may be the most significant human right, because times of war and conflict result in the worst conditions for individuals and the gravest abuses.

Underlying notions of peace and state authority have been very strong assumptions about territorial sovereignty. As the World Court observed in the *Corfu Channel* case and as has been repeated in every attempt by the UN to pronounce the rights and duties of nations, "between independent States, respect for territorial sovereignty is an essential foundation of international relations."[6] While armed incursions into another nation, interferences with its government, and the exercise of authority over its territory are the most obvious challenges to a state's sovereignty, they are not the only ones. One of the difficulties of sovereignty is that, ultimately, it transcends national territory. As state authority has come to expand beyond national boundaries, sovereignty has increasingly meant that international law must respect such values as the dignity of nations[7] and their economic and cultural autonomy.

The international law value of sovereignty is thus many ideals rolled into one. It is fundamentally an urge for order. The international community needs an organizing principle for its operation. States and sovereignty have offered that principle for nearly five centuries. By channeling and managing conflict and mediating between the rights and interests of subgroups and individuals, states were able to lay claim to primary authority and responsibility in the international community. In return, international law was called on to legitimize this arrangement and strengthen it. This postmedieval order has now come around nearly full circle, and state monopoly on power in international relations has been profoundly challenged. Strong theories of sovereignty as a rigid form of territorial control have thus given way to weaker claims to independence, autonomy, and respect. They may ultimately be gravitating to the simplest assertion of all: that international actors of the same type be treated equally. The rallying cry of sovereign equality, once so powerful, may be merely an argument (considered below) for equality and neutrality, not just for states but for all international actors.

In a similar fashion, the value of peace in international law is actually no less than four discrete objectives. To achieve international society has meant that a delicate balance be struck with the internal political and social order of individual states. This has been the singular task of the law of nations, one that it accomplished to a surprisingly effective degree. States can be particularistic: their internal political order can sometimes depend on exclusion, on aggression, and on difference. The rules of state relations have managed to transform this particularism into cooperation. Friendship has been achieved through the translation of hospitality practices into the institutions of diplomacy. Likewise, states have been made tolerant by rules of conduct that permitted the movement of people, goods, and services across boundaries. Trust is possible through the rituals and forms of making faith through treaties and alliances. Finally, restraint came to be exercised by states even in wartime as a consequence of self-interest and concern for order.

These are the essential ingredients of community, a notion and principle that is at the theoretical center of modern international law. The development of peace as a fundamental value of international law is the story of the creation of a nascent society, one with a political structure and legal sensibility bearing on the creation of communities and constituents that aspire to universality.

Many of the specific doctrines of diplomatic and consular relations and of treaty negotiation and termination have embedded within them a profound concern for state behaviors that reflect friendship, trust, and tolerance. Among the functions of modern diplomatic establishments are "promoting friendly relations . . . and developing . . . economic, cultural and scientific relations."[8] The inviolability of diplomatic missions[9] is among the most ancient and traditional aspects of peaceful relations between states[10] and reflects a fundamental value of international law, keeping open communication even between potentially or actually hostile countries. Likewise, the mechanisms for concluding treaties among states are a total vindication of consensual diplomacy and negotiation. Countries are invited to participate in treaty-making processes, translating political commitments into legal obligations enforceable under the rule of *pacta sunt servanda* and good faith.[11] States' ability to unilaterally terminate agreements or to modify their essential provisions is sharply limited in the VCLT.[12] Such actions typically result in open rupture of relations between countries and thus need to be controlled.

Peace and sovereignty, as international law values, are premised on the maintenance of order and legitimacy in international affairs. Such a characterization certainly does not mean that rules made in pursuance of those values are necessarily conservative and tend toward preservation of the international status quo. While this topic will be considered in more detail in chapter 10, it is enough to indicate here that international law was doctrinally dynamic in the period (prior to 1945) in which sovereignty and peace were the dominant objectives of international legal order.

Competing Values:
Fairness, Humanity, and Democracy

Counterpoised with the goal of order in the international community is the objective of justice. But *justice* in the sense it is used here is not simply a restatement of natural law visions for international law. Instead, it has come to mean a definitive grouping of particular values underlying international law rules. Unlike sovereignty and peace, these competing values are not necessarily seen as pervading the entire complex of international law doctrine. Rather, they operate at more discrete levels. For that reason, it is possible to identify these values at work with more clarity than is possible for the ostensibly central objectives of international law.

The objective of fairness in international law has, for example, a long and convoluted pedigree.[13] It began life as a central postulate of sovereignty, the equality of states under international law.[14] This was the logical correlate of absolute territorial sovereignty enjoyed by states and was codified in such documents as the 1970 Declaration on Friendly Relations and Cooperation among States:

> All States enjoy sovereign equality. They have equal rights and duties and are equal members of the international community, notwithstanding differences of an economic, social, political or other nature.
>
> In particular, sovereign equality includes the following elements:
> (a) States are juridically equal;
> (b) Each State enjoys the rights inherent in full sovereignty;
> (c) Each State has the duty to respect the personality of other States.[15]

This formal (and circular) expression of sovereign equality as a juridical condition attached to states as subjects of international law led also to a significant substantive insight: international legal rules should have neutral and general application. The essence of fairness in this conception is that international law rules apply equally to all international actors. This directive of moral and political neutrality in international lawmaking is, however, often at odds with the articulation and extension of other values. In this way, sovereign equality has merged with two other principles. One is reciprocity: obligations (either customary or treaty based) are symmetrical. A state's performance of an international law rule extends only as far as other actors' willingness and ability to comply. The other principle is nondiscrimination. As the International Law Commission has observed, the notion that states should not differentiate in the treatment they extend to other polities is a general rule that follows from and is inherent in the sovereign equality of states.[16]

We know that these conceptions of fairness and equality in international relations can be either a regressive hindrance or a utopian fallacy. Taking reciprocity first, exceptions have been made to the formal symmetry of treaty obligations when the conventions at issue are intended to protect human rights and not to advance sovereign interests. The World Court eschewed reciprocity as a value when it rejected "the maintenance of a perfect contractual balance between rights and duties"[17] for the application of certain human rights instruments. To have embraced a position of true sovereign equality in such circumstances would have meant that the extension of human rights values would have been sacrificed.

As for nondiscrimination, states are uniquely privileged in customary international law to afford different kinds of treatment and respect to their neighbors. International actors may be juridically equal, but the reality of international life is quite different. In addition, a host of treaty regimes are crucially premised on having different rules apply to different categories or groupings of states. The structure of membership on the UN Security Council—the central organ for maintaining international peace and security—is based on granting the veto power to a select handful of Great Powers. In a very different context, many international environmental regimes embrace a double standard in which nations of the developing world are exempted from many substantive obligations and pollution-control targets. The fairness of the Security Council veto or environmental double standards is hardly relevant: none of these regimes would have been feasible without legally recognizing differences in states' relative military and economic power.

If international law has been suspicious of uncritical applications of the reciprocity and nondiscrimination principles, it has also been hostile to many other obvious forms of expression for fairness and equality. Most distributive justice arguments have fallen flat. For example, the New International Economic Order of the 1970s was an attempt at remaking the landscape of international economic relationships and their legal bases.[18] The 1973 UN Declaration on Permanent Sovereignty over Natural Resources and the 1974 Charter on Economic Rights and Duties of States were drafted to propound new rules of customary international law. Among the features of these resolutions were provisions allowing states to expropriate the assets of foreign investors and to have those states themselves establish the "appropriate" compensation to be paid and (in case of a challenge by the foreign owner of the property) to have the disputes resolved only in domestic courts. Needless to say, these alterations to the prevailing customary international law rules were opposed by economically developed, capital-exporting nations (as noted in chapter 3 in the context of UN resolutions as a source of law). In a similar vein, articulation of the "common heritage of mankind" principle was regarded as merely a thinly veiled attempt to transfer control to the developing world of resources as varied as deep seabed manganese nodules, Antarctica, the moon, and forms of intellectual property rights.[19]

International tribunals have also made clear that while they can perform an equitable function in dispute settlement, they are not at liberty to fashion outcomes that serve redistributive ends. One good example of this reluctance was the World Court's reaction to an argument made by a party to the *Tunisia-Libya Continental Shelf* case.[20] The two countries were involved in a heated dispute regarding ownership of offshore oil and gas deposits, and Tunisia made the brazen suggestion that because it was poor and Libya was already rich with oil wealth, Tunisia should be given the benefit of some questionable methods of demarcating the two countries' respective continental shelf areas. This argument was stonily rejected by the World Court, which acidly commented, "Equity does not necessarily imply equality. There can never be any question of completely refashioning nature."[21] It is perhaps also for this reason that concepts of intergenerational equity, which have been extensively mooted in the academy,[22] have been slow to be incorporated in specific international law doctrines. Even while international law may embrace fairness and equality as a value, such objectives cannot remake political or economic realities, change historic or biological facts, or alter the essential character of the international community.

Ideas of fairness and equality have worked a significant influence not as grand statements but within the interstices of international law rules. To take but one example of microlevel applications of equality, consider the doctrine of proportionality—the idea that legal consequences should be gauged to the overall relevance of certain key facts. Proportionality is a form of utilitarian justice and can properly be considered by moral philosophers as a manifestation of fairness. Proportionality appears in many disparate international law doctrinal clusters. In each instance, it operates as a check on the application of what would otherwise be a harsh general rule.

In some of its manifestations, it is a sweepingly broad proposition. In the international law concerning countermeasures, uses of force, and the conduct of military operations, proportionality requires that international actors take action in rough response to their adversaries' actions.[23] While there is no obligation to play merely a game of tit for tat (common in some low-level diplomatic contretemps), proportionality often serves as a brake on escalation, or the too-quick movement of events. Proportionality can thus be an adjunct of necessity and can serve the interests of humanity, values that will be considered presently.

In another application, proportionality imposes a "narrow tailoring" requirement for state action, as in the permissible derogation of human rights instruments in emergency situations. A critical provision of the 1967 International Covenant on Civil and Political Rights (ICCPR)[24] is article 4, which allows a party to depart from its obligations under the Convention, provided that (1) it is a time of "public emergency which threatens the life of the nation," (2) the derogation is "strictly required by the exigencies of the situation," and (3) certain core rights are preserved. Proportionality thus becomes a surrogate for interest balancing (in the ICCPR example, offsetting the rights of individuals with those of society), and is an example of contextual justice in the same way as the international law rules against abuse of rights.

Proportionality can appear in international law doctrine as a technical rule of decision. For example, in the determination of conflicting claims to maritime zones, the length of a state's coastline is compared with the amount of ocean area it has acquired under a particular delimitation (usually derived by use of a mechanical rule of equidistance). This proportionality ratio can then be adjusted to achieve an equitable result as called for under customary international law and the 1982 UN Convention on the Law of the Sea.[25]

Proportionality, therefore, has pervaded many international law doctrines by acting (1) as an aspiration for situational justice and restraint, (2) as an expression of interest balancing, or (3) as a technical "double check" on other rules. These are different forms of fairness and equality, but each is more likely to find practical application than in any general articulation of these principles. By way of contrast, the value of humanity in international law is less amorphous and more limited.

Protection of human dignity as an objective of international law had its first expression in the laws of war. The origins of such concerns may stretch back to the biblical Near East or to post-Vedic India. Whether this value was first articulated as chivalry and a code of arms for medieval European elites or as an affirmative notion of protecting innocents from the horrors of combat hardly matters.[26] Nevertheless, attitudes of humanity were largely disregarded in the brutal religious wars in Europe (including the Thirty Years Wars) that saw the birth of modern nation-states as well as in the European conquest of colonial realms beginning in the sixteenth century. Limited conflict in Europe during the eighteenth century saw a partial renewal of these values, but the beginnings of total war in the Napoleonic period largely erased those gains.[27]

Only at the birth of the twentieth century—the bloodiest and most destructive in history—were principles of humanity expressly embraced as an objective of contemporary public international law. This transition has rightly been traced to the 1907 Hague Peace Conference and to the negotiation of a codification of the Laws and Customs of War on Land. While generally regarded as a successful project (despite the cataclysmic conflicts that followed), its significant impact was in recognizing the need for transforming the laws of war from a static body of law (intended to create a level playing field of mutual expectations for combatant nations) to a system of protections for innocent victims of conflict. This posed a problem for the delegates at the Hague, a difficulty elegantly solved by a Russian diplomat and international lawyer, F. F. Martens,[28] in the addition of a preambular clause to the treaty: "Until a more complete code of the laws of war can be drawn up, the High Contracting Parties deem it expedient to declare that, in cases not covered by the rules adopted by them, the inhabitants and belligerents remain under the protection and governance of the principles of the law of nations, derived from the usages established among civilized peoples, from the laws of humanity, and from the dictates of public conscience."

In the human rights revolution that followed World War II, the fundamental ideal of the Martens clause was validated. As has already been observed in chapter 1, the Allied powers had settled on counts of indictment against the German leadership that included "crimes against humanity."[29] Indeed, in the first World Court decision after the war, higher ideals of humanity were recognized. In the *Corfu Channel* case, the United Kingdom asserted that Albania had illegally mined certain straits used for international navigation. Even though no treaty was applicable and binding against Albania, the Court discerned "elementary considerations of humanity, even more exacting in peace than in war."[30]

After World War II, discussion of humanity as a value in international law shifted into a rights discourse, particularly concerned with the freedoms that individuals could claim even against their own governments. Not surprisingly, this has made quite incoherent much consideration of promoting human dignity as an objective of international law. Those who espouse views of rights as "negative liberties"—protecting individuals from the overweening power of government—have tended to ally themselves with the notion that the only relevant freedoms are the first-generation civil and political rights. By way of contrast, some legal thinkers view second-generation economic, social, and cultural rights as necessary demands or entitlements that individuals can legitimately claim of their government. When one confronts more abstract third-generation rights of a clean environment or peace, the difficulties multiply further. Finally, fourth-generation rights of groups and peoples—whether of indigenous populations or distinct ethnic or linguistic minorities—return the international law of human rights to a posture (common before World War II) that international law should be less liberal and more communitarian in its appreciation of the value of human dignity.

Notions of humanity have come to pervade international law doctrines in many areas and have certainly been perceived as the chief
alternative to an international system motivated by concerns for sovereignty and peace. Nevertheless, there are clearly many strands of
thinking about human dignity, and it cannot sensibly be regarded as
a monolithic value. It can be an adjunct to the principle of restraint
and peace. Human rights can be individual or group centered, liberal or communitarian. Protection of human dignity can be accomplished through creating a protective zone around the individual, free
from government interference. Alternatively, the full potential of human beings may only be realized through the fulfillment of effective
claims to economic, social, and cultural public goods.

Selection of any of these particular sticks in the bundle of ideas
we call humanity necessitates significant substantive choices for the
doctrinal content of international law. It is ironic that among the
values that compete at the moral-philosophic center of international
law, human rights are most contentiously disputed as being artifacts
either of false universalism or dangerous relativism. Rights discourse
is often seen as a surrogate for the transmission or refusal of Western
liberal and individualistic constructs. Human rights are also viewed
as necessary adjuncts for the propagation of certain economic or social systems. Far from being neutral in content, many doctrines and
rules that flow from particular human values are regarded as danger-
ously freighted.

All of this presages a newly emerging objective of international
law: representative democracy. Briefly introduced in chapter 3, a new
"democratic entitlement" as a value in international law carries with
it many pitfalls and opportunities. In one sense, it would appear to be
the ultimate form of Western cultural hegemony: imposing on the
rest of the world what is viewed by a small group of powerful nations
to be a characteristic and essential form of political governance. Seen
in this way, it would be a repudiation of other values in international
law, particularly sovereign equality. Until now, international law has
been studiously agnostic about the form of governments with which
states, as members of the international community, identify. This
neutrality was enshrined in the basic instruments dealing with the

rights and duties of states, with such pronouncements as "Every State has the right to independence . . . including the choice of its own form of government" and "Each State has the right to freely choose and develop its political, social, economic and cultural systems."[31]

Democracy as a distinct value in international law doctrines began to emerge in the mid–nineteenth century, partially as a product of the tumultuous period of the 1848 revolutions in Europe. One early manifestation was in the political-offense exception to extraditions of criminal suspects. This was originally conceived in the nineteenth century as a way for liberal democracies to avoid surrendering dissidents to authoritarian regimes. Once a political offense exception was recognized, efforts were made to limit it. For example, *attentat* clauses were included in some extradition treaties, providing that the murder of a head of state or head of government or of a member of such person's family was not to be regarded as a political offense.[32] In addition, some extradition treaties specifically exclude anarchists or those who "envisage the overthrow of the bases of all political organizations." Other conventions declined to extend the political offense exception to a common crime, even if it had a political motivation or purpose. These variations of the political-offense doctrine manifestly attempted to reflect sentiment about the permissible scope of political opposition in any society and the reactions of the international community to such legitimate opposition.

In a similar way, the act-of-state doctrine has been viewed as a surrogate for representative democratic values. The doctrine is a prudential rule of decision recognized in the United States and United Kingdom that disables judiciaries of one country from "sit[ting] in judgment on the acts of the government of another, done within its own territory."[33] An important corollary of this rule of abstention is that courts should defer only to the acts of governments that can fairly be characterized as representative democracies. Authoritarian and totalitarian regimes, according to this theory, should not receive such comity or a "margin of appreciation" from other nations' courts. Values of democracy have thus come to influence practical determinations of the competence and jurisdiction of domestic institutions.

Finally, discussions of democracy in international law are intimately connected with concerns about legitimacy and peace. Insofar as international law has states at its doctrinal center, representative democratic attributes can confer internal legitimacy on governments that not even the principle of self-determination could. If all national regimes were so buttressed, an international legal order that to a large degree is still state centered will likewise be augmented. Also to the extent that there is truth in the canard that democracies never go to war, this new value may promote the objective of international peace and security.

Discussions of a "new" democratic entitlement in international law may be pursuing another sort of ideological agenda. If values of humanity and human dignity are indeterminate—subject to a critique of moral relativism and Western cultural hegemony—then representative democracy may offer a partial, procedural antidote. Domestic determinations of social preferences and the allocation of public goods will be deemed more legitimate under international law standards if made by the institutions of representative democracy. In short, democracy as a value in international law provides a partial process solution to concerns that human rights obligations will dictate certain social and political outcomes. Of course, representative democracy does not solve problems arising from distinct and disenfranchised minorities in particular societies. Nor does it address consequent countermajoritarian difficulties. But the attitude may be that democracy serves an important role as an objective in international law in raising the legitimacy of communitarian forms of human rights.

Background Values: Necessity, Cooperation, and Rationality

There is thus a subtle interplay among fairness, humanity, and democracy as values in international law. The combination of these principles has offered a powerful philosophic alternative to state-centered objectives of peace, order, and sovereignty. Even so, that is still not the full extent of the picture of international law's constellation of objectives. Certain ideas defy easy categorization as either state-centered or human-centered values.

Among these anomalous motivations underlying the behavior of international actors is necessity. More than a Machiavellian raison d'état, necessity is the notion that states and other subjects of international law rules will seek to adjust their conduct to achieve legitimate but pragmatic ends. This does not always serve as a carte blanche for states to act in any way they desire, even if contrary to law. Indeed, necessity has served as an important restraining impulse for state behavior.[34]

This has certainly been seen in the context of war and conflict. Self-defense, for example, has always been recognized in custom as a permissible basis for initiating armed hostilities. The question was whether a state could, in its sole judgment, decide that it was justified in initiating armed force. In the famous *Caroline* incident, the United States conceded that Great Britain had been entitled to use force and invade part of New York in 1837 to disrupt a group of rebels who were planning on attacking Canada. Secretary of State Daniel Webster observed that an anticipatory reaction is permissible in those situations where the "necessity of that self-defense is instant, overwhelming, and leaving no choice of means and no moment for deliberation."[35] In this diplomatic correspondence, the British government agreed that it was also incumbent upon itself to show that its armed response was proportional to the threat it perceived and the necessity of the situation. These conditions of imminence and proportionality remain important background rules for use of force in self-defense under the UN Charter system. Rhetoric of imminence and necessity was likewise employed by the United States as part of its justification for the quarantine of Cuba in 1962 and its invasions of Grenada and Panama in the 1990s. In less momentous circumstances, necessity provides the essential guiding principle for forced confiscations of neutral vessels by belligerents[36] and the practice of hot pursuit on the high seas.[37]

For every instance of necessity being used as a ground to extend the freedom of action of international actors, there are occasions where it is used to restrain behavior. When Francis Lieber in 1863 drafted the first fully articulated code for the laws of war,[38] he viewed necessity as a significant check on a belligerent's right to engage in whatever military strategy, operations, or tactics it chose. Necessity has thus become something that nations must justify. When combined with principles of proportionality (discussed above in the context of fairness), necessity has most often been seen as a surrogate for restraint, objectivity, and moderation in the content of international law rules.

If necessity operates as a cautionary principle on the outer margins of state conduct, the value of cooperation reflects progressive and functional impulses within the interstices of the system. Not merely a means to peaceful coexistence between international actors, functional cooperation within the international community has become its own goal, its own objective. Doctrines and rules of international law have thus been developed that specifically advance an agenda of world order and integration along a broad spectrum of activities.

Many of these have arisen in the context of growing trade and economic interdependence among nations. Viewing trade relations among states as reflective of comparative advantage—a growing pie that benefits all participants—is certainly better than the mercantilistic zero-sum game that was common in thinking until the mid–twentieth century. Finally, functional cooperation is viewed as a necessity—common problems, resources, and opportunities confront the entire international community and need to be addressed in a uniform and harmonious fashion.[39] No nation can, for example, avoid the consequences of ozone depletion or global depression.

Economic interdependence has always had its detractors, and international law has been no exception in this regard. Economic cooperation has become a central issue of foreign policy for states. In a similar way, discussions of environmental protection for nations have none too subtly been converted into disquisitions on "environmental security." By elevating questions of economic and environmental interdependence to the level of national security raises the stakes in the discourse and places a greater premium on the selection of appropriate rules that allocate economic power and entitlements.

Technology and culture have always figured at the center of progress narratives, and again, international law has followed that larger trend. The increasing pace of technological development as an agent of global integration has been well remarked. Likewise, the feared homogenization of global culture is seen as an inevitable by-product of relentless technological and social forces. All of these elements of globalization contribute today to a deep ambivalence to what was regarded even a decade ago as a central virtue of international legal order.

Nevertheless, functional cooperation remains a vital objective of international law rules and processes. Counterpoised with a communitarian vision of peaceful and productive relations is a brand-new value of rationality in international law. Just as cooperation seems to be globalism's reformulation of peace, rationality would appear merely to be a rehash of fairness as a value in international law. As is often the case, appearances can be misleading.

Rationality recognizes that the international community operates in conditions of what John Rawls would call "moderate scarcity"[40] and thus requires a fair allocation of those resources. Yet the functionalist vision of limitless progress and growth is disputed in a rationally bounded international community. Indeed, the central metaphor for the rational management of international public goods and common resources is not a progress narrative at all: it is the dark tale of the Prisoner's Dilemma.[41] This sour mood is barely lightened by the application of the Coase Theorem, which postulates that members of a community engaged in a dispute involving conflicting property rights can negotiate the most economically advantageous and efficient solution by themselves. International actors can thereby bypass altogether the legal and judicial apparatus provided that two conditions exist: (1) the transaction costs associated with negotiations are zero and (2) the legal rights and obligations of the parties are clearly established.[42] While functionalists espousing values of cooperation foresee the creation of global regulatory systems beyond mere framework instruments, those who see rationality through the lens of economics are rather less sanguine.[43]

Increasingly, though, international law rules are being influenced by values of rationality. In just one branch of the discipline, international environmental law, a veritable complex of doctrines have been fashioned around this objective. The "polluter pays" principle was an explicit recognition that environmental contamination was a type of externality that one nation could impose on another. The purpose of international law was thus to remove that artificial and unfair burdening. A duty to inform and consult was seen as a way to increase transparency and lower transaction costs in international environmental negotiations.[44] Finally, in planning activities that might have an environmental impact, the question arises about how to factor uncertainty into this process and about the propriety of using cost-benefit analysis. If a planner is not sure whether a certain activity might be dangerous to the environment, should it be allowed to go forward while hoping for the best? A number of international environmental instruments promote the use of the precautionary principle (or its less rigorous counterpart, the precautionary approach),[45] which requires that when in doubt, protective concerns should prevail and permission for the activity should be denied.

Framed as I have done so here, neither necessity nor cooperation nor rationality tends toward imposing a particular political or social ideology on the content of international law rules. Janus-faced, these values have a modern, abstract appeal that might help to explain why many international actors seem to be preferring them to the older core values of peace and sovereignty and their newer but heavily freighted competing concerns of fairness, humanity, and democracy. The structure of international law discourse is at stake in this debate about international law values. It is ironic that the best illustration of which values really matter in international law comes not through neutral and dispassionate discussion of the merits of these objectives but, rather, through the collision of these values as reflected in particular doctrines.

RECONCILING CONFLICT THROUGH PARADOXES

Thinking about the paradoxes inherent in international law values is certainly important. I must say at the outset that one can overplay this inquiry into an absurdly critical exercise of characterizing all international law rules as internally incoherent, ideologically charged with meaning, or doctrinally inconsistent. The truth is that most sets of international law rules are reasonably influenced by one or more of the values (or clusters of objectives) I have described above but are hardly riven with incongruities. Where paradoxes seem to rise to the surface of important international law doctrines, it is important to notice them.

In my map of the various objectives that underlie international law doctrines, it would be easy to imagine that the most likely vectors of conflict would be between the demarcated domains. Tradition-bound values of order, peace, and sovereignty would, under this view, clash with competing "new" objectives of humanity, fairness, and democracy. The background goals of necessity, cooperation, and rationality would add to the mix by engaging in a game of shifting alliances—periodically supporting one side or the other in this metaphoric battle for the discipline's heart and soul.

An example of a paradox of this sort goes to the issue of rules for determining state identity. In my discussion of the subjects and objects of international law in chapter 4, I referred to the competing declaratory and constitutive theories of recognition of states. Those who believe recognition by other states is a requisite, or constitutive, of statehood clearly embrace attitudes reflective of peace and cooperation in international affairs. Of what possible use is the concept of statehood if it cannot lead to functional cooperation? If a dispute about recognition of states arises in the context of an insurgent and separatist movement forming a new nation at the expense of an existing one, values of peace and order are implicated. If a democratic government is overthrown by illegal means, another nation's decision to recognize the new regime may be influenced by fears of promoting authoritarian juntas.

At the other extreme, declaratory theories of state recognition that hold that statehood is purely objective—an entity has the criteria of being a state or it does not—seem to be less freighted with values. That is not the case: the values are just different. Necessity, sovereignty, and order are embraced when the decision is made to recognize a state or government that has been formed de facto by means that would offend other international law objectives.

In a similar vein, different modes for interpreting treaties (considered in chapter 3) carry with them strikingly different values. A teleological approach, which emphasizes the identification of an essential object and purpose for an agreement and the full effectuation of that purpose, manifestly espouses values of necessity, cooperation, and peace in international relations. It is better, under this view, to give a treaty regime full effect (even in the absence of unambiguous state consent) than to run the risk that the regime will fail at the expense of peaceful relations. Any rule—even a bad rule—is better than no rule.

By contrast, a restrictive rule of interpretation, one gracious to state sovereignty and to the order and expectations of the parties, may well produce a *non liquet*. As the World Court has noted, "When States make statements by which their freedom of action is to be limited, a restrictive interpretation is to be called for,"[46] and "if the wording of a treaty provision is not clear, in choosing between several admissible interpretations, the one which involves the minimum of obligations for the parties should be adopted."[47] These statements envision an international order in which the participants' sovereignty and freedom of action are paramount. To the extent that treaty regimes can cabin that discretion, they should be construed narrowly. The very exercise of treaty interpretation thus raises doubts about the nature of sovereignty and cooperation in international affairs.

The examples just drawn from recognition doctrine and treaty construction illustrate conflicts between sovereignty and necessity, order and cooperation. Traditional international law concerns appear to be in conflict, not alliance, with new background principles. So far left out of the picture are the competing values of fairness, humanity, and democracy, yet close examination of these ideals indicates that they can be internally contradictory.

This chapter has already mentioned fourth-generation human rights of groups and peoples. Aside from being in tension with a traditional, liberal formulation of individual rights as being "negative" liberties from undue government interference, group rights pose a different—and more fundamental—challenge to international law values. The rights of discrete and insular communities could well conflict with principles of representative democracy. This has been particularly evident in disputes surrounding distinct language minorities in certain political cultures. Language separatism—whether in Quebec or Belgium or Spain—has posed special challenges in reconciling international law values of humanity and democracy.[48]

Perhaps even more contentious have been concerns about the rights of indigenous peoples.[49] This subject touches on a point of great shame for international law doctrine. To the extent that international legal theory of the sixteenth and seventeenth centuries justified the treatment of native peoples in the Americas, Africa, and Asia as less than human and opined that their lands were forfeited to conquering European powers as a *res nullius*, international law carries a heavy moral burden. The battle today is not over any residual role of power or sovereignty justifications for the suppression of the aspirations of native peoples. Rather, the questions arise as to the proper restitution to be made to these groups as well as the appropriate protection that should be afforded to these peoples' unique ways of life. These disputes tend to conflate values of human dignity, democracy, and equality.

The international law of state responsibility has embedded within it a comparable paradox, one that has challenged the legitimacy of this area of international law and greatly hampered its evolution.[50] An individual who lives in a foreign country is expected to abide by the laws of the host state, yet when that person is injured by the host government, she is free to seek diplomatic protection from her state of nationality. Foreigners thus appear to have the best of both worlds: they expect to travel and conduct business in other countries on conditions of equality, but when adverse events occur, they are free to seek their own nation's protection. This sense of unfair advantage to persons living in another country is why the international law of state responsibility has been criticized as an instrument of coercion in the hands of nations engaging in new forms of economic imperialism.

Central to this debate are two competing visions of how a nation should treat foreigners living in its midst. One view is that a host government should, within recognized limits, treat aliens in the same way as it would treat its own nationals. This is the principle of equality. The other view is that there is an international minimum standard of treatment, a threshold below which no "civilized" nation should drop. These two ideals have collided in spectacular fashion, as in the case of Harry Roberts. Roberts was a U.S. citizen who was arrested in Mexico on charges of armed robbery. He was thrown into a Mexican jail for eighteen months awaiting trial. Roberts was confined in a small cell with about thirty-five other prisoners. The United States argued before a special claims commission, established to resolve disputes with Mexico, that the conditions of Roberts's incarceration violated Mexico's international responsibilities. Mexico rejoined that Roberts was entitled to the treatment afforded Mexican nationals: Mexican jails were overcrowded, but Roberts had not been singled out for bad treatment. The General Claims Commission rejected this argument, holding that Mexico had violated the international law of state responsibility. Roberts's treatment was depressingly substandard, and the commission articulated a universal test of "whether aliens are treated in accordance with ordinary standards of civilization."[51]

Fairness and humanity have thus appeared to conflict in some international law doctrines, even though both of these values have been properly associated with new alternatives to central paradigms of sovereignty, peace, and order. Nor are new background principles immune from this mutual animosity. While rationality has been seen as a central component of many new areas of international legal regulation, particularly of the global commons and environment, this has not gone unchallenged.

Common resources lead to management disputes, precisely because the assets are held in common. Known as the "tragedy of the commons," this is the observation that things owned by everyone (say, a village green or mutual fishery) are conserved by no one.[52] No single actor has an incentive to forswear adding extra sheep to graze on the green (and thus protect the grass) or to halt overfishing. Under this theory, common resources are inevitably degraded and destroyed over time. There appear to be only two alternatives to this tragedy: divide up the resources (and thus grant individual property interests in the asset) or depend on explicit institutions and rules to manage it. International law has relied on variants of partition and management strategies for many international common resources. Sometimes these approaches are mutually contradictory and incoherent. Rationality in managing a common resource can thus conflict with fundamental fairness or equality.

Rationality and cooperation can also come into bitter conflict. One example of this is the recognition that the most potent tool for protection of the entire environment is linking enforcement mechanisms to the global trading order. The first pathbreaking international instrument to do this was the 1973 Convention on International Trade in Endangered Species (CITES).[53] CITES's solution to the problem of rampant poaching of endangered animals and harvesting of rare plants was also economic—remove incentives for profit by eliminating the trade in these items.

CITES has been hailed as an international law success story, and, indeed, it has managed to control some of the worst forms of abuse. Poaching of African elephants, for example, has dropped because the trade of ivory, irrespective of source, has been banned. This has caused problems, though, for the handful of countries that manage elephant herds by granting proprietary rights in the resource, a sort of "partition" model. Villages that had been conserving herds and expecting the proceeds from sales of ivory harvested from animals that die of natural causes have been bitterly disappointed. In any event, CITES's trade strategy for environmental protection has been replicated in a vast network of agreements, ranging in subjects from sales of tropical timber to high seas fish stocks.

Today at least, the global trade regime has been bitterly criticized by environmental advocates who maintain that it unnecessarily punishes the unilateral acts of environmentally progressive nations. When the United States imposed import restrictions on tuna caught by foreign fishermen with insufficient regard for the safety of dolphins (which swim with tuna and are often killed when nets are thrown), the affected nations sought relief before the institutions of the General Agreement on Tariffs and Trade (GATT) and, later, the World Trade Organization (WTO). In a series of decisions,[54] GATT-WTO panels have ruled that nations may not unilaterally impose trade restrictions on tuna caught with dolphin (or shrimp caught with turtles) or unreasonably require heightened environmental protection as a condition for trading in their markets (such as rules against certain fuel additives or hormones in beef). The difficulty is that much recent international environmental lawmaking has been made by progressive states, with the international community following behind. WTO's requirement that environmental restrictions on trade can only be imposed multilaterally may delay some needed innovations. However, it will ensure that once consensus is reached, effective international enforcement through global trade disciplines will be available.

Rationality—as a surrogate for progress in the development of international law norms—can thus be seen to conflict with principles of cooperation, which tend to promote lowest-common-denominator diplomacy and "race to the bottom" economics.[55] The trade-environment conflict is one reflection of this paradox. Likewise, rational outcomes are not necessarily fair. Questions of global distributive justice may well be on a collision course with other international law objectives. Indeed, some UN bodies have already observed that treaty protections granted for intellectual property rights (such as patents on seed varietals or copyrights on folklore produced by indigenous peoples) directly conflict with human rights to food, health, cultural identity, and scientific progress.[56]

I save for last the most profound paradox in international law's goals. While certainly generating intellectual curiosity (and a substantial scholarly literature), the conflicts I have so far described tend to implicate either marginal doctrinal concerns or expected value choices. None of these seem to debilitate international law or deny it any essential vigor. Some of these paradoxes we can readily live with and embrace, just as many other legal systems have accepted similar disparate results in the pursuit of multiple objectives. Some of them, however, push the limits of any system's tolerance for contradiction.

A very real collision between a world public order based on human rights and one premised on state sovereignty arises with the phenomenon of humanitarian interventions.[57] A humanitarian intervention occurs when one nation (or a group) unilaterally invades another country to alleviate or stop human rights abuses by that government. A number of publicists have suggested that if the human rights crisis is truly serious and if the intervening state is limited in its objectives in removing the abusing government from power, then humanitarian intervention might be legitimate under international law. Other commentators, and quite a few states, have asserted, however, that humanitarian intervention could become a pretext for continued meddling in the affairs of nations, particularly those in the developing world. In one disputed doctrine we have a central dilemma in international relations: What matters more, state-centered objectives (peace, order, sovereignty) or values of human dignity?

This is not an abstract or hypothetical concern. Humanitarian intervention is becoming an increasingly used option in international affairs. Whether it was Vietnam's invasion of Cambodia in the 1970s, or Tanzania's 1979 effort to oust Idi Amin in Uganda, or (most recently) NATO's military action to expel marauding Serb forces from Kosovo, humanitarian interventions have captured the headlines and become a central issue of the foreign policies of many nations, Great Powers and small countries alike.

How this ultimate enforcement mechanism of human rights norms (the physical invasion of the offending state and the removal of an abusive government) can be reconciled with other international law rules promoting international peace and security is perhaps an unsolvable riddle in international law today. It remains to be seen whether a doctrine of humanitarian intervention can be substantively defined (exactly how bad does the human rights situation have to be to warrant invasion?), be effectively limited to UN political action, and produce favorable human rights conditions.

Nor have attempts to reconcile competing considerations for humanitarian intervention been successful. It may be facile to say that the ultimate human right is peace. This is sometimes suggested as a way of critiquing a too permissive doctrine of humanitarian intervention. Pretextual invasions will lead to greater human suffering in the aggregate. Likewise, to argue that the interests of state sovereignty

and legitimacy are served by nations invading their neighbors to re-
store respect for human rights may miss the mark. Limiting humanitarian interventions to the collective decision making of the UN
merely transfers the problem of legitimacy and agency to an international institution that may be less competent to shoulder it than
some countries. However one broadens or narrows the doctrine, it is
not really possible to make it serve the interests both of sovereignty
and of humanity.

The riddle of humanitarian intervention lies at the center of international law discourse. It may reflect a handful of true value conflicts in the discipline, and while it would be easy to characterize
the lines of division in expected ways (positivist versus naturalist
sources; state-centered versus human values), the reality is far more
complex and unsettling. The lines of paradox in values of international law cut across expected frontiers. Some of the conflicts do
exhibit tendencies of exacerbating debates between old and new objectives, but others feature battles between values within ostensibly
common groupings.

The real message here is that the sheer multiplicity of values is itself the problem. Without a central, consensual goal and purpose for
international law rules, one would expect conflict to arise. Although
(as I indicated previously) too much can be made of these paradoxes,
they do define sharply the sets of successive underlying values undergirding international law rules.

What is perhaps most surprising is that, notwithstanding these apparent tensions, international law is still perceived to be morally neutral in the content of its rules. When particular international law doctrines are subject to withering critique by certain actors, it is rarely
because of philosophic bias. The developing world may still advance
rules of distributional justice emphasizing notions of fairness and
equality. Human rights campaigners may seek changes in national
practices that reflect principles of humanity and democracy. International environmental advocates articulate arguments in the idiom of
rationality, while global businesses employ the argot of cooperation
and progress. States, still at the center of interests that is international

relations, can maintain an agenda that includes all of these elements plus a number of others that nourish states' legitimacy and expectations.

Despite these multivalent interests and values—or perhaps because of them—the international community tolerates divergent ideologies in the fashioning of international law rules. Values perhaps do not drive the system as much as one might think. The permissible scope of international law norms is constrained less by some grand teleology than by the background noise that constitutes the international legal system. The identity of actors, the ways in which they make law, the sources of obligation, and the techniques for legal process may all matter a great deal more than some ultimate objective.

The legitimacy of international law is only rarely staked on its values. Historically, self-conscious reflection on international law's goals has worked important changes in sources, processes, and doctrines only in times of profound transformation. These periods have included the Westphalian moment and the birth of modern nation-states, the period of high positivism in the late nineteenth and early twentieth centuries, World War II and the human rights revolution, and today's move towards globalism. At other times of quiescence and tradition, values have simply been taken for granted.

The neutrality, coherence, and sophistication of the international legal system have thus been determined more by the relative balance of formalism and pragmatism in the construction of actual international law rules. In addition, the demarcation of the outer boundaries of the system has mattered more than the internal guideposts of material objectives. I will turn next to these considerations.

7 Confines

One of the characteristic features of international law is that it is tightly constricted. Perhaps unique among modern, secular legal systems, international law is conceptualized and defined as much by what is excluded from its remit and mandate as by what is embraced by the permissible scope of its regulations. Although I have spoken of the huge increase within the past century of the legitimate topics of international law rules, one should not be fooled into thinking that international law is boundless in its conception.

Indeed, the realm of international law is constrained by no fewer than three frontiers. The first (and perhaps most obvious) restraint on the range of international law processes and doctrines is national or municipal law, the domain of protected domesticity for state members of the international community. Typically, international law is conceived as being a tiny zone in which the internal law of states does not apply. In this vision, international law and internal law are two mutually exclusive circles in a Venn diagram of power and authority.

It is not just spatially that international law is restrained. A second frontier for international law has variously shifted over time, like a meandering river. Within international law there has always been a division between public and private subjects: a public realm of relations between states and a private zone for transactions between substate actors (particularly individuals and businesses). At times, this division has been sharp: the frontier river has been too wide to ford, and the effect has been to constrict the body of rules that we associate with public international law. On other occasions (such as the present), the river has amounted to a little more than a shallow stream, and there has been a gradual merger of the two aspects of the discipline.

The last frontier for international law can also be characterized as a check on the acceptable scope of its subject matter. It actually may reflect far deeper limitations. The division between law and politics has, in many respects, been historically the most relevant demarcation of international law's domain. There has always been a sense that it is inappropriate—and, indeed, even self-destructive—for international law rules to venture too far in purporting to regulate certain behaviors of international actors that are fundamentally driven by diplomatic and power calculations.

Taken together, these frontiers fundamentally define international law, at least by negative implication. Understanding how the discipline is compelled to keep out of various kinds of issues and disputes is certainly crucial to characterizing its nature and scope.

INTERNATIONAL AND DOMESTIC LAW

The relationship between domestic law (sometimes called municipal law in European nations) and international law is subtle and complex. First, it needs to be borne in mind that international law is substantially influenced by domestic law. That predisposition might be manifested by the elevation of general principles of national law recognized by civilized nations as a source of international legal obligation. Precise rules of domestic law may be interpreted and applied by international tribunals in disputes between states. In addition, as already observed in chapter 1, many international law rules emulate doctrinal pockets from domestic law. In other words, the relationship between international law and domestic law is a two-way street. International law's use of municipal law is, however, constrained by a number of important principles.

The first of these is that a state typically may not (with only very few exceptions) invoke a provision of national law as the basis for refusing to perform an international legal obligation. As U.S. Secretary of State Bayard observed in 1887, "if a Government could set up its own municipal laws as the final test of its international rights and obligations, then the rules of international law would be but the shadow of a name and would afford no protection either to States or individuals."[1] Many international tribunals have emphatically rejected litigant states' arguments that their domestic laws somehow trump international law.[2] Many international courts have likewise declined to follow an "authoritative" interpretation of a custom or treaty made by one of the disputants (and supported by a decision of a domestic court), preferring to independently construe the practice or agreement.

The second important principle governing the role of domestic law in international law is that international tribunals are free to apply and interpret national law as relevant to the international disputes that come before them. For example, the World Court in the *Brazilian Loans* case[3] was obliged to rule on that nation's default on certain loans that were supposed to be repaid in French francs. A significant question was the meaning and effect of French legislation governing the payment of debts in gold or gold value. (The case arose just before the global depression, and many countries were taking their currencies off a gold standard, which obviously affected the value of any debt repayments.) The PCIJ observed that to the extent the loan agreement with Brazil made French law binding on this point, the Court was obliged to ascertain what that law was. Obviously, an international tribunal will reject a ruling of a domestic court if it is self-serving, fraudulent, or erroneous.

It must be kept in mind that the international legal system really is indifferent as to how international legal obligations are enforced in municipal law, provided they are effectively implemented. There has long been a debate about the incorporation of international law into domestic law. The two sides in this polemic have been given the unfortunate names of monists and dualists.[4] Reduced to its essentials, monism is the idea that international law and domestic law are parts of the same legal system, but international law is higher in prescriptive value than national law. Dualism is the position that international law and municipal law are separate and distinct legal systems that operate on different levels, and international law must be incorporated or transformed before it can be enforced in national law.[5]

Although the monism-dualism argument is a favorite topic of conversation among international law academics, it is vital to understand the significance—and limits—of this discussion. For starters, this debate matters only on the domestic law plane. International law simply does not care how a rule of international law is applied in internal law. International law just assumes that all international obligations are carried out in good faith and that state responsibility attaches for the failure to observe a rule of custom or treaty.[6] The monism-dualism divide matters only for a particular nation's domestic housekeeping for recognizing and applying international law rules.

As an example of this, international law recognizes only a handful of instances where a state may rely on its internal law as a basis for refusing to comply with an ostensible international law obligation. Article 46 of the VCLT provides that when one party's ratification of an agreement has been made in a way that violates its domestic constitutional law, and such violation was manifest to the other party or parties, the treaty is null and void. In a sense, this exception proves the rule that states may not rely on their own national constitutions as a way to evade international legal obligations.[7] Or, as the World Court observed, "it is a generally accepted principle of international law that in the relations between powers who are contracting parties to a treaty, the provisions of municipal law cannot prevail over those of the treaty."[8]

Although the precise modalities by which particular domestic legal systems incorporate international legal rules (whether by treaty or custom) is beyond the scope of this chapter, what is certainly relevant here is the manner and extent to which international law defers to forms of domestic decision making. Despite obvious pronouncements that states may not depend on internal law as a ground for outright noncompliance with international norms, the reality is that international law doctrines are routinely structured to afford substantial consideration to the legal effects of domestic law.

Deference in international law rules is often expressed in the argot of comity. Comity was mentioned in a slightly different context in the earlier discussion about the formation of customary international law (in chapter 2). In that setting, comity was the idea that states may engage in a particular course of conduct, but not out of a sense of legal obligation. Nations may thus engage in a practice out of courtesy or respect for their neighbors or partners in the international community. In the circumstances of conflicting claims of state jurisdiction and power, comity means more than mere courtesy and goodwill. As the U.S. Supreme Court observed in the 1895 *Hilton v. Guyot* decision, "it is the recognition which one nation allows within its territory of the legislative, executive, or judicial acts of another nation, having due regard both to international duty and convenience, and to the rights of its own citizens or of other persons who are under the protection of its laws."[9]

In the wider ambit of international law's engagement with domestic law, comity is more often expressed as a margin of appreciation that international tribunals extend to various forms of domestic decision making. Especially in a human rights context, international institutions will defer to positions taken by national governments, even if they superficially appear at odds with international norms. The well-respected European Court of Human Rights has on more than one occasion vindicated a respondent state's defense that it took appropriate actions affecting the freedom or property of individuals, even in arguable contravention of the European Convention on Human Rights.[10] Derogations of human rights norms are thus permissible within a degree of necessity and proportionality.

International institutions are not, however, unreflectively deferential to the legal consequences of domestic acts. Just one example of some cynicism is to be found in ICJ's decision in the *Nottebohm* case.[11] Frederic Nottebohm was born a German national in 1881, but he lived most of his life in Guatemala, becoming one of the nation's largest landowners and acquiring a vast fortune. Nottebohm was a savvy observer of international affairs. In the 1930s, after Hitler's rise to power, Nottebohm realized that Germany would soon be embroiled in a war that would inevitably draw the United States and the Western Hemisphere into the conflict. Nottebohm certainly did not want to be considered a German national and thus an enemy alien in the event that Guatemala declared war on Germany.

As a result, Nottebohm made a plan. At the invitation of his brother, who lived in the tiny—and traditionally neutral—principality of Liechtenstein, Nottebohm became a citizen of that country in 1939. Regrettably, this proved too clever by half. Nottebohm had correctly predicted the chain of events that led the United States and Guatemala into war with Germany in 1941, but he had not counted on the fact that the United States and Guatemala would simply refuse to recognize his Liechtenstein nationality. In the end, his worst fears were realized: Guatemala confiscated his properties.

Liechtenstein sought later to bring a claim on Nottebohm's behalf on principles of state responsibility and diplomatic protection. Yet the World Court refused, ruling that countries did not have complete discretion in granting nationality, and if certain limits were exceeded, other countries were not obliged to respect the grant of nationality. More specifically, the Court said that there must be a "real and effective" relationship between an individual and his state of citizenship, a "genuine link."[12] The Court found as a factual matter that Nottebohm's links with Liechtenstein were too tenuous: he had never really resided in the principality, and his connections were ephemeral. The Court intimated that Nottebohm had duped Liechtenstein into participating in a clever fraud, and Guatemala was not under an international duty to respect it.

Nationality decisions would normally be committed to the sound discretion of domestic laws and institutions. The World Court, ruling in an advisory opinion in the 1920s, indicated that such matters would normally be "within [a] reserved domain" of internal law, subject only to the express treaty obligations a state might undertake toward other countries.[13] In this way, international tribunals treat nationality determinations in much the same way as other state regulatory actions. The *Nottebohm* decision is typical in that it prescribes a substantive threshold that such action must satisfy. If it does—as in the instance of at least a modicum of connection between an individual and state of nationality—then international institutions will otherwise respect it. International law thus sets a very high standard of review for domestic rulings and will only overrule them if they are, in essence, clearly erroneous or manifestly unjust.

Another avenue by which international law keeps out of domestic decision making is through forms of procedural abstention. The best example of this is probably the exhaustion-of-local-remedies rule in the law of diplomatic protection. This is premised on the notion that injured aliens should seek redress from local courts before seeking satisfaction through their own government's espousal of the claim under international law. If a claimant has failed to exhaust local remedies offered by the respondent state, the claim is barred.[14] There are, however, reasonable exceptions to this rule. Claimants are under no obligation to pursue local remedies if to do so would be clearly futile or if the remedies offered are not adequate and effective for relief.[15] The World Court has consistently held over the past fifty years that the rule of exhaustion of local remedies remains alive and well, and unless the requirement has been explicitly disavowed by treaty, the Court will render a claim inadmissible.[16] Nevertheless, the Court recently noted in the *Elettronica Sicula* case[17] that the burden of proof was on the state wishing to show that local remedies had not been exhausted. In that case, Italy was obliged to show that an American company had failed to use fully the remedies afforded by Italian courts. The Court then ruled that Italy had not made that showing.

The exhaustion requirement has quite properly been viewed as a means of limiting individuals' direct access for relief before international institutions. It certainly has been applied consistently in diplomatic protection and human rights contexts. It has not, however, been invoked in situations where treaty rights are being directly litigated as between state parties in their own right (not on behalf of nationals). The exhaustion requirement may also find a reciprocal in the customary international law rule that countries will afford foreign states and their officials immunities in their own tribunals. State immunities certainly are a way that the division between international law and domestic law is maintained and preserved. The privileges and immunities of diplomatic and consular personnel are one obvious illustration of this. Even more pertinently, views about foreign sovereign immunity have evolved as conceptions of the role of state institutions and governments in international relations have also changed, especially over the past two centuries.[18] Attitudes about the immunities of states in foreign courts have also been altered as domestic legal systems have modified the immunities given to their own sovereigns and governments in their own tribunals.

Conceptions of state immunity originally were rather weak. In the seventeenth and eighteenth centuries it would have been extravagant to suggest that monarchs and governments enjoyed blanket immunity from suit in their own nation's courts or in the tribunals of foreign nations. In the early nineteenth century, a significant sovereign immunity revolution occurred, and countries throughout the world began to extend wide immunities from suit to various forms of government institutions. This resulted in the extension of absolute immunity to foreign governments in the courts of various countries,[19] a result that was not really challenged until the mid–twentieth century.

Beginning after World War II, when the role and conception of the state was changing, absolute sovereign immunity came under intense attack. In response to many nations' having widespread and lucrative commercial operations, international law doctrine was required to rethink foreign sovereign immunities. Government-owned mines, transport, and communications; state trading and marketing arms; and national banks and insurance companies were but a few examples of this trend. Obviously, a doctrine of absolute foreign sovereign immunity that protected such government-owned commercial entities from lawsuits for breach of contract or other remedies was profoundly distortive in the competitive marketplace. European courts began to adopt a restrictive form of foreign sovereign immunity that did not immunize the commercial activities of foreign governments.[20] The United States began to move toward this position with the 1952 issuance of a State Department opinion on this subject, known as the Tate Letter.[21] The letter pragmatically concluded that "the Department feels that the widespread and increasing practice of governments of engaging in commercial activities makes necessary a practice which will enable persons doing business with them to have their rights determined in the courts." Within a few decades, state practice—as largely reflected in the views of foreign ministries and domestic tribunals around the world—had shifted to a theory of restrictive immunity for foreign sovereigns that carved out extensive exceptions to claims of immunization from proceedings in other nations' courts.

Immunity doctrines were clearly an important way to prevent the deflection of international disputes into domestic law. Internal law was thus excluded from a central preserve of the law of nations. Ironically, as states, businesses, and individuals became less distinctive in their functions and activities, the level of protection that has been afforded to states in domestic courts has decreased. If the exhaustion requirement keeps international tribunals out of private disputes between individuals and governments, domestic courts have compensated by asserting control over such matters, especially when they have a commercial character.

That leaves the concept of jurisdiction as the central doctrinal mechanism for controlling the relationship between international and domestic domains. It has been considered an article of faith that the competence of international institutions is limited. In contrast, states enjoy a plenitude of authority and are able to freely compete with each other for control of various transactions, relationships, and occurrences having legal consequences.[22]

There is a central dilemma lurking here in matters involving conflicting jurisdictional claims made by states. It arises from the PCIJ's 1927 decision in the *Lotus* case.[23] That controversy, already discussed in chapter 3 in the context of the formation of customary international law, featured France's challenge of Turkey's assertion of criminal jurisdiction over a French national who committed negligent homicide on a French ship on the high seas that injured or killed a number of Turkish nationals. The World Court ruled in that case that France bore the burden of showing that Turkey's exercise of jurisdiction violated international law. This burden allocation was decisive in that case: France could not show a prevailing customary international law that opposed Turkey's exercise of criminal jurisdiction on those facts.

What has come to be called the *Lotus* presumption has exerted a strong influence on the international law of jurisdiction. Under this rule, states are free to assert their jurisdictional competences to the absolute limit that international law allows. When in doubt, this presumption counsels, states are able to insist on their jurisdiction over a particular individual, matter, or transaction. In short, international law is a permissive system when it comes to state jurisdiction: everything is permitted, save that which is expressly—and unambiguously—rejected. Or, as Judge Loder feared in his dissent in the case, "every door is open unless it is closed by treaty or custom."[24]

It does not take much imagination, however, to realize that the *Lotus* presumption and its underlying assumptions about international law and relations can cause very real mischief. If states are atomistic bodies entitled to assert their jurisdiction to the notional limit that international law allows, then conflict will be rife. What is worse, under such a system, States will be obliged to make aggressive and contentious assertions of jurisdiction for fear that failing to do so will constitute some sort of acquiescence or acceptance of another nation's claim of authority. For these reasons, international law has sought to soften the effects of the *Lotus* presumption in a variety of ways.

The most popular of these is to assert that even when a state has a legitimate ground for asserting the effect of its domestic laws on foreign individuals and events, "a state may not exercise jurisdiction to prescribe law with respect to a person or activity having connection with another state when the exercise of such jurisdiction is unreasonable."[25] This challenges the *Lotus* presumption and replaces a muscular system of aggressive assertions of jurisdiction with an approach that requires that any claim of prescriptive jurisdiction satisfy a test of reasonability.[26]

It seems a traditional conception of international law that faithfully and consistently keeps out of the internal affairs of its constituents may well be an artifact of a bygone age. That this rule of abstention has been constitutionalized in various fundamental instruments of international relations may simply be irrelevant. The provision of article 15 of the League of Nations Covenant that barred the organization from ruling on a "matter which by international law is solely within the domestic jurisdiction of [a] party" was regarded as a critical reason for that organization's failure. Even though substantially the same language was incorporated into article 2(7) of the

UN Charter, it was with the crucial caveat that the "domestic jurisdiction" exclusion did not affect the organization's power to take
enforcement actions against states that had breached the peace or
otherwise threatened international peace and security. Under both
the Covenant and Charter, international law has the *compétence
de compétence* to determine its own boundaries with domestic law.
Within the institutional culture of the UN, the "domestic jurisdiction" exclusion is now regarded as a dead letter.[27]

Globalization is certainly accelerating this trend to further blur the
edges of international and domestic domains. The dualist truism that
international law is separate and distinct from domestic law—a position especially embraced by Anglo-American jurisdictions—seems
under withering attack. The practical adoption of human rights instruments that regulate government conduct toward citizens is one
example, with Great Britain having just effectively implemented the
European Convention on Human Rights as its written bill of rights.
Alternatively, economic regimes such as the WTO, NAFTA, and European Union are dissolving sovereignty to an extent not seen in centuries.

International law thus seems poised on a knife edge in determining its relationship with the internal laws of its state constituents.
International tribunals and institutions continue to show a high degree of deference to domestic decision making, even while formal
doctrines barring these institutions from reviewing such matters are
ignored. Jurisdictional boundaries between the two zones are constantly being transgressed from each side. Domestic courts are asserting competence over disputes that would have, as little as a generation ago, been assigned for resolution to international mechanisms.
Conversely, international panels are making decisions that touch on
national sovereignty (particularly in such areas as human rights, environmental protection, and economic regulation) that would have
previously been regarded as out of bounds.

The vertical feel of the entire monist-dualist debate—with national
law ostensibly answering to a higher but inchoate set of international
norms—is being radically altered. What is emerging is a horizontal model in which international and domestic rules, processes, and

institutions are situated side by side. The boundary is not a brick wall of national sovereignty and international deference, hermetically sealed. Rather, the barrier is permeable, and the two domains interact, sometimes continuously, in the formulation of new rules of conduct or the resolution of particular disputes.

PUBLIC AND PRIVATE LAW

For the last century and a half, international law fundamentally has defined itself through an internal schism. As Jennings and Watts's latest edition of Oppenheim puts the matter, public international law "governs the relations of states and other subjects of international law amongst themselves," while private international law is those rules, found in domestic law, to "resolve problems which, in cases between private persons . . . involve a foreign element." Or, in other words, "public international law arises from the juxtaposition of states, private international law from the juxtaposition of legal systems."[28]

While the distinction between public and private international law appears intuitively obvious, it is important to realize that it was a relatively recent construct in the intellectual history of the discipline. Prior to the mid-1800s, the concerns of private actors operating in a transnational context were considered a legitimate part of the law of nations. The medieval *ius commune* included rules for the handling of commercial and maritime disputes as well as the hereditary and military perquisites of European nobility. Private international law did not become recognized as a separate legal discipline until the nineteenth century. Before then, conflict of laws had been largely resolved by reference to an objective law of nations that was powered by natural principles.

The birth of conflict of laws and private international law was made possible only after the announcement of the supremacy of municipal law. This declaration required many profound changes in the thinking about the way law affected foreign persons, relationships, and transactions. Not only was natural law repudiated in favor of positive statutory and judicial authority, but comity—arguably the motive force for the earlier vision of international law—was also buried. The eulogy was provided by Joseph Story in the first published treatise on the subject of conflict of laws, which appeared in 1834:

[W]hatever force and obligation the laws of one country have in another, depends solely upon the laws, and municipal regulations of the latter, that is to say, upon its own proper jurisprudence and polity, and upon its own express or tacit consent. . . . It has been thought by some jurists, that the term, "comity," is not sufficiently expressive of the obligation of nations to give effect to foreign laws, when they are not prejudicial to their own rights and interests. And it has been suggested, that the doctrine rests on a deeper foundation; that it is not so much a matter of comity, or courtesy, as of paramount moral duty. Now, assuming, that such a moral duty does exist, it is clearly one of imperfect obligation, like that of beneficence, humanity, and charity. Every nation must be the final judge for itself, not only of the nature and extent of the duty, but of the occasions, on which its exercise may be justly demanded. And, certainly, there can be no pretence to say, that any foreign nation has a right to require the full recognition of its own laws in other territories . . . where their moral character is questionable, or their provisions impolitic.[29]

Justice Story's statement was both cliché and revelation. Based on an imperfect reading of earlier publicists (including Grotius and Ulricus Huber),[30] Story's argument implicated the question of whether a nation's law was truly supreme within its frontiers. No one had forgotten that sovereign equality made the laws of all nations equally deserving of recognition and enforcement. The interjection of individuals into the state system, with their own rights and obligations, demanded a first principle of conflict of laws, and Story supplied it. A state was under no compulsory obligation to enforce a foreign right or responsibility. For purposes of good order, a state could do so, but if it refused to enforce such a right or responsibility, no adverse public international law consequences would follow.

In the course of the late nineteenth and early twentieth centuries— the period of high positivism I have narrated already in this volume—

the divide between public and private international law widened. As they separated from each other, they coalesced around new subjects and objects, and the individual's position in the nation-state system was changed forever. In the realm of private international law, where municipal law was supreme, the right to avail oneself of a foreign defense or cause of action flourished, but always under the watchful glare of the state's overweening sovereignty.[31] The state was under no obligation, at least respecting public international law, to recognize those rights or duties. In the world of public international law, where sovereign equality and sovereign autonomy combined to endorse the rule of comity, individuals' standing within their own states was not (until later) considered a proper subject of international concern. Even when it was, individual rights were only rarely vindicated completely.

Conflicts doctrine had its own conception of human rights long before human rights became fashionable in international relations. The privilege of having one's actions and decisions, one's very lot in life itself, governed by a relevant and applicable law was as profound and important as any other right. Moreover, people wanted that law to be the positive product of a representative government with which they had, in some way, affiliated themselves. Private international law thus had its own human rights revolution long before the public sphere did.

The division of the discipline into two segments thus served significant progressive objectives. The old law of nations, caught in the grips of profound positivism, was quick to relegate many topics of regulation to the private domain. By the middle of the twentieth century, public international law came to be gradually liberated from those positivist confines. As the activities of individuals became subject to international legal regulation, the traditional divide between public and private international law began to close.

Significant distinctions do, however, remain, and some of these are not merely relics of abandoned ideas. One of these affects the application of the sources of international law. Truly international regulation of private international law subjects typically can only be achieved via treaty, not through customary international law. In combination with a protected zone of domestic jurisdiction, states can be charged with violations of duties to individuals arising under private international law only when those obligations are expressly incorporated into a convention. Adjudication of such private disputes before international tribunals is, therefore, quite exceptional.[32] On a related point, concession contracts concluded between states and private parties are rarely accorded the status of treaties, and, absent some special mechanism for adjustment by an international institution, their breach will not be remediable in a public international law context.[33]

Finally, there remains the problem alluded to by Story as impelling a domestic-conflicts doctrine in opposition to the law of nations: the unwillingness of states to entertain foreign causes of action or to enforce foreign judgments. Most domestic jurisdictions in the world still flatly decline to enforce the public law of foreign sovereigns, especially in the realm of penal, revenue, and confiscatory regulations. This rule dates as well to the late eighteenth and early nineteenth centuries[34] but continues to enjoy great currency today.[35] Because of this principle, public international law was compelled to adopt a panoply of uniform law projects, carried out through conventions negotiated by standing bodies. In addition, it has necessitated a host of rules for mutual cooperation between states to regulate such matters as law enforcement, extraditions, and judicial assistance for legal proceedings.

As the dividing line between domestic and international jurisdictions has shifted, so has the boundary between public and private concerns. We may well have reached the point of recognizing a substantial reunification of the two branches of the discipline. International institutions are increasingly concerned with ordering relations and transactions between individuals and businesses from different countries. This augmentation in prescriptive jurisdiction is being matched by an equally aggressive effort to extend the competence of international dispute settlement bodies. Mixed arbitration, involving one governmental party and one (or more) private actors, is growing in popularity.[36] The continued use of multinational public enterprises (business consortia with governments as their stakeholders) also has meant that state entities should, as a matter of fairness, be treated like private business actors.

The public-private distinction offered only an illusory frontier for international law. This construct was the necessary creation of a law of nations that was enduring an intensely positivist and dualist phase and may have been rightly seen as an avenue for progress and doctrinal safeguarding of the legitimacy of the discipline. But once the legal system further matured and refined, it was inevitable that the false conflict between state and private actors in international relations would be exposed, just as the hermetic seal between international and domestic systems was punctured.

INTERNATIONAL LAW AND POLITICS

That may well leave only one true barrier for international law to confront. As suggested in chapter 1, it is the ultimate heart of darkness for the discipline, the definitive battle with the Other. International law has, from its intellectual formation, been counterpoised with international politics. If diplomacy is the art of the possible, then international law is the rule of the certain. If international politics is dynamic, international law is static.

Even within the international law academy and college, there has always been a deeply harbored sense that international law is bounded by political realities, and it dare not intrude into those counsels. In the intensely controversial *South West Africa* cases, Judge Sir Gerald Fitzmaurice observed, "We are not unmindful of, nor are we insensible to, the various considerations of a non-juridical character, social, humanitarian and other, which underlie this case; but these are matters for the political rather than for the legal arena. They cannot be allowed to deflect us from our duty of reaching a conclusion strictly on the basis of what we believe to be the correct legal view."[37] An irony should not be lost here. In what was probably its nadir, the World Court later adopted the legal posture recommended by Fitzmaurice and consequently refused to adjudicate the dispute involving South

Africa's illegal occupation of South West Africa (Namibia) because the applicant countries lacked standing to bring the claim. This was despite the fact that both Ethiopia and Liberia had been members of the League of Nations, which had issued the original mandate for South West Africa that South Africa had allegedly violated. As it turned out, only the Court's standing was damaged by this decision,[38] and, because of it, countries from the developing world avoided the ICJ for nearly two decades.

If international jurists occasionally engage in self-abnegation, forswearing the political realm while paying homage to the purity of legal considerations, other practitioners and decision makers are not as scrupulous. In one notorious instance, the repudiation of international law values was wrapped in realist rhetoric and bromide. When asked about U.S. actions toward Cuba during the Cuban Missile Crisis, Secretary of State Dean Acheson—a well-regarded international lawyer—responded, "I must conclude that the propriety of the Cuban quarantine is not a legal issue. The power, position and prestige of the United States had been challenged by another state; and law simply does not deal with such questions of ultimate power—power that comes close to the sources of sovereignty. I cannot believe that there are principles of law that say we must accept destruction of our way of life."[39] The only thing that is shocking about this statement is its frankness. The normal rhetoric of international law is neutral and dispassionate. States virtually never resort to an explicit claim of might makes right. Closer examination of Acheson's remark reveals that its veracity has withstood the test of time. The World Court, nearly a third of a century later, acknowledged that the use of nuclear weapons would potentially be lawful "in an extreme circumstance of self-defence, in which the very survival of a State would be at stake."[40]

These two vignettes clearly illustrate that the perceived division between the legal and political realms of international relations may be more palpable and real than any barrier of domesticity or privity. Rhetoric aside, many international law doctrines and processes carve out a protected realm of outcomes determined by diplomacy and negotiation, not by legal considerations or determinations. In a very real sense, international law confronts its evil twin of politics by uniquely privileging certain types of decisions as beyond the law.

Many international law doctrines, for example, emphasize negotiated settlements as the avenue for reaching legally significant results. Under the law of the sea, nations are obliged to negotiate delimitations of maritime zones that may be in dispute. This is not mere hortatory language. The 1982 UN Convention on the Law of the Sea makes negotiation—or an attempt at an agreed settlement—a requisite for further application of legal principles (including equidistance and special circumstances).[41]

In disputes involving nonnavigational rights to international watercourses,[42] international law has charted a middle course between extreme positions taken by states. Imagine a scenario in which a river traverses two nations. The upper riparian (the state where the river begins) wants to build a dam for irrigation or power production. Construction of the dam will cut the expected flow of water to the lower riparian farther downstream. Decisions from international tribunals have indicated that in such situations, neither state has automatic priority for its claims. Instead, there is "natural community of interest"[43] in the river resource, and an equitable result should be worked out through good-faith negotiations between the disputants. The arbitral tribunal's 1957 decision in the *Lac Lanoux* case[44] certainly emphasized the requirement of coriparian states to consult and negotiate in good faith concerning their mutual water resources.

Closely related to a structural obligation of good-faith negotiation is the idea of creating a separate international duty for states to consult and notify other nations about environmental issues and emergencies. Such a duty has been inferred from general principles and customary international law for many years, and some treaties certainly have specifically codified this duty. After the Chernobyl atomic reactor disaster in April 1986, there was international outrage at the Soviet Union's failure to promptly notify European states of the impending nuclear fallout. In what was probably a record of some sort, in six months the International Atomic Energy Agency in Vienna had concluded the Convention on the Early Notification of a Nuclear Accident. This treaty set forth the kinds of disclosure that are required with nuclear accidents and provided for the submission of disputes to the World Court.

If anything, the duty to consult and notify is part of a larger phenomenon in international lawmaking: the international community taking steps to address a problem only after an authentic disaster. This kind of crisis diplomacy and style of legal negotiation is not, however, an optimal way to proceed in making a cohesive body of international law. Yet such a political approach has been replicated in many negotiating settings, particularly in the environmental sector. Diplomats purposefully assign particular issues to contingent baskets, awaiting later events that will necessitate revisiting the issue and demanding resolution.

Another aspect of this political dimension to many international lawmaking exercises is more subtle. Diplomats and lawyers have been astute in employing scientific, technological, and economic realities as a way either to impel action or to restrain it. These are often seen as exogenous factors, regrettably outside the control of political negotiators, and often constitute a hidden subtext for many treaty-drafting projects or the state practices that lead to customary international law. A significant constraint for international law has been when these considerations have been merged with politics. One notorious example should suffice.

Caught up in the negotiation of the 1982 UN Convention on the Law of the Sea were fist-sized lumps of manganese, cobalt, nickel, and copper known as manganese nodules. These are found on the deep seabed, under miles of water, and far from shore. Beginning with an innocuous speech by Malta's delegate, Arvid Pardo, before the UN General Assembly in 1967, the international community became entranced with these nuggets. Seeing a ready source of valuable, strategic minerals there for the taking, developing nations lobbied hard for the deep seabed minerals to be declared the common heritage of mankind. Delegates subsequently negotiated to fashion a set of international law rules to exploit this resource. And what a baroque regime it was: elaborate articles on production limits for seabed mining; complex regulatory systems, including the creation of an international mining company (called the Enterprise); mandatory technology-transfer requirements; and detailed institutional arrangements with the creation of a new International Sea Bed Authority.[45]

There was just one problem: no technology existed—or has been developed—to recover manganese nodules from the deep seabed. More importantly, the mineral economics are such that there has been absolutely no incentive to develop such proprietary technology. In short, the deep seabed mining provisions of part XI of the convention were a fiasco. This aspect of the law of the sea negotiations illustrates the absurdities of lawyers and diplomats negotiating ahead of the curve of science, technology, and economics. The elaborate provisions of part XI were utterly irrelevant and fanciful and later had to be changed. Regrettably, this same kind of groupthink also befell the negotiators of outer-space, Antarctic mineral, shipwreck-management, and climate-change regimes. While international lawyers should take pride in developing creative legal regimes, to do so in advance of practical certainties is folly. On occasion, international law can unintentionally increase the drag coefficient on progress in the face of technological change.

So far, what have been narrated here are cautionary tales. International law processes are exposed to great peril when they intrude into political domains or activities beyond the current understanding of the legal participants. International law also recognizes certain purely political acts that are not subject at all to legal challenge. This creates a safe harbor of state conduct that permits the smooth operation of essential legal rules, many of which are at the doctrinal core of the discipline. By segregating law from politics, international law is inoculated from contamination by political considerations.

For example, host nations are under an obligation to protect the privileges and immunities of foreign diplomats stationed in their countries. Hospitality has its limits, however. By far and away the most politically explosive issue surrounding diplomatic immunity is when envoys (or their families) quite literally get away with murder or engage in activities inconsistent with their diplomatic status (a polite phrase for espionage). Since diplomats have absolute immunity from the receiving state's criminal jurisdiction, when an envoy commits a serious crime, the receiving state can only demand either that the sending state waive his immunity or that he immediately leave (this is called being declared persona non grata, or, in diplomatic argot, being PNGed). Most importantly, the host state's decision to PNG a diplomat is unqualified, and the 1961 Vienna Convention on Diplomatic Relations makes clear that a state may do so "at any time and without having to explain its decision."[46]

Likewise, states have the ultimate power to reject the reservations to multilateral treaties made by other nations. Even if such reservations satisfy the bare minimums that international law imposes—such as that they do not violate the fundamental object and purpose of a treaty—that does not mean that other countries are required to acquiesce. Such reservations still constitute a counteroffer that other states, in their unfettered political judgment, can accept or reject.[47] In a similar vein, international law may stipulate the legal effects of recognition or nonrecognition for other states or governments. It most certainly does not dictate the political attitude that a country must adopt in relations with a new member of the international community.

International law is generally hostile to the position that international actors can demand certain entitlements or political favors from each other. Despite talk of an international human right to development, the dispensation of foreign aid remains in the sound political discretion of states. Similarly, there is no international law requirement for states to diplomatically espouse the private claims of their nationals. That is a matter for political judgment and diplomatic adjustment. Certain forms of mutual legal assistance between nations, most notably extradition in the face of particular defenses, may be freely withheld without any adverse international law consequences. The fundamental conception of comity is traditionally framed as a course of conduct that is pursued merely as an act of grace and without any sense of legal obligation. Finally, states are free to respond to another nation's illegal acts with legal, if unfriendly, countermeasures, even if such responses are not entirely proportional to the original conduct.[48] Such a decision to escalate a dispute by using legal countermeasures (retorsions) is a purely political one.[49]

If it sometimes seems that there is a close correlation between a topic that is political and one that is domestic or private, that is not necessarily so. Just as international law came to recognize that how a government treats its own citizens has both a legal and international dimension, other rules could be similarly transformed in the future. The structure of international dispute-settlement mechanisms makes such transmutations possible, although not likely.

The availability of low-grade forms of facilitation for dispute settlement is another aspect of political processes at work in international law. Conciliation and mediation may be premised on application of a rule of law in the resolution of a dispute between two or more countries, but it is hardly a legal or binding process insofar as either of the parties can walk away. When the UN secretary-general or another international leader offers his or her "good offices," the resolutions often have the flavor of political expediency and quick-witted pragmatism.

Even when a dispute reaches the rarified legal realm of the ICJ or an international arbitration, a number of doctrines can restrain the tribunal from rendering a decision. Over nearly eighty years, the World Court has developed a number of prudential grounds for finding a case inadmissible and thus declining to decide it. For example, the Court will dismiss a case if its subject matter has become moot, as when in the *Nuclear Test* cases France unilaterally declared that it would no longer conduct atmospheric testing.[50] Although the Court was careful to say that it would remain seized of the issue (in case the French changed their minds), the dispute was, for all intents and purposes, concluded. Likewise, the ICJ will not decide a case if the dispute is not sufficiently ripe, or well developed.[51] Somewhat more controversially, the Court will dismiss a case if indispensable parties are missing from the litigation.[52]

Interestingly, the Court has flatly rejected other forms of admissibility challenges, most notably arguments that the Court should avoid certain forms of political questions.[53] Despite the attitude of Judge Fitzmaurice, reflected earlier, the ICJ seems unwilling to draw a bright line between the domains of international politics and law. Such a demarcation would be unnecessary and institutionally foolish for the Court because many other doctrines and principles are extant that permit it sensibly to avoid deciding certain matters without appearing cowardly in doing do.

Even while the political limits of international law appear to be the most insuperable and confining, they may be slowly dissipating. One might legitimately wonder whether any idea, or set of principles, can effectively restrain international law (assuming it even wants to be circumscribed). The public-private distinction should properly be regarded as a vestige of a historic period that has little relevance to the dynamism and integration of contemporary international life. In a similar way, the international-domestic divide began to be breached with the human rights revolution, and the gap has been progressively closing with the successive waves of globalizing developments.

Nevertheless, it would be a profound mistake to envisage international law unbound. Without the limits of domesticity, privity, and politics, international law might have profound difficulties in delineating itself. If hitherto the international legal system has defined itself by a set of negations—it neither intrudes on domestic law nor prescribes for private transnational actors nor substitutes for international politics—it may be difficult to conceive of it as a purely positive system for a community of international actors. If international law has no limits, it may well have no function or purpose.

8 Formalism and Pragmatism

I have already discussed how the development of international law is typically presented as a progress narrative. There is a prevailing sense that international law has evolved from a primitive regime to a sophisticated legal system. While there is some truth in this, thinking exclusively about international law in an evolutionary way can be deceptive and misleading. Already in this volume I have taken issue with those who would portray international law as fully replicating national legal systems or meeting some millenarian rendezvous with world government. Instead, international law has to be understood on its own terms as reflecting unique constituencies, values, processes, and institutions.

This dynamic tension can best be seen in efforts to generally characterize the form and function of international law doctrines. Certainly within the last half century, international law has been presented as a progressive legal system. Progressivity has two aspects. One is in the actual substantive content of international law rules and the extent to which they reflect broad-minded, cosmopolitan and dynamic values for the international legal system. Part of this conspectus was essayed in chapter 6, and the remainder of that project will be completed in chapter 10. The other aspect of progressivity has more to do with the structure and form of international law rules than with the tangible substance of the doctrines, and that is my present task.

An apparent common ground of agreement among jurists and decision makers, academic lawyers, and international relations theorists is that international law has recently managed to transform itself from a formal to a functional legal system.[1] While the etiology of this pragmatic turn can be traced to the writings of Gentili in the late sixteenth century,[2] the modern roots of the transformation are usually laid in the emergence of a functional world order. In the words of Wolfgang Friedman, "It is in [the functional] direction . . . that the main hope lies for the development of an international legal system that will correspond to the needs of a society which is anachronistically divided into [many] 'sovereign' states, but which is, for the fateful questions of survival or extinction, indivisible. Unless social and legal organization catches up with the physical and technological realities of our time, the prospects for survival are slender indeed."[3] Whether one sees functional pragmatism as the natural outgrowth of the demands of international life or as the result of a systems analysis of international law,[4] it is hard to disagree with Harold Maier's observation that "[i]nternational law is nothing if it is not pragmatic."[5]

IN PRAISE OF FORMALISM . . .

I would readily concede that formalistic doctrines may well be the exception today in international law. I believe, however, that it goes too far to relegate those formalisms to the dustbin of history and to conclude that a progressive international legal regime would be better off if it systematically purged itself of these kinds of rules. It may well be, as the PCIJ observed in the *Mavrommatis Palestine Concessions* case, that the "Court, whose jurisdiction is international, is not bound to attach to matters of form the same degree of importance which they might possess in municipal law."[6] Nevertheless, many of the formalisms that currently exist in international law doctrine serve significant purposes and may promote important policy values. Some of the formalisms are connected with the confines of international law (just discussed in the preceding chapter). Others are premised on long-standing customs and usages of the international community, not just on eccentric treaty provisions. Finally, where certain formalist rules have softened and transmuted over time, they may continue to exercise extraordinary significance.

Structural Formalisms

Some doctrines in international law are imbued with what I would call a structural formalism. The subjects-objects division in international law discourse, considered in chapter 4, can certainly be regarded in this manner. The formal distinction between international legal actors and legitimate topics of international legal regulation casts a strong spell over many issues bearing on sources, processes, and institutions. Of all such categorical distinctions, this may have been the one that earned formal legal analysis a bad name among publicists. One defining characteristic of formal rules in any legal system is that they are self-proving and often mask a subjective selection of important values by members of the legal community.[7] What appears to be a neutral and dispassionate rule can thus be nothing more than a bald bid for power. While formalism often gets confounded with law as an autonomous discipline,[8] such structural typologies as the subjects-objects division clearly affect determinations of which entities count in a legal system, what norms matter, and who wins or loses in particular disputes.

A similar form of structural formalism is the divide between the international law of peace and that for war. This has quite a pedigree, tracing its origins back to Gentili's *De Jure Belli* (published in 1598) and Grotius's *De Jure Belli ac Pacis* (1625). It was always understood in international law scholarship and practice that the fundamental nature of state relations changes with the outbreak of hostilities. It was as if there were some binary code embedded in all international law doctrines. Treatises certainly reflected this schism until the mid–twentieth century,[9] although beginning in the early 1800s formal recognition was given to the status of neutrality as a position intermediate between war and peace.[10] So ingrained is the distinction between war and peace that certain international law rules in one sphere are formally precluded from having effect in the other. The 1969 VCLT, which provides rules for every aspect of treaty making and enforcement, specifically disclaims an intent to "prejudge any question that may arise . . . from the outbreak of hostilities between States" and provides that "the rules of customary international law will continue to govern such questions."[11] A whole panoply of treaty regimes are specific in not prescribing rules that would affect matters of international peace and security under the UN Charter. Thus, even though the formal distinction between an international law of peace and of war has dissipated, the practical consequences of these two conditions of state relations continue to be manifest.

As might be expected, some structural formalisms in international law impinge on the sources of international legal obligation. The purpose of these formalities is to ensure predictable and ostensibly neutral selections of rules to resolve disputes. Some of these have deeper meanings. As discussed in chapter 3, divergent treatment has been given to global, regional, and special customs. Silence by states during the formation of these various types of usages has been given different legal consequences, with lack of objection equated with acquiescence for global and local customs and with rejection for regional usages. As already intimated, this formalism structures a particular vision of international lawmaking processes by effectively promoting the role of the World Court in pronouncing uniform rules at the same time as giving tribunals the freedom to simply decide a particular dispute.

On a more micro level, much of the law of treaties has a distinctively formal feel, particularly with rules regarding treaty formation and especially on such matters as the powers of treaty negotiators, expressions of consent to be bound, and entry into force.[12] Especially important in the VCLT are norms that are structured as "default rules," which the parties are free to opt out of but otherwise will stand as their intent. Having such background rules reduces the transaction costs of much treaty negotiation and provides clear grounds for adjudication of disputes. The VCLT's rules of treaty application—particularly in regard to territorial scope and nonretroactivity[13]—are good examples of this sort of rule formalism. The last kind of formalism exhibited in the VCLT is an attempt to superimpose a regularity of terminology on difficult-to-characterize doctrines. Not merely an example of codification at work, the VCLT's treatment of grounds for treaty invalidity and termination imposes doctrinal rigor and conditions results.[14] While some of these formalisms have been drawn from domestic contract analogies (an exercise fraught with some danger), others have been developed through the unique experiences of the international community.

Doctrinal Formalisms

While these structural formalisms have imparted some flavor to international law as a discipline, most commentators tend to focus instead on those doctrines that appear to be driven most by formal distinctions and considerations. Some of these are, indeed, historical anachronisms. In his discussion of the ways that states acquire territory under international law, Ian Brownlie notes, "Many of the standard textbooks, and particularly those in English, classify the modes of acquisition in a stereotyped way which reflects the preoccupation of writers in the period before the First World War."[15] He and other publicists savagely attack this kind of "orthodox analysis" as being grossly simplistic and incapable of producing coherent results. What thus characterizes these doctrinal formalisms is that an entire cluster of rules appears to be motivated by a single, overriding typology, and imposition of that schematic produces widely varying outcomes.

An excellent example of this is the international law doctrine of state succession. State succession occurs when there has been a fundamental transformation in the identity of the state itself, not its government. Characterizing the precise nature of the state succession is absolutely crucial for understanding the proper rule of international law to cover the situation.[16] The legal consequences of these various changes of identity have been poorly understood and largely remain governed by customary international law (chiefly expressed through national court decisions and the positions of governments in response to various events). The UN ILC has drafted two treaties that attempt to codify this area of law, but they have met with little success. The 1978 Vienna Convention on State Succession in Respect to Treaties[17] and the 1983 Vienna Convention on State Succession in Respect to State Property, Archives, and Debts[18] have drawn only a handful of adherents and may not be a completely reliable guide to this area of international law.

State succession is formalist in the sense that it depends for its coherence on a series of characterizations, which produce a gridlike decision tree. First, one identifies the kind of question (succession for treaties, nationality of individuals, property, debts, or delicts) and then the nature of the succession itself. The 1978 convention distinguishes carefully between successions involving part of a state's territory, newly independent countries, and unification and separation of existing nations. Each category is presented with a general rule and then further elaboration for particular situations. The same methodological approach is taken with successions in respect of state property, archives, and debts. Some scholars reject the idea that these categorical distinctions are "terms of art carrying with them clearly established legal consequences, nor are they sharply differentiated."[19] Nevertheless, this formal approach has permeated the entire doctrine and probably explains its lack of coherence.

Other doctrinal formalisms share this strong schematic flavor. In the laws of war and international humanitarian law there has until very recently been a strong doctrinal distinction between internal or civil wars and truly international conflicts. For instance, UN Charter article 2(4)'s prohibition on use of force may not necessarily extend to bar interventions in support of one side in a strictly internal conflict. The distinction also resonated in international humanitarian law. Although the 1948 Geneva Conventions have been widely ratified, serious concerns have arisen as to their application in certain kinds of situations. For example, it has remained unclear whether the protections of the Geneva Conventions applied only to individuals involved in international conflicts, as opposed to civil wars. In reality, civilians tend to be brutalized more in internal conflicts. Common article 3 of the Geneva Conventions attempted to extend the reach of the treaties to civil wars, and this was later acknowledged by the ICJ in the *Nicaragua* case.[20] In a further development in 1977, two additional protocols were negotiated for the Geneva Conventions, and they apply its protections to most internal conflicts and wars of national liberation (although not to situations of "internal disturbances and tensions, such as riots, isolated and sporadic acts of violence").[21]

These principles and distinctions were recognized by the International Criminal Tribunal for the Former Yugoslavia (ICTFY), established by the UN Security Council in 1993 to "try those persons responsible for serious breaches of international humanitarian law committed on the territory of the Former Yugoslavia."[22] As part of the broad pattern of international law's holding individuals responsible for their own acts, especially in the wake of Nuremberg and the Nazi atrocities, the ICTFY has had the opportunity to clarify and apply many aspects of international humanitarian law. In one decision,[23] the ICTFY's Appeals Chamber rejected a defendant's claim that the tribunal lacked jurisdiction over him because his alleged crimes occurred in the course of an internal conflict and thus were not covered under the Geneva Conventions, Protocols, or customary international law.

Formalistic categories are thus dissolved by practical developments in international law, yet they retain substantial vitality. Additional examples of this would include the realm of state immunities for various sorts of public officials. This area of international law makes sharp distinctions between such actors as heads of state or of government, diplomats, consuls, representatives to international organizations, agents on special missions, members of a nation's armed forces, or employees of state-owned commercial instrumentalities.[24] These are, of course, functional distinctions based on the character and duties of the respective type of official. They are nevertheless played out in formal categories.

Formalism for state succession, state immunities, and the laws of war has the look of a matrix of various contingent options leading to no sure conclusions. Formalities for other areas of international law are presented more as a spatial continuum producing clearer outcomes. The best illustration of this kind of doctrinal formalism is found in the law of the sea, where many rules seem to be structured around what may appear to be arbitrary and peculiar distinctions. Essential to understanding the contemporary law of the sea is recognizing the legal construction of maritime zones emanating out from shore.[25] These zones matter: certain activities that are permitted by a coastal state within its territorial sea or contiguous zone (out to twenty-four nautical miles) are absolutely prohibited beyond that. The legal outcome of a law of the sea dispute could very well turn on the precise location of certain critical events.

If these zones sound mystifying (and they are to most international lawyers), keep one simple point in mind. The closer to shore that a particular activity or resource is located, the more likely it will come under the control, jurisdiction, or regulatory authority of the nearest coastal state. Conversely, the farther one moves from shore, the more coastal state authority decreases until, presumably, one reaches a point (the high seas) where it ends and total freedom of the seas prevails. This spatial continuum is inextricably linked to the conflict between nations with predominant maritime interests and those states that desire to secure access to maritime resources close to their shores. Formal doctrines thus serve to mediate these disputes by imposing, almost literally, lines in the water that reflect different legal regimes.

This doctrinal formalism is reflected at the micro level by very detailed and technical formulas for ascertaining the baselines on which the various maritime zones are measured.[26] If the general structure of an international law doctrine is imbued with formalism, it is likely that such will be repeated in the more and more specific iterations of the rule. It would do no good for the law of the sea to have a formalist construct of maritime zones yet have vague and open-textured standards for the practical ascertainment of the extent of those zones and the application of rights and duties within them. This is not to suggest that the law of the sea is entirely formalistic. It is not, and some pockets (such as rules for delimitation and management of resource conflicts) generally eschew formalism. For its broadest organizing principles, however, the law of the sea depends on a formal construct of rights and duties.

The international law of state responsibility offers a final example of a doctrinal formalism that operates on a continuum. Depending on the nature of the conduct affecting the rights of aliens, international law will impose different standards of care on host states. One historically common class of international claim went by the name "denials of justice." These claims arose in situations where the host state's law enforcement system or judiciary failed to operate properly, and, as a consequence, a foreigner's rights were affected.[27] In the *B. E. Chattin Claim*, where the United States–Mexico General Claims Commission ruled that the procedural defects in the claimant's show trial (including the failure to be informed of the charges, the lack of oaths for the witnesses, and the long delays) amounted to a denial of justice.[28] With the advent of definitive standards of criminal justice—often contained in international human rights instruments—there is almost a strict liability standard for a host state's failure to follow those rules, although that might be softened somewhat by a tribunal's granting of a margin of appreciation to a respondent state.

At the opposite end of the spectrum for a host state's standard of care for foreigners is the failure to protect claims. Here, nations are being charged with an omission. The standard adopted by most international tribunals is some form of due diligence: a state is required to exercise the same care in protecting foreigners as it would in protecting its own similarly situated nationals. In the *William E. Chapman* claim, for example, a claims commission ruled that Mexico had failed to grant the police protection for a U.S. consul (who had earlier been threatened by a private Mexican citizen) that it would for one of its own officials and was therefore liable.[29] In a case before the Iran–United States Claims Tribunal, the plea of an Iranian national that he had been subjected to private harassment and threats by Californians was rejected under the due diligence standard.[30] The remaining types of international claims—such as wrongful expulsion, contract breaches, and outright expropriations or regulatory takings—are reviewed under more traditional tort standards of negligence or contractual forms of breach.

State responsibility toward the persons and property of aliens thus reflects a sliding scale sort of formalism. Positions are staked out on a doctrinal continuum rather than in a more rigid matrix or decision tree. Thinking about these doctrinal areas for international rules remains formal, despite strong functional rationales for the norms. In this way, formalism and pragmatism mix and blend with each other. The structure and terminology of rules appear formal, while the content and direction of the norms have been subtly changed by developments exogenous to the legal system.

. . . AND TWO CHEERS FOR PRAGMATISM

As I have already suggested, pragmatism now seems to have won its battle against formalism. But why exactly does the international legal system need to be pragmatic? One would think that formalism would better serve the interests of international constituencies, which crave regularity and seek an underlying legitimacy for international relations under a rule of law. Nevertheless, there are few defenders of formalism in much of the academic literature. Formalism is often regarded as antithetical to functional values in international law.[31] Because formal doctrines are brittle and may reflect anachronistic values and ideas, formalism, it is posited, cannot really satisfy the needs of the international community. In this trope, pragmatism and functionalism are equated.[32]

Most of the doctrines we identify as being pragmatic are so for reasons that have nothing to do with their functional character. Rules can be pragmatic when they are the products of repeated, negotiated compromise. No great objects are being served by such norms; they simply reflect international actors' desire to advance some particular interests. Conversely, pragmatic doctrines may actually be indicative of deep-seated tensions between international law values and may be the only avenue by which those paradoxes are practically resolved. Pragmatism is thus impelled by practice and rarely by theoretical concerns.

Pragmatism in Custom and Treaty Law

As a consequence, few international law doctrines are systemically pragmatic. These are typically confined to issues arising with international law sources. Already mentioned in chapter 2 was a material uniformity standard for demonstrating the objective element in customary international law formation. As the World Court observed in the *Military and Paramilitary Activities* case, it is unnecessary to prove complete consistency of a practice, and indeed, it is permissible to presume that deviations from a usage are reflective of a violation and not the emergence of a competing norm.[33] This has been construed as a rule of reason. International tribunals are at liberty to identify certain state behaviors as reflective of customary international law while discounting other behaviors.

Treaty law reflects the same flexibility. The open-textured rules of treaty interpretation achieve that effect. So does the possibility of oral agreements and unilateral declarations, despite the temptation for international law to impose a formalistic equivalent of a Statute of Frauds or a doctrine of contractual consideration. In a similar move, both the ICJ and VCLT recognized the existence of "objective" regimes, treaties deemed to bind even nonparties. Although this constituted a sharp departure from domestic contractual analogues of privity, it was vital to achieve recognition for certain global institutions or decision-making processes.[34] The Vienna Convention's requirement that after signing a treaty, states are under a duty not to take steps that would "defeat [its] object and purpose" prior to formal ratification and entry into force[35] is likewise a sensible compromise recognizing that there are often substantial delays between treaty signings and full application. While states are free not to complete the ratification formalities, this rule allows treaty regimes to build a momentum of informal observance even prior to entry into force. Without unduly constraining states' freedom to contract, this rule removes some friction from the treaty-making process.

Another rule in treaty law reflects both systemic concerns and fundamental paradoxes in international law values. One ground for termination of treaties is known as the doctrine of fundamental change of circumstances, or *rebus sic stantibus*.[36] The idea here is that when the conditions that led to the conclusion of a treaty change fundamentally, then one party or another can unilaterally terminate the agreement. Such a doctrine has the potential of being utterly destructive of good faith and predictable observance of treaty obligations. It has nonetheless persisted in treaty law because of the need for a mechanism of peaceful alteration of treaty obligations that are no longer considered desirable. The League of Nations Covenant even embraced the idea that the international community could reconsider "treaties which have become inapplicable, and [those] conditions whose continuance might endanger the peace of the world."[37]

Pragmatism entered the picture when diplomats and lawyers were compelled to cabin this potentially expansive doctrine. The VCLT carefully sought to limit its use by requiring the satisfaction of a multipart test. Article 62 requires that (a) the change must be fundamental, (b) the change must be unforeseen by the drafters, (c) the assumption of the old circumstances must have been "an essential basis of the consent to be bound by the treaty," (d) the new circumstance must radically transform the obligation for the party seeking termination, and (e) obligations are yet to be performed under the treaty (and may not involve territorial boundaries).

As one might suspect, no state has successfully justified a termination of a treaty for changed circumstances under the article 62 standard. The only credible attempt to raise a *rebus sic stantibus* justification in the World Court failed miserably. Iceland had concluded a 1961 exchange of notes with Britain, agreeing that Iceland could claim a twelve-nautical-mile fishing zone; if Iceland later wished to increase that claim, the matter would have to be adjudicated in the ICJ. This proved to be a bad deal for Iceland. Later developments impelled states to claim up to two hundred–mile zones. In 1971 Iceland unilaterally extended its zone to fifty miles, and Britain sued in the ICJ. Iceland protested that its acceptance of ICJ jurisdiction in the 1961 notes was an unenforceable promise because of changed circumstances. The Court vigorously rejected this challenge to its jurisdiction,[38] ruling that while the change in the law of the sea may have been fundamental and unforeseen, it did not radically transform Iceland's obligation. Iceland was obliged to submit its increased zone to the Court, which subsequently rejected at least part of Iceland's claim.

Pragmatism as Negotiated Compromise

A last example of pragmatism in treaty law is the World Court's decision in the *Reservations to the Genocide Convention* opinion.[39] This struck a significant compromise between two extreme positions: a state's absolute right to condition its acceptance of treaties and the principle of perfect contractual parity for convention parties. This was more than a "split the baby" solution for the World Court or for international law. Pragmatically rejecting extreme positions means that a middle ground for doctrine needs to be elaborated. International law has often advanced by rebuffing extreme bright-line rules reflecting conflicting notions of state sovereignty and instead substituting a pragmatic alternative standard that is then solidified in state practice and treaty. The VCLT later did just that by partially codifying the ICJ's requirement that reservations not violate the object and purpose of a treaty.[40] This pragmatic approach has been vindicated by decisions that have held that particular nations' treaty reservations violated an instrument's object and purpose, while other rulings have upheld restrictive reservations.[41]

Other significant areas of international law doctrine have been developed in precisely the same way. Consider, for example, the evolution in rules for claiming territory (already discussed in the context of intertemporality in chapter 5). The doctrine of effective occupation was enunciated by international authorities to replace the older rule that permitted symbolic discovery alone to serve as the basis for title. This transformation was the product of negotiated compromise in the late 1800s, the high-water mark of European colonialism, and it was intended as a means to avoid unnecessary conflict.[42] Pragmatic elaboration of the effective-occupation rule was left to international institutions adjudicating particular disputes. Tribunals ruled that effective occupation meant rather less when at issue are small, isolated islands or territories subjected to harsh conditions (as in the Arctic).[43] Conversely, effective occupation required a higher degree of control for areas subject to fierce colonial competition (as in the African hinterland).

Doctrinal pragmatism on the subject of territorial claims gradually was transformed into a flexible institutional ethic for the management of one vast international common space, Antarctica. In the early twentieth century, nations that had ambitious scientific expeditions to the Antarctic began to make actual territorial claims to that polar region. These claims depended on assertions of discovery or more spurious notions of contiguity but certainly were not supported by any credible evidence of effective occupation. The way in which states have purported to perfect territorial claims in Antarctica has a formal, even comic, aspect. The Chilean and Argentine governments flew pregnant women to Antarctica, had them deliver babies there, and then recorded in the children's passports the place of birth as their "Antarctic Territories." The United States and Britain engaged in a 1934 diplomatic correspondence over the propriety of issuing postage stamps and operating a radio station in the Antarctic.[44]

The practical solution for competing Antarctic claims was developed in the 1959 Antarctic Treaty,[45] which for all intents and purposes "froze" national claims to sectors on the Southern Continent. As long as that treaty remains in force, no nation can assert a territorial claim to Antarctica. At the same time, the Antarctic Treaty System demilitarized the region and established a unique form of condominium regime to manage activities and resources there. The Antarctic Treaty Consultative Parties, which include all states that have a scientific presence in Antarctic, meet regularly to develop regulations for the safe and friendly use of the continent. These have included regimes for the management of fishing resources in the Southern Ocean as well as a comprehensive environmental protection protocol.

The functions of significant international institutions are typically promoted through pragmatic doctrines. As discussed in chapter 3, the World Court has often been called on to provide pragmatic solutions to institutional difficulties encountered by the UN. In the *Certain Expenses* opinion, this manifested itself in an enunciation of a pragmatic rule of institutional governance: dissenters could not rely on separation-of-powers arguments to defeat an exercise of authority by the organization but, rather, were limited to arguing that the action was entirely ultra vires.[46] In the *Namibia* opinion,[47] the ICJ used a form of intentionalist and pragmatic reasoning to hold that despite the Charter's clear text, a permanent member of the Security Council did not need to vote yes to be considered as "concurring" and that an abstention did not act as a veto. To have cleaved to a textualist interpretation would have rendered hundreds of previous Security Council resolutions and decisions invalid. Pragmatism can thus serve a significant function in effectuating the intent of international actors and recognizing their actual practices.

Negotiated pragmatism is often the result of muscular diplomacy. These interactions often take place on the margins of state sovereignty, especially with conflicts over jurisdiction. The controversial aspect of the jurisdictional basis of territoriality does not arise with respect to persons and things within the forum's territory. Rather, the problem occurs when a state wishes to exercise jurisdiction over a person or thing located outside that nation's territory when that person or thing causes effects inside that state's borders. This is known as the objective territorial principle or, more descriptively, the effects principle. This is simply illustrated by the scenario of a gunman located just a few feet inside the territory of one nation who fires a weapon into another country and injures someone on this side of the border. If this sounds fanciful, consider a German decision of 1889 in which a French national, standing on a hillside in France, shouted "Vive la France!" and was later prosecuted for sedition in Germany because his declaration was heard across the frontier.[48] It is no surprise, therefore, that some of the most contentious cases of disputed jurisdiction have arisen when one state purports to exercise jurisdiction on the basis of the effects principle.

Beginning in the 1970s, some countries (most notably the United States) aggressively sought to expand their ability to prescribe conduct extraterritorially by liberally asserting the effects doctrine. Other major trading nations—Canada, Europe, and Japan—vigorously opposed what they regarded as an untoward and illegal extension of U.S. prescriptive jurisdiction over competition, securities, and other regulatory matters. In the late 1980s, however, the Europeans shifted their thinking and began to give qualified support for the use of the effects doctrine.[49] This time it was in vindication of the European Community's own competition policies and directives. The effects doctrine is thus becoming a more widely recognized aspect of the jurisdictional basis of territoriality.

Pragmatism is thus a quality that can be exercised by all sorts of international decision makers. Tribunals and treaty regimes have together promoted flexible doctrines in avoiding sovereign disputes and promoting rational resource management. In prescriptive jurisdiction matters, the determinations of domestic legislators and policy makers tend to count, with only limited review by international bodies (although the process of globalization, especially through the WTO, is changing that). By way of contrast, the pragmatism exhibited in the construction of the organic charters of international institutions seems more internalized to those organizations and less relevant to wider international law doctrines. The important point here is that pragmatism is not merely a doctrinal phenomenon but a style of international decision making.

So far, negotiated pragmatism in international law doctrines seems to be utterly consistent with principled yet flexible attitudes in the international community. In some instances, though, international decision makers have used pragmatism to reach merely a safe result, one that might be chosen by the disputing actors behind a Rawlsian "veil of ignorance" but with otherwise little to recommend it. In such instances, a pragmatic doctrine may superficially appear to lead to a just result, even while significant substantive values or procedural safeguards are sacrificed.

To return to another example drawn from the wide body of practice for territorial disputes, maritime delimitations have raised principled concerns about pragmatic jurisprudence. The creation of maritime zones under the law of the sea brought with it the need to demarcate these zones when nations dispute their boundaries. With so much at stake—valuable fish stocks, critical oil fields, and strategic locations—the odds of nations being disposed to use force to assert their claims to maritime real estate vastly increase. The same principles that are implicated in territorial disputes also apply to maritime delimitation, although they are often amplified. For example, title to well-positioned islands has become a major issue for international relations. Control of a small island can generate hundreds of thousands of square miles of territorial seas, contiguous zones, and exclusive economic zones (EEZs). The 1982 Law of the Sea Convention does try to moderate this result somewhat by providing that rocks incapable of supporting "economic life" cannot generate an EEZ. But without further defining its terms, this provision is itself problematic.

When coastal nations are in proximity to each other, as either opposite or adjacent states, real problems arise. The 1982 Law of the Sea

Convention stipulated an "equitable solution" for maritime delimitations of continental shelves and EEZs.[50] This has meant in practice that an equidistance line might be the start of the process, but that line can be altered by relevant circumstances. What the appropriate circumstances are has been decided by international tribunals. These have included giving special treatment to islands, especially in circumstances where those of one disputing nation are located just offshore of the other state. The Greek isles right off the coast of Turkey and Britain's Channel Islands off France are just two examples. A number of tribunals have chosen to give half or quarter effect to islands of one nation located in close proximity to another.[51] This really is a "split the baby" solution to what would otherwise be an intractable dispute of sovereignty.

Pragmatism as Value Conflict

There is also a dark side to pragmatism in international law. This arises when the state actors doing the negotiating achieve their ends at the expense of other constituents of the system. Pragmatism in international law can often cover profound conflicts in values.

For example, a problem common to both universal and regional human rights systems is what to do when individual rights conflict with the perceived safety and well-being of the state. If human rights law reflects an accommodation between state sovereignty and individual dignity, how is that balance struck in times of crisis? This raises the problem of derogation of human rights instruments in emergency situations. A critical provision of the 1967 International Covenant on Civil and Political Rights (ICCPR) is article 4, which allows a party to depart from its obligations under the convention provided that (1) it is a time of "public emergency which threatens the life of the nation," (2) the derogation is "strictly required by the exigencies of the situation," (3) certain core rights (such as the right to life, the prohibition of torture and enslavement, and freedom of thought and conscience) be preserved, and (4) notice of the derogation be communicated to other parties.[52]

The derogation provision of article 4 was essential for the passage of the ICCPR. States wanted to protect their freedom of action in times of emergency. The ICCPR's provision was drawn from a regional human rights system: the 1950 European Convention on Human Rights,[53] article 15 of which is virtually identical. That clause has been construed by the European Court of Human Rights in a way that allows a margin of appreciation for governments to declare national emergencies but also imposes substantial restrictions on derogations. In *Lawless v. Ireland*,[54] that court ruled that Ireland was justified in declaring an emergency in the wake of Irish Republican Army attacks and that detention of suspects for limited periods without trial was "strictly required by the exigencies of the situation."

There are two silver linings in this dark cloud of a pragmatic solution to state recognitions of human rights for citizens. One is that states must be open and transparent in their violation of human rights: in announcing a derogation, they are subjecting themselves to international scrutiny and the mobilization of shame. Additionally, the derogation clauses of the ICCPR and European Convention indicate that certain rights can never be violated, and these rights are comparable to *jus cogens* norms.

Pragmatism can often mask value paradoxes by seemingly harmonizing concerns for sovereignty, fairness, and rational resource use. In the law of nonnavigational uses of international watercourses, states often staked out extreme positions. In a typical situation, two coriparians would be in conflict over allocations of water from the river. An upper riparian might claim that it was entitled to do whatever it wished with the river resource as it flowed through its territory, even if that meant denying the downstream state substantial quantities of water or severely degrading the quality of the river. Lower riparians would likewise claim entitlement to the last drop of water that would flow through their territory in a natural condition. Needless to say, the law on this subject would not have progressed far if these incompatible positions were embraced.[55]

Aside from announcing a "natural community of interest"[56] for river resources and requiring good-faith negotiations between the disputants, international law was relatively slow to add specific content to these general principles of river management. One significant step was the 1966 publication of the Helsinki Rules by the International Law Association,[57] an NGO of academic international lawyers. The rules prescribed some specific criteria for balancing and weighing competing interests, such as (1) geography and hydrography of the river basin, (2) past utilization and economic needs of the riparians, and (3) the most efficient use of the water resources. These were later amplified in the official work of the UN's ILC, and the international community is currently reviewing Draft Articles on Non-Navigational Uses of International Watercourses. These codifications have already been applied by international tribunals.[58]

Pragmatism can thus take the shape of free-form standards in a middle range of potential outcomes, with the extremes representing alignment with one significant international law objective or another. Another example of this arises in the context of international economic law and environmental protection. Equality, fairness, sovereignty, and rationality all compete in producing pragmatic doctrines that allow developing nations to either opt out of stringent environmental standards under many treaty regimes or receive preferential treatment under global trading disciplines.[59] As with the negotiation of derogations under human rights instruments, this explicit double standard was regarded as diplomatically essential to secure the concurrence of nations that would otherwise dissent to a regime or persistently object to the formation of relevant customs. In this way, pragmatism is deliberately used to obfuscate fundamental differences between national negotiating postures. The general attitude embraced by such doctrines is that time will serve to harmonize those positions. A pragmatic rule serves as a sort of doctrinal placeholder, allowing for later convergence.

In a similar fashion, pragmatic concerns have impelled increased access by individuals and business enterprises to forms of international dispute settlement that would not have been available even decades ago. Most international tribunals are open only to adjudicate the causes of states or those individual claims that have been espoused by a government. More recently, a handful of institutions— including the U.S.-Mexican Commissions of the 1920s, the Iran–United States Claims Tribunal, and some investment-dispute mechanisms—have been opened to individual claims without government sponsorship. Many states have recognized that it is better to allow individuals direct recourse to international justice mechanisms than to always require the elevation of disputes to an interstate diplomatic level.

Sovereignty concerns and individual rights have thus been conciliated through pragmatic procedures. Effectuating a direct right of access for persons and businesses has necessitated some alterations to technical rules of diplomatic protection and international claims practice. For example, the rule used to be that individuals who were dual nationals could not bring a claim against either of their states of nationality. This harsh result was modified over time by international tribunals that adopted a test of dominant and effective nationality: a dual national could bring a claim against one of her states of nationality, provided it was not the dominant and effective one.[60] In an extremely contentious dispute, the Iran–United States Claims Tribunal ruled that dual Iranian-American nationals (almost all of whom were associated with the hated regime of the Shah of Iran) could nevertheless bring claims against Iran for expropriated assets as long as the claimants could show that their dominant and effective nationality was that of the United States. They could make that showing by proof that the United States was their habitual residence, the center of their economic interests (and business assets), and the locus of family ties and political participation (including voting) as well as providing other evidence of attachment (particularly speaking English and being acclimated to American ways).[61]

If the claims of dual nationals have posed difficulties for international tribunals, those of business associations (including partnerships and corporations) have been particularly troublesome. The Algiers Accords that created the Iran–United States Claims Tribunal in 1981 specifically adopted a rule at variance with custom,[62] allowing claimants to bring claims on behalf of any corporation in which U.S. nationals owned 50 percent or more of the capital stock. In addition, individual shareholders were permitted to assert claims against Iran if they had some form of controlling interest in an entity affected by the Iranian government's actions. Finally, partnerships were allowed to file claims as long as any partner was of an eligible nationality. In each of these circumstances, the tribunal would often prorate the value of the claim to reflect the relative percentage of the business entity controlled by U.S. citizens.

The doctrinal evolutions in the law of diplomatic protection and of international environmental protection tend to affiliate pragmatism with progress. Flexible doctrines are negotiated to achieve compromise or to leave open the possibility of future breakthroughs. Pragmatic positions occasionally have a cyclical flavor to them, as with the evolution of standards of compensation for expropriated or nationalized property. The Hull-Hay correspondence of the 1930s articulated a custom for "prompt, adequate and effective" compensation for nationalized property.[63] Precisely because of the long association of state responsibility law with colonial and imperial politics, it came under withering attack during the period of decolonization in the 1950s, 1960s, and 1970s. Newly independent former colonies asserted that the then-existing customary international law of state responsibility was not of their making and assertively bid to change it. The primary vehicle chosen for this transformation was a series of UN General Assembly resolutions.

These resolutions were collectively known as the New International Economic Order (NIEO) and were an attempt at remaking the landscape of international economic relationships and their legal bases. The 1973 UN Declaration on Permanent Sovereignty over Natural Resources and the 1974 Charter on Economic Rights and Duties of States were drafted to propound new rules of customary international law. The key features of these resolutions were provisions allowing the expropriating state to establish the "appropriate" compensation to be paid and (in case of a challenge by the foreign owner of the property) to have the disputes resolved only in domestic courts. Needless to say, these alterations to the prevailing customary international law rules were opposed by economically developed, capital-exporting nations. (This lack of consensus was later noted by the arbitrator in the *TOPCO* arbitration, discussed in chapter 3.)

The NIEO initiative coincided with a time of rising commodity prices and wholesale expropriations of foreign businesses in the developing world (particularly in such extractive industries as mining and petroleum products). The pendulum, however, was bound to swing again, and by the 1980s, commodity prices collapsed, and developing nations in South America, Africa, and Asia were once again hungering for foreign investment. Having been once harmed by host government expropriations of foreign properties, capital-exporting nations insisted on placing the law of state responsibility toward aliens on a firmer footing. Since that time, such countries as the United States, Japan, and France negotiated bilateral friendship, commerce, and navigation treaties with developing states, including specific provisions on the rights of foreign nationals to live and work in those countries. In additional, a new form of international agreement, bilateral investment treaties, has been created to address very particular issues of investment protection, including detailed rules for compensation in the event of expropriation or nationalization as well as valuation of certain kinds of business assets (most notably, intellectual properties).

It may be that the wheel will turn again, and a new pragmatic solution will be sought to the perennial problem of investor protection and the conflicting objectives of sovereignty, equality, and fairness. Especially difficult questions arise about when a government action becomes a taking compensable under international law. Legally savvy states do not nowadays outright confiscate foreign property in their territory. Instead, they might engage in forms of "creeping" expropriation by limiting foreign investors' ability to control their enterprises by restricting their ability to repatriate funds or accounts (often through foreign exchange controls). These kinds of restrictions, unless they accumulate to the point of an irreversible interference with the foreign investor's property rights, are often not regarded as alone constituting a compensable taking. States may also engage in what appear to be completely innocuous and unassailable forms of regulation—perhaps the imposition of taxes or of environmental protections—and these will not necessarily be regarded as expropriations requiring compensation under international law. An international tribunal early in the 1900s ruled that imposition of a series of license fees that had the effect of forcing the claimant to close a business were not an expropriation.[64] Nevertheless, recent decisions of institutions created by NAFTA and the WTO are revisiting this significant question of regulatory takings in international law.

Pragmatic international law doctrines can either accentuate or obscure conflicts between the values undergirding international legal regulation. The internal structure of many of the particular doctrines reviewed in this chapter reveal a number of pragmatic strategies. One group would attempt to resolve technical disputes by literal, split-the-difference outcomes, justified by some appeal to situational justice or fairness. Another set of rules shows a willingness to defer important decisions to a later day of reckoning. A last cluster of pragmatic norms eschews extreme positions and deflects outcomes into a middle ground of a case-by-case application of sensible standards. Many forms of pragmatism pander to state-centered interests, while a small minority extol other values. The overall feel of pragmatic rules is one of a necessary evil—a utilitarian approach that is ready to concede advantage to states in the interstices of international lawmaking.

It seems that pragmatism, like formalism, has many demeanors. It is not easy to distinguish those that are gracious from those that are unsettling. One thing is for sure, however: to regard the evolution of international law doctrines as an inevitable transformation from formal to flexible structures, rigid rules to pragmatic principles, would be a serious error. The reality of contemporary international law is that it is a subtle admixture of these two styles of legal analysis and rule making. It would be hard to imagine an effective international legal system that was too quick to get rid of certain types of formalisms, especially with the certainty and legitimacy they conferred. It may be, to recast Thomas Jefferson's conciliatory statement, "We are all pragmatists; we are all formalists."

The interior life of international law doctrines will remain poised between formal and pragmatic constructions. That is not to say, however, that gains are unlikely to be made in advancing the substantive content of those norms or improving their consistency with overriding values of the system. Progress has come to international law, and its tempo has beaten faster and faster. It is just that progress is rarely manifested in an easy transition from formalism to pragmatism. It remains to examine the mechanisms by which international law rules are observed, along with the general tenor of the system's conservatism or progressivism. These questions will be taken up in the remaining chapters.

9 Enforcement and Compliance

The ultimate test of international law is how well it manages conflict between states and other international actors. So far, this volume has demonstrated that international law, while primitive in some respects, has some attributes of a fully formed legal system—with clear sources and methods, a diversity of subjects and objects, and the ability positively to interact with domestic legal systems. Even so, international law would be a failure if it could not adequately meet the needs of the international community in constructively resolving the problems that arise in international affairs. The only real way to measure the success of the international legal system is by its ability to resolve peacefully those international disputes.

Regrettably, the gauge of international law's success in managing conflict traditionally has been skewed. The enforcement of international law often has been viewed as implicating fundamental issues of war and peace. When state relations are strained, or (if the worst happens) hostilities break out, some defect of international law is typically blamed. It would be as if the very integrity of a domestic legal system were challenged or questioned with every murder, every act of depredation, every nuance of lawlessness. That may be an impossible standard to meet, and international law flunks that test more readily than any other legal system.

That is why international law's success in managing conflict among its constituents may have to be measured by a different yardstick. Traditional models of enforcement will have to give way to more contemporary notions of compliance. By the same token, consent mechanisms for the use of dispute-settlement procedures may have to be modified to bring states and other international actors directly before international institutions. In addition, questions of standing (identifying what parties can complain of an international law violation) will have to be clarified.

VERTICAL AND HORIZONTAL ENFORCEMENT

International law always has been preoccupied with how it enforces its rules.[1] Two enforcement models traditionally have been offered. One can be described as vertical, where respect for international legal norms is somehow enforced from above. Such enforcement mechanisms have been exceedingly rare in international legal history. Indeed, the occurrence of such top-down enforcement has usually been the product of circumstances that are typically antithetical to an authentic state system for international law: hegemony or proto–world government. Even imagining such vertical processes tends to require an embrace of naturalist motivations of religious belief or political ideology to justify them.

As a practical matter, collective security regimes—of the sort one would expect in any thrust toward vertical enforcement of international law—have been virtual failures. The Covenant of the League of Nations, adopted in 1919 as part of the Treaty of Versailles that ended World War I, ushered in the first global system for collective security and protection of international peace. The primary feature of the Covenant system was a compulsory dispute-settlement mechanism (operated by the council of the League), to which states had to submit as a condition preparatory to initiating hostilities. If a nation jumped the gun and began a war before the League institutions had the chance to adjust the dispute, then that party would have violated Covenant article XVI, and the League council could recommend action against the aggressor. The critical weakness of the League Covenant was the requirement of unanimity in the council to trigger collective security, and, even when that was achieved, member states still had the option of whether to use force against the aggressor. This accounts for the League's notable inability to deter aggression by Nazi Germany, Fascist Italy, and Imperial Japan in the 1930s.

The UN Charter's attitude toward international law enforcement was at once more legal and pragmatic than the League's. Charter Article 2(4)'s proscription of use of force is the prime directive of modern international law, although states have struggled to establish the outer limits of that obligation and any potential exceptions. Legal controls on resort to armed conflict can only be as successful as the underlying collective security regime that the UN manages. States will only refrain from aggression if they have the certain knowledge that breaches of the peace will be the subject of immediate economic sanctions and, much more importantly, decisive military response by the wider international community.

The Charter system's original intent was to prevent or suppress dangerous regional powers from militarizing and challenging the authority of the Great Powers. The system of collective security under the Charter was never intended to address Great Power conflict or rivalries acted out between the proxies of the Security Council's permanent members. The Charter's plan was that the Security Council would, in the face of an act of aggression, declare a violation of the Charter under article 39 and then order all UN member states to impose economic sanctions or other penalties. If such sanctions are ineffectual in reversing the unlawful conduct, then the council can, under article 42, order the mobilization of air, sea, or land forces. UN members are obliged not to give any support to the outlaw nation. Under Charter article 43, states were supposed to have negotiated agreements with the UN to provide military contingents for the UN's use under the command of the Security Council and its Military Staff Committee. No such agreements have ever been concluded, and thus, on those few occasions when the UN has ordered an enforcement action under chapter VII of the Charter, ad hoc coalitions of forces have been assembled for the task.

It is fair to say that the entire collective security mechanism of the UN Charter was nullified during the Cold War. The Security Council literally could not act against aggressor nations because, almost inevitably, each one was a proxy of either the United States or Soviet Union, and thus the Americans (and their allies) or the Soviets could be counted on to veto any responsive resolution. The only exception to this Security Council gridlock was the serendipitous action taken by the UN at the beginning of the Korean War. The Soviets had been boycotting the council and were not there to cast the necessary veto of the enforcement action.

Security Council inaction profoundly disappointed the international community in the 1950s and 1960s. In response, the UN General Assembly began to assert its authority to order certain kinds of actions without Security Council approval. Thus was born the use of UN peacekeeping forces, authorized under chapter VI of the Charter. Developed by the dynamic UN Secretary General Dag Hammarskjöld of Sweden, the first uses of peacekeepers occurred in the aftermath of the Middle East Suez Crisis in 1956 and the 1960–63 Katanga Rebellion in Congo. Essential to the creation of the UN Emergency Force for the Sinai and the UN Force for the Congo was permission for their deployment by the host states. Unlike enforcement actions against malefactor countries, which can only be ordered by the Security Council acting under chapter VII, peacekeeping forces, established and funded by the General Assembly under chapter VI of the Charter, are consensual (with the permission of the host state).

Even under the ostensibly more ambitious collective security regime of the UN Charter, enforcement may well be a misnomer. Aside from the peculiar post–Cold War confluence of events that led to the UN's forceful response to Iraq's 1990 invasion of Kuwait and some isolated interventions in such "failed states" as Somalia and Haiti, the organization may not be capable of playing an enforcement role. If the UN is the only international institution today that can make a legitimate claim to acting as a vertical enforcer of international law, such may be impossible, and—make no mistake—the only law that would be enforced under such circumstances would be that which implicates values of peace, security, and humanity. Vertical enforcement is virtually nonexistent in the pursuit of other international law objectives.

Horizontal enforcement is where actors in the international legal system take it upon themselves to vindicate their rights and obligations. Countermeasures, or self-help, are a necessary part of any legal system that lacks strong vertical enforcement, like the international community.[2] There is no world policeman to command or coerce obedience to international law rules; instead, states and other actors rely on a combination of mechanisms to win respect and compliance with these duties. Countermeasures traditionally have been divided into two categories: forcible (involving recourse to armed conflict) and nonforcible (not involving military power).

If viewed primarily as a horizontal system, the chief task for international law is to channel and control the muscular aspects of international life. It may well be inevitable that states will participate in this struggle for law. The only question is how to make this competition constructive and civil and not degenerate into atavistic conflict, a return to a metaphoric state of nature. One of international law's vital features is a cluster of doctrines that tend to manage, not suppress, countries' legitimate attempts to aggressively vindicate their international legal rights and duties.

One aspect of these rules can be seen in the law of treaties. An extremely contentious issue in treaty law arises when one state purports to unilaterally suspend or terminate an obligation in an international agreement. A situation where this arises is when one party to a treaty believes that another state has breached the obligations of the agreement. The natural reaction in such circumstances is for the offended state to suspend or terminate the treaty. International law clearly recognizes the right of a state to terminate a treaty if another party has breached its obligations under the agreement. Customary international law and VCLT article 60 have added an important caveat: a nation cannot terminate the treaty unless another party has materially breached a provision "essential to the accomplishment of the object or purpose of a treaty."[3]

In other words, a trivial or accidental breach of a treaty obligation does not give grounds for unilateral termination. Indeed, under this rule, if a party anticipatorily terminates a treaty, believing the other side has committed a material breach, but later finds it was wrong in that belief, then it will be regarded as the party in breach. Of course, just because a state believes a treaty partner has committed a material breach does not necessarily mean, in practice, that termination will be forthcoming. It might just spark a renewed round of diplomacy to heal the rift.

A related context of restraint occurs when a state is obliged to re-spond to another nation's ostensibly illegal conduct with an unlawful act of its own. Most commentators agree that nonforcible reprisals remain necessary to promote respect for international obligations. Without some kind of threat to take action (even illegal action) in the face of unlawful conduct, many countries will flout international law. Under this vision of a muscular international law, we need a bit of punch and counterpunch to persuade recalcitrant nations to respect their duties under custom or treaties. At what point does a system of countermeasures become too energetic and in fact contribute to in-stability and conflict in international relations? In addition, if coun-termeasures are chiefly used by the rich and powerful nations of the world, does that mean that weaker states are reduced to a position of meekly acquiescing to the demands of their more powerful neighbors or simply forgoing their remedies when their rights are violated?

Perhaps the best illustration of this dynamic of countermeasures can be seen in the *Air Services Agreement* arbitration of 1978 be-tween the United States and France.[4] The underlying dispute arose in connection with a 1946 bilateral Air Services Agreement between France and the United States. These treaties regulate every aspect of scheduled commercial aviation between two nations. Under the 1946 agreement, an American airline, Pan Am, was given the right to operate a scheduled route between Paris and London. Because of aggressive subsidies being provided by the French government to Air France, Pan Am desired to substitute a smaller plane for a 747 aircraft on the route, what is called a change in gauge. The 1946 treaty was arguably silent or ambiguous as to whether an air carrier could sub-stitute a smaller aircraft. The French government steadfastly refused, and the basis for the refusal ranged from assertions of national honor (for Pan Am to fly anything smaller than a 747 into Paris would be an affront) to the more pragmatic reason that Air France rather enjoyed the prospect of forcing its competitor to run a grossly unprofitable route. Finally, the French dropped all pretenses and simply compelled Pan Am to cease its flights to Paris.

At this juncture, the U.S. government proposed arbitration as a way to resolve the dispute. For nearly two years, the French refused this invitation to resolve the dispute in this manner. Finally, the

United States made a reprisal in the form of suspending Air France's Paris–Los Angeles route, long established under the 1946 agreement. This got the French government's attention, and France finally agreed to arbitration. The two questions submitted to the panel were (1) whether Pan Am could change gauge, and (2) whether the United States could unilaterally suspend Air France's route to Los Angeles. The first matter was quickly resolved in favor of Pan Am, but the second question implicated the international law of countermeasures.

The arbitral tribunal first had to respond to France's suggestion that because the 1946 agreement provided for arbitration, it was impermissible for the United States to engage in unilateral self-help measures. The tribunal ruled, however, that France had stonewalled the arbitration process, and only the U.S. retaliatory move terminating the Los Angeles route brought France to the negotiating table. In short, the tribunal ruled that countermeasures were a necessary part of the punch and counterpunch often needed in international relations for states to decide to submit their disputes to arbitration or some other method of binding settlement.

The tribunal did indicate, however, that there was a risk of escalation in any use of countermeasures. France conceivably could have cut off Pan Am's New York–Paris run, and then the United States could have retaliated by economic sanctions outside of the air sector, and so on. Nevertheless, the tribunal ruled that the U.S. response in terminating Air France's Los Angeles run—although a violation of the 1946 agreement—was a permissible and proportional response to France's earlier refusal to allow Pan Am to change gauge. Despite its endorsement of nonforcible reprisals as a means of enforcing international law rights, the tribunal did observe that once an effective dispute-settlement mechanism was triggered, all countermeasures should cease. In this case, once the arbitral tribunal had jurisdiction over the matter, neither France nor the United States could take unilateral measures without the panel's permission. The ICJ made a similar ruling in 1980, validating the U.S. freezing of Iranian assets in response to the takeover of the U.S. embassy in Tehran.[5]

The holding of the *Air Services Agreement* arbitration permits a wide ambit of discretion to states that believe themselves to be victims of an international law violation. They may proportionally seek to punish the offender by engaging in their own retaliatory response—a response that would itself be illegal but for the earlier unlawful act of the other side. This rule precisely matches the VCLT principle that only where there has been a material breach of an agreement can another party terminate or suspend performance. This means that states must be cautious in taking the first step of what may later be characterized as an anticipatory breach. Both of these rules are intended to give states the option to respond to the perceived illegal acts of other nations, but only within a limited scope. Such retaliations also carry the risk that a later arbitration might rule that there had been no initial violation or material breach and that, therefore, the responder's actions were the first to cross the threshold of illegality.

The last sort of doctrine in international law's cluster of rules to control conflict arises in the use of force context and thus provides a final horizontal counterpoint to vertical means of enforcement. The ICJ addressed these issues in one of the most contentious and controversial cases it has ever decided: *Military and Paramilitary Activities in and against Nicaragua.*[6] The case arose out of U.S. efforts to destabilize and topple the left-leaning Sandinista government in Nicaragua in the early 1980s.

The heart of the dispute decided by the ICJ was the U.S. assertion that it was permitted to use force against Nicaragua (whether in the form of support for the contras or direct action) because it was engaging in collective self-defense on behalf of El Salvador. El Salvador, the United States argued, was the victim of an armed attack by Nicaraguan-backed rebels. The ICJ rejected this defense, based on its reading of UN Charter article 51 and the background rules of customary international law for *ius ad bellum.*[7] The Court found, as a matter of fact, that El Salvador had made no formal request to the United States to engage in collective self-defense against Nicaragua. Without such an appeal, the Court reasoned, collective self-defense could not be invoked. In short, international law does not give states the right to foist assistance on an unwilling partner. This makes sense, but on the facts of the *Nicaragua* case, it was manifest that El Salvador had been on record as believing that insurgent forces were being supported by the Nicaraguan Sandinistas and had requested aid from the United States to repel that intervention.

The ICJ went on to make, however, the crucial ruling of the case. It held that, in any event, Nicaragua's aid to the El Salvadoran rebels had not risen to the level of an armed attack under Charter article 51. The Court found that the United States was the first to cross the trip wire of an armed attack, and, therefore, the United States was found to be the aggressor under article 2(4).

This rule—similar in structure to the VCLT's provision on material breach and the *Air Service* arbitration's principle of countermeasures—requires that a state be cautious in reacting to a potential international law violation by another nation. For if a country does not fully appreciate the situation, it might later be found to be the breacher, violator, or aggressor. International law thus permits self-help measures for its constituents but proceeds to cabin overly muscular enforcement in all potential arenas of conflict: treaty breaches, reprisals as countermeasures, and uses of armed force as self-defense. In each instance, the structure of international law rules counsels moderation and discretion.

RIGHTS AND REMEDIES

One of the key characteristics of international law is that it often features a notable lack of connection between rights and remedies. Unlike many modern legal systems, international law seems comfortable with the position that some of its norms may confer rights, the violation of which may well be irremediable. While this may seem oxymoronic—after all, a right is definitionally something that can be enforced—this insight may cut to the quick in defining the nature of international law as a legal system.

The rights-remedies disconnect is partially the result of an international legal system that lacks strong verticality in its enforcement mechanisms. When compliance with norms cannot be coerced from above by a purely positivist, Austinian sovereign, it is entirely possible to imagine that certain expectations created by a legal system (a softer way of referring to a right) may go unfulfilled. Furthermore, the lack of effective remedies in international law may be even more reflective of the confines of the system. To the extent that international law remains bounded by considerations of domesticity, privity, and politics, it is certainly not surprising that truly effective and autonomous enforcement mechanisms may be lacking.

This is particularly true at the intersection of domestic and international realms of competence and within the interstices of legal and political disputes. For intensely dualist countries, it is entirely possible to imagine that obligations contained in agreements with international application may not have domestic effect. One court observed in the United States that to "imply a cause of action from the law of nations would completely defeat the critical right of the sovereign to determine whether and how international rights should be enforced in that municipality."[8]

Domestic tribunals and agencies are thus often disabled from directly applying the norms contained in custom and treaties to concrete disputes brought before those institutions. This blocks a significant avenue of redress for international actors seeking a remedy for violations, even though one might wonder whether domestic courts (not many of which embrace principles of judicial independence) are up to the task of enforcing international obligations. In any event, barring recourse to domestic institutions may also have a strong political aspect. States may have a strong incentive not to see international disputes resolved in forums that are beyond the states' direct control.

Another example of politics limiting effective international remedies can be seen in the context of execution of judgments against foreign sovereigns and their instrumentalities. Even for those nations that have adopted the customary international law doctrine of restrictive immunity for foreign states—thus permitting suits to be brought in their courts for commercial or similar, nonsovereign conduct—it remains exceedingly difficult to collect on such a domestic judgment. This has caused substantial miscarriages of justice. In one case, Chilean secret agents entered the United States in 1976 and murdered a Chilean dissident and his American companion in a car bombing in

Washington, D.C. The families brought suit under the U.S. Foreign Sovereign Immunities Act[9] and prevailed under the tort exception to immunity, despite Chilean arguments about having the "discretion" to assassinate opponents in the United States. When it came time to enforce the $5 million judgment, however, problems arose. The only Chilean assets the plaintiffs could find in the United States were the property of the Chilean national airline. A court later ruled that under the immunities act's narrow drafting, the airline was a separate entity from the Chilean government and that, in any event, it was by no means clear that the property to be executed against was related to the underlying political murder. The Second Circuit Court of Appeals acknowledged that this left the plaintiffs with a "right without a remedy."[10]

Because of all of these limitations on domestic institutions, international law in the past century has been preoccupied with the development of international tribunals and other judicial mechanisms for the resolution of disputes.[11] One of the crucial features of contemporary international law certainly has been the evolution of these institutions (many of which were discussed in chapter 3 insofar as their pronouncements are considered as law). We have a continued role for interstate public arbitrations (including claims tribunals) as well as private commercial arbitration.[12] New commissions have been monitoring and enforcing international human rights and humanitarian law norms. Tribunals for vindicating individual responsibility under international law, including the just-established International Criminal Court, will likely play a significant role. In addition to such global adjudicatory bodies as the World Court, we have specialized bodies (of which the International Tribunal for the Law of the Sea is a good example) as well as institutions created by regional organizations.

We may well have reached the point that these institutions are proliferating and are not being effectively coordinated to produce a coherent body of law. Are there too many international courts competing with each other for a narrow jurisdiction and a limited docket of cases? This has been suggested,[13] but I cannot really credit this criticism. These institutions have been created by the demands of the international community. Using a market metaphor, those dispute-settlement mechanisms that prove their worth will survive and flourish. Those that have been fashioned in anticipation of a need that has not materialized will wither away and die. If anything, there is a greater demand today for coordinating the decisions of international tribunals with those of domestic courts.

One aspect of the proliferation of dispute-settlement mechanisms offers a definite benefit to the international community. International actors are in a position to choose from a veritable Chinese menu of options, ranging from the casual and nonbinding (including conciliation, inquiry, and mediation)[14] to the formal and judicial (including arbitration and adjudication). Some treaty regimes (like the 1982 UN Convention on the Law of the Sea) were elaborately structured around this premise. This has given rise to stages of successive settlements of the same dispute. A matter may be submitted to mediation with the good offices of an international figure (the UN secretary-general being popular), and if that solution fails to satisfy, the parties may seek more formal and binding processes. A recent cause célèbre—involving France's nuclear testing in the South Pacific and its attack on a Greenpeace vessel in a New Zealand harbor—went through no fewer than three stages of settlement.[15] We are now witnessing a sort of ratcheting-up phenomenon for dispute settlement, where multiple and (sometimes) parallel mechanisms are being employed.

Despite this, the consent model of international adjudication remains preeminent for states. This has meant that countries cannot be haled before international tribunals without their approval, somehow manifested. This was part of the original bargain in creating the PCIJ in 1920 and remains the central precept of jurisdiction by its successor, the ICJ. Cases before the World Court are largely confined to disputes specially submitted (via a *compromis*) or under a treaty that so provides. Use of the so-called compulsory jurisdiction, under the optional clause of the ICJ statute,[16] has been disappointing, to say the least.

One need not look far for the reason for the relative unpopularity of optional-clause jurisdiction. Filing an article 36 declaration exposes states to suits brought by any other nation that has filed a similar declaration. That would invoke the Court's jurisdiction over disputes that may not even be in a state's contemplation when it makes its declaration, and, in many cases, countries have been quite queasy about making such broad, advance concessions. Virtually none of the states that have made an article 36 declaration have accepted the ICJ's jurisdiction unconditionally. Article 36(2) establishes an incredibly broad ambit for disputes covered by a declaration—almost anything involving the content of international law obligations (including treaty interpretations) and remedies for the breach of such a duty. Most countries have, therefore, applied substantial reservations to their acceptances.

Attempts to transform the consent paradigm of interstate dispute settlement into a truly compulsory and binding process have, for the most part, failed. It would be a mistake to think, however, that the entire structure of international dispute settlement is flawed. If anything, it is more robust today than it has been in the past half century. As of this writing, the World Court's docket consisted of a staggeringly large number of cases—twenty-four. Of these, four were boundary cases. Of the remainder, one involved environmental issues, two concerned treatment of aliens, two dealt with aerial incidents, and the rest implicated uses of armed force (in such global hot spots as the Persian Gulf, Africa, and the Balkans). Arbitration of disputes through ad hoc institutions is also incredibly popular today.

Nevertheless, the key remedial defect in international judicial process remains in satisfying the demands of nonstate actors. The really critical question is whether the rights of individuals and business enterprises can be vindicated in a structure of international law that still, to a great degree, emphasizes states and sovereignty. Two broad mechanisms have been developed over time. The first was the international law of diplomatic protection, where a nation asserts its right to protect the interests of a national by bringing an international claim against a state that has injured that person's rights or interests. States are under no moral or legal obligation to espouse the claims of their nationals, and the most serious drawback to the concept of diplomatic protection is the assumption that a state other than the country of nationality will have injured the individual. It is true that persons traveling or conducting business in foreign countries are sometimes treated in ways that are contrary to the law of state responsibility to aliens. Most often, however, one's own country is the perpetrator of abuses, and the procedures of diplomatic protection and international claims have no relevance where an individual has a complaint against his own state of nationality.

That is why the international law of human rights was formed, the development that clearly placed the individual in a status of rough parity with states as subjects of international law. Originally, how a state treated its own citizens was of no concern to international law. Today, a vast body of global and regional standards has developed, along with an array of enforcement mechanisms to vindicate individual human rights. Some of these are rarely invoked. These include such approaches as the 1948 Genocide Convention's referrals to international political organs (the UN Security Council) and tribunals (the World Court). By way of contrast, the approaches available under the 1967 ICCPR combine reporting and transparency activities and a limited form of UN Human Rights Committee review of direct petitions. Regional human rights systems, particularly in Europe and the Americas, have evolved the most sophisticated—and judicial—means of human rights enforcement.

There remain, nevertheless, deep dissatisfactions with the availability of judicial remedies for individuals' claims. Procedural doctrines (like exhaustion of local remedies) often conspire to block access. Even where international judicial recourse is available, the effective range of remedies may be severely limited. International tribunals are, for example, split on whether a state can be properly ordered to render specific performance (or restitution in kind) to cure a human rights abuse or remedy a breach of contract. In a more commercial context, lost profits are often included as a form of contract damage, although these are often attacked by respondent states as inappropriately speculative. Interest on awards is more and more common, although grants of attorneys' fees or punitive (exemplary) damages are virtually unheard of.[17]

The rights-remedies disconnect is unlikely to be resolved any time soon in international legal practice. The drawbacks inherent in the structure of international dispute settlement have been further re-

vealed by new forms of conflict, the resolution of which has shifted
from self-help measures to institutional remedies.

STANDING AND COMPLIANCE

Aside from increasing access to and the effective range of international remedies, there remains the matter of whether judicial approaches offer the best results. Many people have speculated that the
better way to enforce international law obligations is through quasi-
regulatory regimes in which international actors themselves have a
larger role in fashioning appropriate responses, as opposed to the traditional model of third-party judicial settlement. The creation of epistemic communities of experts who will guide and manage suitable
resolutions to disputes[18] would inevitably be part of this process.

Significant problems of legitimacy lurk here, and the resolution
of environmental and trade disputes offers two good examples. Even
though international institutions (such as NAFTA chapter 11 investment-dispute and WTO trade panels) are being vested with an increasing amount of authority, the lack of openness or transparency
of these mechanisms has been hotly criticized. What has been most
often criticized is the lack of political accountability of most forms
of international dispute settlement. These mechanisms have been de-
rided as a means by which cosmopolitan elites can transfer unpopular
kinds of decisions (typically of a distributive character) to international forums and thus deflect attack from themselves, all the while
supporting this globalizing agenda at the expense of local, authentic
values.

When narrated in this way, international law enforcement becomes
entwined with the most optimistic hopes, and most visceral fears, of
world order under law. At bottom is the question of which constituencies count in the international community and of how their voices
should be heard in decision-making processes. Standing to vindicate
international law rights and duties and to participate in the actual
mechanisms of enforcement has again become a central concern. Not
merely a rehash of an arid subjects-objects debate in international le-

gal theory, standing goes to the very heart of how international law rules are practically followed.

In a traditional formulation, rights and duties run between international legal actors in a binary, symmetric, and reciprocal manner. The paradigmatic international law norm was to have been found in a bilateral treaty, replete with perfect contractual equilibrium. Customary international law, like multilateral treaties of a legislative character, raised more difficult problems in identifying the appropriate stakeholders in a dispute, but these were still quite manageable. With the growing diversity of international law subjects and the emergence of dispute areas that were largely impervious to traditional notions of sovereignty, it was inevitable that the circle of parties that could enforce certain norms would be expanded.

As mentioned in chapter 5, notions of an expanded *ius standii* were related to forms of nonconsensual lawmaking: *jus cogens* customs, *erga omnes* obligations, and objective regimes. Additionally, *actio popularis* are those violations for which any member of the international community can seek redress.[19] In a 1966 decision, the World Court declined to allow "the equivalent of an 'actio popularis,' or right resident in any member of a community to take legal action in vindication of a public interest. . . . a right of this kind . . . is not known to international law as it stands at present."[20] But the latest set of Draft Articles on State Responsibility, prepared by the UN International Law Commission, indicates that the "obligations of the responsible State . . . may be owed to another State, to several States, or to the international community as a whole, depending on the character and content of the international legal obligation and on the circumstances of the breach, and irrespective of whether the State is the ultimate beneficiary of the obligation."[21] Some international tribunals seem prepared to recognize a wide constituency of claimants for certain types of obligations. Expanding the ambit of international obligations will invariably create pressure to augment forms of dispute settlement mechanisms and to make them available to nonstate actors.

For all of these reasons, the rhetoric of international law has subtly shifted from obedience to compliance, from compulsion to legitimacy, and from authority to transparency. The transition began, in some measure, with Louis Henkin's famous observation that "almost all nations observe almost all principles of international law and almost all of their obligations almost all of the time."[22] This spawned a growing literature, in both academic international law and international relations circles, on the noncoercive ways that international law rules are followed.[23] More importantly, the idea of compliance has shifted expectations among international actors themselves, building a culture of compliance with international norms. The empirical evidence suggests that compliance with international law rules is, indeed, the usual way of things. Violations of international law rules are the exception and are regarded as aberrant situations that deserve to be notorious and widely condemned.

As has been suggested throughout this volume, to demand that international law govern a peaceful and just international community—one that is completely free of conflict, disputes, and lawlessness—simply asks too much. For starters, it assumes that law in any culture can completely control society, and this it cannot do—nor should it. In any political society, law serves the interests of the constituents, not the other way around. More significantly, a society that is free from strife is no community at all. International law has grown and developed through conflict. Sometimes the dynamic has been a subtle struggle for law, but, on occasion, muscular competition for rights and obligations in the international legal system has led to outright hostilities.

The challenge for international law is the extent to which it can manage conflict without the usual tools available to other legal systems: vertical enforcement, coercive measures, and reliable remedies. It cannot be doubted that international law dispute settlement has notably matured in the last century. For the foreseeable future, however, it will be characterized by horizontal mechanisms, self-help, inadequate remedial structures, and uncertain coordination with domestic regimes.

This is not to suggest that international law tolerates high levels of noncompliance with its rules. It does not. International actors routinely and vigorously denounce every perceived slight by a neighbor, object to every bid for an unwanted rule, and complain of every violation of an accepted norm. For particular circumstances, mounting challenges can influence the behavior of the malefactor. Even if the unlawful behavior is not reversed, the incident may lead to further efforts to progressively develop uncertain areas of doctrine. Cumulatively, this process of protest (and its reciprocal, acquiescence) lies at the heart of the self-correcting mechanisms of international law enforcement and compliance.

When it comes to implementing its rules, what is distinctive about the international legal system is how much it has made with so little. In conditions that might legitimately be likened to a Hobbesian state of nature, international law has nonetheless managed to structure an international community, build expectations of order and compliance, and preserve a high degree of liberal freedom of action for its constituents. It is a remarkable achievement. What remains to discover is whether international law is regarded substantively as a force for good or for ill in international life.

10 Rectitude and Ambition

Conservatism and progressivism have been oddly paired throughout much of international legal history. As considered in chapter 3, the international community has defined itself in various ways over the past five centuries. This process of definition and self-reflection has meant that international law has had to serve many purposes and achieve numerous objectives. The demands of international life have meant that international law has often been obliged to sacrifice coherence and progressivity on the altar of expedience and expectation.

There has been a cyclical character for many of the signal developments of international law. As observed in chapter 1, the most significant changes made in international law doctrines, processes, and institutions have followed the bloodiest conflicts. It is as if the international community schizophrenically follows episodes of national atavism with global utopianism. Epochs of relative stability for international law rules seem invariably to be followed by short periods of frenzied reform across many sectors of international relations and for many doctrinal pockets. Far from being a progress narrative, international law may well be a circular dialectic.

Likewise, international law has never been consistent in expressing an unalloyed desire either for stability or for change. Much that has been discussed in this volume has tended toward a conclusion that international law rules are meant to promote security of expectation among international actors. For a community that remains as primitive as that for international relations, it is no surprise that the systemic value that would be treasured above all else would be certainty. Yet much in recent history suggests that international law has attempted in a variety of ways to manage and structure legal change.

Treaty doctrines such as "fundamental change of circumstances," or *rebus sic stantibus,*[1] are certainly one example. Rules concerning intertemporal law try also to mediate the consequences of necessary changes in legal rules over time (as described in chapter 5). These relatively narrow legal doctrines are part of a larger insight, captured in article 19 of the League of Nations Covenant, that the international community is obliged to manage the conditions of peaceful change. The very contemporary concern about "treaty congestion"—that we literally may be the victims of our own success in prescribing too many rules without effective understanding or enforcement of those norms—may be some vindication of Cicero's maxim, *summum ius summa iniuria:* the more law, the less justice.[2]

CONSERVATISM

In many respects, the anachronisms of contemporary international law tell us more about the nature of the legal system than its progressive achievements. Conservative doctrines seem oddly out of place in an international community that we describe as dynamic and changing. Why, the question must be posited, do such rules continue in force? What purposes do they serve? Just as many formal international law doctrines maintain the confines of the discipline or reflect certain state-centered values, so too with some conservative doctrines. But not all rules exhibiting rectitude or caution necessarily mirror formalism or paradox.

If that were the case, we would probably characterize as conservative any rule that privileges the role of states as international legal actors. Yet to do so would mean that we would damn with faint praise the doctrinal core of international law—including much of sources discourse, the law of treaties, and rules of international intercourse, jurisdiction, and liability. The current condition of international life is that states remain first among equals as international actors. We assume, for example, that only states can conclude treaties or prosecute hostilities. While there is a growing body of conventional and customary law to the contrary (such as the capacity of interna-

tional institutions to enter into treaties or national liberation movements to wage wars), the presumption remains for staking out a preserve of unquestioned state competence and power in international
relations.

Another conservative doctrine is the broad holding of the *Lotus*
case that everything is permitted in international law, save that expressly and unambiguously barred. It is no accident that this is regarded as the locus classicus of a truly liberal world order in which
states have total freedom of action, or, as Judge Loder wrote, "every
door is open unless it is closed by treaty or custom."[3] To use another
metaphor, this is the Wild West: self-reliant actors (states) do what
they can, or what they must, to survive, the only limit on their autonomy being their consent to be bound.

At first blush this does not seem conservative at all: it is downright
anarchic. This kind of liberalism can properly be seen as a position
of rectitude. While specific applications of the *Lotus* doctrine are no
longer current in the context of jurisdiction, especially with the introduction of a "rule of reason" in states' assertion of jurisdictional
authority,[4] the *Lotus* rule lives on in many forms. Most significantly,
it is perpetuated in the principle of consent in the formation of international law rules. While competing, nonconsensual sources of law—
such as *ius cogens* and objective regimes—are increasing in popularity, they are still kept in check by the strong sentiment that states
cannot be made to follow rules when they have not somehow agreed
to them.

Some conservative doctrines are specifically intended to promote
stability of expectation in international relations where it matters
the most. Questions surrounding the very constitution of nations,
their hermetically sealed sovereignties and borders, and the maintenance of peace between these polities count among these prime directives. That is why, despite the rhetorical appeal of self-determination
as a doctrine in international law (one that confers legitimacy on
what would otherwise be the doubtful place of states at the center of
world order), a "right of peoples" has never been permitted to sanction
wholesale rebellions, civil wars, or irredentism. Doctrines of recognition and state succession have been elaborately designed to deny such

breakaway regimes much legitimacy unless their claim to power and authority is unassailable as a matter of fact.

An ever-present problem for international law is what to do with entities that are created in violation of legal norms. This often arises from impermissible military conquests in which the victorious state declares a sham entity to gain some kind of political or diplomatic advantage. One notorious illustration of this was the creation by Japan of the puppet state of Manchukuo in northern China after the illegal Japanese invasion of that country in 1931. The League of Nations refused to accept Manchukuo as a state, and this incident prompted the United States to enunciate a principle (known as the Stimson Doctrine) that it would not accept the forcible creation of entities in violation of international law. This same principle motivated the UN to refuse to accept the membership applications of Transkei, a black homeland or Bantustan created by the white minority government in South Africa in the 1970s as a way to deflect criticism of that government's racist policies.

If recognition and state succession doctrines are fundamentally conservative—in the sense that they tend to nurture a status quo of political power—so, too, are rules of territorial acquisition. International law, for example, embraces a peculiar aspect of the European colonial legacy. It recognizes the (often) artificial boundaries that colonial powers in South America, Africa, and Asia drew between administrative units or rival territories. Under this doctrine—*uti possidetis*—the modern states of Latin America are obliged to follow the original Spanish and Portuguese colonial boundaries (dating back to 1800), just as current African nations must follow the old English, French, German, and Portuguese lines. Although there is a manifest contradiction between the principle of decolonization and the application of *uti possidetis*, the World Court has at least rationalized its use by observing that "maintenance of the territorial status quo . . . is often seen as the wisest course . . . to avoid a disruption [and promote] the essential requirement of stability."[5] Once again, a bad rule seems preferable to no rule at all.

International law's emphasis on stability and security may readily account for the conservatism of doctrines surrounding acquisition and control of territory. For obvious reasons, title to territory based on military conquest is certainly not a legitimate ground today; however, what about lands acquired long ago by force? Likewise, certain transfers of territory made by treaty of cession still remain controversial. (Spain, for example, still disputes British control of Gibraltar, acquired by treaty in 1713, as does Cuba with U.S. title to Guantanamo Bay.) Nevertheless, international law tends to exalt stability over justice, at least when it comes to the resolution of disputes that potentially could escalate into armed conflict. This is certainly not an extravagant fear, what with Argentina's 1982 invasion of the Falkland Islands (Malvinas) and Iraq's 1990 invasion of Kuwait.

Conservative doctrines can show up in the oddest places in international law. Some reflect a serendipity of historic events or are impelled by very real needs of the international community. Conservatism in international law rules can be an expression of Burkean traditionalism or pragmatic instrumentalism. A good example of conservatism as tradition is the rule of flag-state supremacy in the law of the sea. In granting access to foreign vessels, coastal states will often restrain themselves in the exercise of jurisdiction. In a number of cases, domestic courts have concluded that the coastal state cannot either exercise criminal jurisdiction over the crewmen of foreign vessels who commit crimes on board a ship in harbor or otherwise apply domestic law to shipboard activities.[6] The only departure from this custom—when the crime is murder and offends the "peace of the port"—rather proves the rule. In all other situations, coastal nations defer to the flag state to exercise control over all aspects of life on board the ship, including enforcing law and order.[7]

International law over the past four hundred years has evolved a number of mechanisms to temper and manage freedom of the seas. One of these is the rule (like that of aircraft registry) requiring that all vessels have a state of registry, a "flag state." The flag state is charged with the responsibility of overseeing and regulating all aspects of the ship's construction, design, equipment, and manning and with ensuring that the vessel is in compliance with international standards.[8] Flag-state control is taken so seriously as to result in a literal race to the bottom, with shipping concerns rushing to identify the jurisdiction that will regulate them the least. Another mechanism for enforcement on the high seas is the right of visit exercised by warships. Certain activities are prohibited on the high seas and thus are grounds for stop and seizure. The formalities of flag-state control are religiously respected, and short of suspicion of the commission of some universal offense (piracy or slave trading), the vessels of one state will not stop the ships of another, no matter how compelling the cause.[9]

While flag-state authority can certainly be justified as a practical vindication of freedom of the seas, it is better understood as historic tradition that has yet, over a half millennia, to be challenged by a better rule. Some international law processes reflect states' singular unwillingness to burden themselves with undue obligations. Exemplary of this has been the slow creation of liability and compensation regimes that would require states to pay for environmental damage they might cause. Pursuing this lawyerly approach to international environmental management is to simply make all the questions turn on answers of state responsibility. States are obviously reluctant to make rules that will require them to pay for their environmental misdeeds.

Nor have background rules of customary international law helped in this process. There is a substantial division in authority regarding the relevant standard of liability for environmental harms. Language in the *Trail Smelter* arbitration is suggestive of a strict liability standard, provided that the damage is of "serious consequence" and the injury is established by "clear and convincing evidence."[10] The 1972 Stockholm Declaration was also indicative of a possible strict liability standard. But other sources, including the World Court's 1949 *Corfu Channel* case,[11] might stand for the proposition that a state must be aware that it is causing environmental damage and fail to take steps to halt it. This would be more consistent with a fault, or negligence, standard of liability. A cynic might think that international law is deliberately incoherent on this issue. The truth is, it serves state interests by being cautious in framing these sorts of doctrines.

Other international law rules have been subject to more cyclical perturbations. Standards of compensation for national expropriations of foreign investment have fluctuated with the relative power gradients of capital exporting and importing countries. Nevertheless, the longer trend has been to adhere to a conservative—and pragmatic— position that states are free to nationalize foreign investment and property but must pay fully for it.[12] The traditional rule can admit progressive exceptions, although these usually manifest themselves as arguments going to the appropriate valuation of expropriated entities. International law rules can be conservative, even while having traditional pedigrees or pursuing pragmatic ends.

This applies as well to the institutions of international lawmaking. We tend to regard international institutions as progressive, organic entities that grow and change as conditions dictate, but that is often not the case. Most institutions have respected the sentiment expressed by Judge Hackworth in his dissent to the *Reparation for Injuries* opinion: there is danger in giving international institutions too free a rein in deciding their objects and purposes beyond the scope of their constituent charters and the corporate will of their members.[13]

A telltale marker of conservatism in international organizations is the privileged place of the Great Powers in the structure of both the League of Nations and UN. After all, the UN Security Council remains the ultimate lawmaking authority in the international community, as long as it is able to act under chapter VII of the Charter and without the veto of a permanent member. This reflects a significant pragmatism: coordinated action by the UN, in pursuit of international peace and security, would be impossible without at least the acquiescence of the world's most powerful nations. When the council performs its functions under chapter VII, it acts as a political body unconstrained by legalities. No judicial review of Security Council decisions on the maintenance of international peace and security is likely to be possible.[14] This reflects a conservative sentiment that there are limits to law and judicial institutions, and these ought to be respected as much in international contexts as in domestic, constitutional ones.

In a similar fashion, the consent principle for state participation in international adjudication reflects deep-seated conservatism. That a nation may not be haled before an international dispute settlement mechanism without its consent—somehow manifested—remains a crucial limitation on the jurisdiction of institutions like the World Court. Even when the Court is able to hear cases, some aspects of its procedures and practices hearken back to an earlier time in international dispute settlement. According to the Court's Statute, in any case where one (or more) of the parties is not represented on the bench by a judge of its nationality, that litigant can appoint a judge ad hoc.[15] A holdover of the practice of party-appointed arbitrators, ad hoc judges almost invariably vote in favor of the legal arguments advanced by the state that named them. This has come to be expected, although judges ad hoc may exercise some subtle influence on the Court's deliberations, especially in cases where the legal issues may turn on the interpretation of treaties written in an arcane language or on a fuller understanding of particular local laws or customs. Limits on third-party interventions in ICJ proceedings also reflect conservative concerns that litigation before the Court ought to remain, as much as possible, in the hands of the parties.[16] Despite the Court's ostensible appearance as an independent and neutral adjudicatory body, there is still a perception that it serves merely state interests in resolving particular disputes and that its function in articulating world law is secondary or even peripheral.

A last form of institutional conservatism is reflected in the limited forms of relief available before international dispute-settlement mechanisms, irrespective of their character or function. The rejection of specific performance as a remedy on the ground that it would be unseemly and futile for an international tribunal to order a state to take or forswear certain action, particularly corrodes respect for those institutions. When individual rights are notionally vindicated in international forums, the relief granted often appears grudging and circumspect.

Conservative doctrines can reflect state-centered conceptions of international relations, promote stability of expectation, continue anachronistic customs or treaty norms, or fulfill institutional roles. Whatever their particular function, conservative rules tend to help in demarcating limits for the legal system or build confidence in certain kinds of substantive outcomes. In this respect, conservative rules may project a kind of rectitude and wisdom that every legal system needs to function and sustain itself. There are, of course, some conservative doctrines without which we would certainly be better off. These are rules that have only a dubious link to a characteristic feature of international law as a legal system: its sources, techniques, values, or limits. International rules are, therefore, not bad because they are conservative; rather, they are bad because they fail effectively to bolster a significant structural component of the system or to advance an important objective.

PROGRESSIVISM

What has international law accomplished? If to recognize conservative doctrines is to understand the continuing limits on the international legal system, then to see its progressive achievements is to gauge the scope of international law's ambition. Such a review is necessarily historic and generic, touching on the broadest aspects of modern international relations under a rule of law. The emphasis here must also be on those aspects of international life that were truly altered or changed by legal developments, not those that transformed themselves by exogenous influences. While this may falsely distinguish political from legal change, it is still a contrast worth making. Giving voice to international law's triumphs should not deflect attention from its failures, many of which have been gleefully described in this book. It is, nonetheless, an appropriate way to nearly conclude this volume.

International law's first gains were on the ocean. While the legacy of transmarine European colonial expansion and competition from 1500 to 1820 was problematic—if not outright destructive for the native peoples it touched—it also marked an important shift in international cooperation. European powers engaged in unrestrained hostilities on land in Europe (the Thirty Years War and later wars of dynastic succession being fine examples) managed to develop a body of international law through conflict at sea. Naval warfare was progressively legalized by a customary process of customary law observed in domestic royal decrees and decisions of admiralty tribunals to adjudicate vessels and cargoes taken as prize in war.[17] This was the first consistent example of domestic institutions self-consciously following a law of nations observed by other states. Indeed, the body of prize law was vast and intricate, setting a standard of sophistication and coherence that subsequent international law doctrines would emulate.

This led to international law's first achievement of a humanitarian goal. This was the legalized suppression of slavery and the slave trade in the early 1800s. This would not have been possible without international law having first made subtle doctrinal changes in the law of the sea and high seas freedoms. The active suppression of piracy in the eighteenth century was certainly a significant precursor, although the prime objective of that initiative was the protection of colonial and mercantile systems of dominance.

The abolition of the slave trade illustrated some vital features of progressivism in international law. Many of the signal achievements in international law have been made at the behest of just one country or a small group of countries, often (it seems) against the implacable opposition of the remainder of the international community. Great Britain's campaign against the slave trade in the early 1800s, although partly impelled by domestic politics and a flexing of naval might, was certainly one of the most altruistic human rights initiatives of all time. As a great progressive leap forward, it was also accompanied by a jump in doctrinal sophistication for international law. Today's notion of universal jurisdiction can trace its intellectual lineage to that period. While, as mentioned in chapter 1, the unilateral application by British and American courts of universal jurisdiction over French and Spanish slavers was blocked by positivist scruples, the victory was consummated with treaty undertakings by all maritime states to suppress the slave trade.

The abolition of the slave trade reflects a paradigmatic structure for all international law "revolutions."[18] Forceful leadership is taken by a handful of prominent states that care deeply about an issue and are prepared to stake much in bidding a new rule of international conduct. Then a significant advance is made in an international law doctrine, without which political and diplomatic change would be impossible. It may be that an old rule is swept aside or, more typically, subtly altered to accommodate new conditions. This is often accompanied by a significant addition of new values of international legal regulation or new structures and processes to support preexisting objectives. The last stage of the process is the move to consensus, a slow and inexorable change by international actors to recognize the new paradigm.

A similar progression can be seen in the decolonization movement, which accelerated after the conclusion of World War II. Cracks in colonial structures became apparent after World War I, and one of the first legal interventions made to manage the process of decolonization was in the Covenant of the League of Nations, which established a system of mandates for former German colonies that would guide non-self-governing areas, in various stages of development, to full independence.[19] Only with the formulation of the concept of self-determination of peoples was decolonization able to grasp at a legal justification, however. With the exhaustion of colonial powers after World War II, it was necessary for the UN Charter to establish decolonization as an objective of the organization and to require a trusteeship system that would apply (in principle) not only to the colonies of nations defeated in the war but to all countries.

The widespread decolonizations in Africa and Asia in the 1960s and 1970s, as wrenching and disruptive as they were to those peoples, would have wreaked havoc on the international system but for progressive innovations in international law. The task was nothing less than the quick integration of scores of new states into the international order and the accommodation of an international society that doubled and then tripled from its numbers in 1945. This doctrinal innovation was largely manifested in the legal system's sources and methods. Rules for ascertaining custom had to be modified, as were important treaty law principles (such as the permissibility of reservations to multilateral conventions). The World Court was obliged to suppress regional custom for fear that newly emerging states would simply opt out of the process of global lawmaking. By way of compromise, international actors recognized significant changes in the law of state succession by granting newly independent former colonies a blank slate of treaty obligations while requiring that these new states be bound by customary rules.[20]

The history of decolonization in the twentieth century illustrates a situation where international law was mostly reacting to political developments rather than directly guiding them. Nevertheless, the role for law remained crucial, especially in allowing the international community to respond to radical changes in its constitution and structure. While we live in a postcolonial world, international law remains significant in this area. Concerns about failed states and the propriety of humanitarian interventions by the international community to correct human rights or political abuses by governments has been likened to the mandate and trusteeship systems of old. Despite international law's cosmopolitan image, international law's progress has been as much measured by its engagement with the periphery as by its association with the metropoles of Europe, North America, and the northern Pacific.

That leads to considering a unique late-twentieth-century achievement of international law: the development of international infrastructures for a wide array of global regulatory challenges. Whether it is international transport issues (including shipping and aviation), global communications, science and health concerns, or international economic relations, legal structures and processes have pervaded all aspects of international life. Whether regarded as creatures of treaty or as more organic regimes, these infrastructures have come to dominate functional cooperation between international actors. Even realist international relations theorists have grudgingly conceded the legal component of these structures, even if state participation in them may well be driven by self-interest.

In a related vein, international law has systematized cooperation in the management of common resources. This process of legalization can be seen in such varied contexts as demands for systematic cooperation and consultation for boundary waters, the long history of the law of the sea, condominium regimes for Antarctica and cyberspace, and the thick regulatory schemes for management of international environmental problems. It would be easy to dismiss this development as being impelled by the necessity of managing these common resources. That would ignore the hard law that can be found in the interstices of these infrastructures. Whether it is the growing custom and jurisprudence of nonnavigational uses of international watercourses or the elaborate bureaucratic regime of deep-seabed mining, the response of the international community to problems posed by the global commons can rightly be characterized as legal.

If the foregoing were all that international law could boast as achievements, it might properly be criticized still as epiphenomenal, tangential to influencing the kinds of conduct that really matter in international relations. One might think that international law has served merely as a cover for states' demands in international life or only to grease the wheels of inevitable change. Certain recent developments in international law speak to a desire that the system fulfill the expectations of all of its constituents, states and nonstate actors alike. International law's withdrawal of legitimacy for aggressive war as an instrument of national policy certainly reflects this. Begun with the League Covenant but consummated only with the UN Charter, the prime directive of Charter article 2(4) stands as a testament to a legal ordering of international relations. Even if one regards such legalism (as within either Woodrow Wilson's or Franklin Roosevelt's conception) as naive, the core of the international community's contemporary constitution certainly embraces the principle that aggression outside the constraints of the Charter is unlawful. The fundamental notion is that states may need to defend muscularly their rights and to bid new rules, but there are legal limits on their recourse to armed force to do so.

Even more extraordinarily, international law has penetrated a realm that one would intuitively think is beyond the pale of regulation: imposing restraint in the conduct of hostilities between states. If anything, this is a very old theme in international relations, and with the cataclysmic conflicts of the twentieth century, it has become especially relevant. Whether framed as disarmament, limits on the use of particular weapons or tactics (even of the ultimate armament, nuclear devices), or the protection of civilians and innocents in conflict, international law has exercised a degree of influence one would have hardly expected in this field. It is perhaps the ultimate expression of the international community's growing maturity that restraints in warfare should be seriously respected. This development reflects a belief that international life is continuing and that, in a sense, all international actors are repeat players. The violators of today can easily become the victims of tomorrow. And, indeed, the worst violations of international humanitarian law in the past decades have been by actors that have considered themselves at the margin of international life as pariah states or felt that (quite literally) they had nothing to lose in committing atrocities.

International law's recent repudiation of impunity may stand as its greatest testament. The inability of state leaders (or the heads of non-state polities, such a liberation movements) to claim immunity for their violations of international norms surely rates as a vital development in international legal life. The ultimate repudiation of Machiavelli's raison d'état and the prince's prerogative, the Nuremberg trials after World War II were (as mentioned in chapter 1) a watershed event for international affairs. More recently, the operation of the Yugoslav and Rwandan criminal tribunals (created by the UN Security Council to punish the genocidal abuses and war crimes that occurred in both sets of domestic conflicts) has sent an important signal to the international community that internal human rights abuses may be treated as breaches of the peace and prosecuted accordingly.

The temporary and political nature of these tribunals concerned many states and motivated suggestions for the creation of a permanent International Criminal Court (ICC). In July 1998 the Rome Statute of the ICC was signed by many nations (although the United States has yet to ratify and is continuing to review its possible participation in the court). The ICC's critical innovation is a permanent judicial institution and prosecutorial staff, standing available to commence investigations of suspected genocide, war crimes, and crimes against humanity (in essence, the original London Charter indictment counts).[21] If a nation is unwilling or unable to initiate a prosecution against one of its own nationals, then the ICC's jurisdiction can be triggered. This was seen as preferable to a political decision made by the UN Security Council to initiate proceedings, especially given that the council's delicate makeup might frustrate such a vote.

The ICC has properly been regarded as the last element in establishing a rule of law for individual responsibility in international affairs. Although the ICC has many flaws that need to be addressed, it certainly represents the international community's aspiration that individuals are endowed under international law with both significant rights and important obligations.

As a response to the impunity of those who would flout international law, the creation of the ICC may not be as important as an even more recent event: the well-publicized case brought by Spanish prosecutors against former Chilean head of state Augusto Pinochet. In a very significant decision,[22] the British House of Lords ruled that Pinochet had no immunity from extradition and subsequent prosecution for human rights abuses committed by his government after Chile had agreed to be bound to particular human rights norms. The British government ultimately declined to extradite Pinochet to Spain, ostensibly on grounds of his ill health, although Pinochet was later subjected to investigation by Chilean authorities.

The creation of international adjudication institutions has been a highly visible phenomenon and has produced a widely noted perception of achievement for international law. To some degree, this has been deserved. The establishment of the World Court in 1920, the use of claims-settlement institutions to resolve major crises (such as the Iran–United States Claims Tribunal created in 1981), the foundation of international criminal tribunals, and the employment of trade and investment dispute bodies all manifest the international community's seeming commitment to a rule of law. Nothing is more symbolic of international order—or more corrective of the Austinian critique of international law—than well-functioning international tribunals of established jurisdiction whose judgments are routinely obeyed.

As I observed in the previous chapter, international law's great achievement is not so much in the creation of institutional devices as it is in building a culture of compliance for international norms. The regular workings of international tribunals simply raise an expectation of formality, due process, and integrity of the proceedings and the respect to be accorded to their outcomes. International courts cannot confer legitimacy or strength on the international legal system it could not otherwise summon through its internal sources, methods, processes, and doctrines.

Perhaps, then, the more significant achievement of international law has been its efforts to make the workings of international relations more open and transparent. One effect of this has been to demand a higher level of accountability by international actors. Although periodically ignored, the requirement under both the League Covenant and UN Charter that treaties between nations should be registered and openly published[23] prohibits networks of secret agreements that could inadvertently be triggered to cause conflict (as occurred with the outbreak of World War I in 1914). Openness of international relations also allows the internal processes of political accountability and democracy to work within states and thus to present a popular check on abusive, militaristic, or aggressive domestic policies.

The democratic deficit about which international law needs to be most concerned is the perception that it remains the exclusive preserve of state prerogative, a cult of protecting hidden mysteries that only elite cosmopolites can divine. In the twentieth century, states have ceased to be the sole subjects of international legal rules and have made possible the application of norms of conduct to a wide range of individuals, institutions, and businesses. This has democratized law for international relations and opened vast vistas of practice opportunities for legal advisers around the world. The entire phenomenon of globalization is largely about making international legal rules relevant to the everyday lives of human beings across national boundaries, socioeconomic divides, and cultural affinities.

The great accomplishments of international law thus neatly dovetail with its abiding conservatism. The international legal system is rightly seen as ambitious, because without such aspiration it is unlikely that it could serve its purpose in fulfilling the needs of the most demanding set of law consumers in the world today: a fully constituted international society of nations, transnational enterprises, and individuals engaged in life across boundaries. The rectitude and caution of many international law doctrines simply reflects practical realities implicated in most aspects of international interaction: the continuing desires and functions of state sovereignty, the relatively high transaction costs of cooperation, the confines of international legal order, and the conflict among the system's values and objectives. Conservatism and progressivism combine to produce a substantive mix of international law doctrines that are, at one and the same time, coherent and pragmatic, impervious to and reflective of change, and respectful and disdainful of the limits of legal imagination.

11 Skepticism and Exuberance

This volume has attempted to chart international law's trajectory over the past centuries and to describe its current strengths and weaknesses as a legal system. In the final pages, it is worth reflecting on international law's progress in overcoming substantial obstacles in fashioning a global order based on a rule of law.

An important theme of this book has been to properly characterize attitudes about international law and to assess its evolution as both a learned discipline and a practical means of influencing international behavior. This effort is complicated because the international legal system periodically has been afflicted with bouts of profound distrust and uncontrolled enthusiasm. Just in the twentieth century, international law oscillated between widely held regard (at the turn of the century and the interwar period) to ill-disguised hostility (during the Cold War). In the last decade, both skeptical and utopian strands of thinking about international law have been evident, although post–Cold War evaluations of international law have tended to be quite positive.[1]

Skeptical attitudes about international law have always been prevalent, and one might legitimately think that they arise from the nature of the international legal system itself. Of modern legal systems that are non–faith based, international law appears to be alone in being largely detached from a spatial context. One cannot locate international law in a particular territory or isolate its attributes in reference to the unique characteristics of a place. While it is easier to place international law in a temporal setting, it is difficult to speak of its grand historic traditions or, indeed, of any strong, historically determinate aspects of its processes, doctrines, or institutions. If international law is intellectually detached from geography and history, it is denied the sustenance that other legal systems enjoy.

For these reasons, international law is often regarded as alien and apart, divorced from a "real" community that would confer on it needed legitimacy. Much of contemporary criticism of international law focuses on its lack of transparency and accountability and its ostensible domination by elite, cosmopolite forces that would seek to use international mechanisms to overturn the legitimate, democratic choices made by domestic polities. In the trope of all politics being local, international law is forever condemned to distrust and irrelevance.

All of this, of course, feeds into the Austinian critique of international law, introduced in this volume's first chapter. Lacking a local flavor, international law is seemingly bereft of the critical features of "authentic" legal systems. According to the skeptics, international law has no intelligible basis of authority and can offer no predictable guidance as to the sources of legal obligation. Because the international community remains ill-defined, the skeptics continue, the processes of international lawmaking must remain indeterminate. Lacking these positivist elements, many groups of doubters (including international relations realists and New Stream scholars) are left to conclude that international law is nothing more than a weakened form of international morality, situated in an imperfect and unfriendly world of sovereign states.

With this intellectual pedigree of international law skeptics, it is hard to believe that international law enthusiasts can prosper—but they have. As if there were some inevitable backlash to critical thinking about international law, utopian views of the subject have been expounded precisely as a reaction to realist skepticism, and this school of publicists and practitioners can point to extraordinary gains for the international legal discipline. The sources of law in the system have been codified and rationalized as well as expanded and diversified to accommodate the role of nonstate actors. There is a greater coherence and sophistication to the technical and substantive methods of determining what the law is and applying it to specific situations. Most importantly, as the universe of legal actors in the system has increased, so has the permissible scope of topics for international legal regulation.

International law's stunning practical successes in the past two centuries have planted seeds of potential discord. One aspect of this is the multiplicity of values and objectives for the legal system, seemingly pandering to newfangled constituents and increased demands. While I have suggested that the paradoxes between these values may be less severe than some commentators have feared, they are nonetheless worrisome and do indicate particular fissures that could split the system apart. Competition among doctrines advancing agendas for peace, human rights initiatives, and campaigns for justice and rationality may become difficult to manage and could enter a collision course with residual objectives of state sovereignty. Moreover, the most important feature of international law to members of the world community—the predictability and neutrality of its rules—may be slowly eroded and sacrificed by this multiplicity of objectives. Our new world order may be a hydra-headed beast in which a diversity of international law values means that none can be well and truly fulfilled.

Another profound challenge facing international law in its current millenarian exuberance is the control of relentless expectations. More is being asked of international law today than at any time in its history. This is, of course, a recognition of its earlier successes and a tribute to its potential as a useful tool of international relations. When one strips the international legal system down to its essential elements, one can be seriously concerned that it is reaching the limits of its operational capacities. Clever lawyers, diplomats, and state leaders can, however, expand those limits by using the well-developed tools of functional cooperation, treaty making, and institution building.

Some primitive features of the international legal system cannot be so easily evaded, nor should they be. The international community's tightly knit membership and the preeminent role given to states is surely one of these. Despite predictions that we are entering a neo-medieval phase in which states will be replaced as the chief international legal actor,[2] this seems as unlikely as a radical move to world government that would (in any event) spell the doom of the international legal system. The strongly consensual aspects of primitive legal systems are a vital strength for international law. The use of custom as a source of international legal obligation and the continuing role of general principles derived from national legal systems are two aspects of these primitive elements. Finally, and most importantly, the exogenous and external bases of obligation in primitive systems (whether they be magic, religion, ideology, or morality) have inoculated international law against succumbing to the disease of excessive positivism, an ailment that would have surely stunted its growth in its early years of development (in the sixteenth and seventeenth centuries) or outright killed it after the world wars of the twentieth century.

If modernity means that international law must take on the mantle of other "real" legal systems, it could prove to be a fatal attraction. The prospect of achieving regular processes and institutions of legislation, enforcement, and adjudication may well be illusory. International law's achievement of both primary and secondary rules of conduct, including H. L. A. Hart's rules of recognition,[3] may have to come though untraditional approaches. More importantly, emulating more mature domestic legal systems may entail the adoption of sources and methods that could lessen international law's ability to respond rapidly and effectively to changes in international life. International law can ill afford to be afflicted with aging doctrines and sclerotic decision making.

The history of international law may well contain a moral of social progress and human betterment. Such victories have been hard won and were by no means inevitable. Rather, this book has suggested a series of cyclical processes and dialectics. Progress in refining the sources of international law, diversifying its fundamental values, articulating the processes of lawmaking, and expanding the institutions of dispute settlement have been slow and halting. Change and ferment have come after crucial moments: the creation of the Westphalian state system in 1648, the period of high positivism in the late nineteenth century, the world wars of the twentieth century, and now the post–Cold War order of globalization.

The tempo of change in international relations has accelerated, and to use Thomas Kuhn's construct,[4] the structure of revolutions in thinking about international law will likely result in further paradigm shifts. Many of these will come as the confines of international law are further degraded over time. We need not anticipate a future of world government or neomedievalism to realize that state actors will be pressed to maintain intact aspects of their internal sovereignty. If the frontiers of domesticity and privity are crossed as international law augments its domain, the final frontier—the separation of law from politics in the construction of world order—may not be far behind. Additional paradigm shifts will occur as novel legal actors are added to the system, as new values and objectives are emphasized, as more difficult topics of regulation are tackled, and as our imagination creates the legal infrastructure to support the global community.

The genius of international law has been reflected in its ability to grow and prosper as a distinct legal system and learned discipline in the most inhospitable of practical and intellectual environments. International relations, and the caustic cynicism it engenders, is an unlikely place for a rule of law to take root, but it has. The challenge for international law's future—as for its past—is to serve a diverse and dynamic community of interests in the world while remaining true to unchanging truths and unyielding aspirations of global peace, prosperity, and justice. The real measure of international law's spirit is how it keeps that faith. If Charles Louis Montesquieu had succeeded in finding a true principle[5] for international law, he would have discovered it in that insight.

NOTES

Preface

1 1 Charles Louis Montesquieu, *The Spirit of the Laws* 6 (1748) [Thomas Nugent trans., rev. ed., New York, 1900].

2 See 1 id. at 161 ("Offensive force is regulated by the law of nations, which is the political law of each country considered in its relations to every other.").

3 See 1 id. at 7 ("The mischief is that their law of nations is not founded on true principles.").

4 To the extent that doctrinal discussion is made in this book, I acknowledge a debt to the leading treatises, including, most notably, Sir Robert Jennings and Sir Arthur Watts eds., *Oppenheim's International Law* (Vol. 1: *Peace*) [9th ed., London, 1996] (referenced throughout as Oppenheim).

1. Authority and Obligation

1 A complete doctrinal history of international law is beyond the scope of this work. For such, see Wilhelm Grewe, *The Epochs of International Law* [Michael Byers trans., Berlin, 2000]; Arthur Nussbaum, *A Concise History of the Law of Nations* [2d ed., New York, 1954]; J. H. W. Verzijl, *International Law in Historical Perspective* [11 vols., Leiden, 1968–96].

2 John Austin, *The Province of Jurisprudence Determined* 127, 201 (1832) [rep., London, 1954].

3 H. L. A. Hart, *The Concept of Law* 214 [2d ed., Oxford, 1994]. But see Glanville L. Williams, International Law and the Controversy Concerning the Word "Law," 22 *BYBIL* 146 (1945).

4 *United States v. La Jeune Eugenie,* 26 F. Cas. 832, 846 (C.C.D. Mass. 1822) (No. 15,551) (Story, J.).

5 *The Antelope,* 23 U.S. (10 Wheat.) 66, 115 (1825). See also *Le Louis,* 2 Dods. 210, 245, 165 Eng. Rep. 1464, 1475–76 (Adm. 1817) (reaching a similar conclusion). See also John T. Noonan Jr., The Antelope: *The Ordeal of the Recaptured Africans in the Administrations of James Monroe and John Quincy Adams* [Berkeley, 1977]; Alfred P. Rubin, *Ethics and Authority in International Law* 97–130 [Cambridge, 1997].

6 *Brown v. United States*, 12 U.S. (8 Cranch) 110, 128 (1814) (Marshall, C.J.).

7 Agreement for the Prosecution and Punishment of the Major War Criminals of the European Axis, Aug. 8, 1945, Art. 6, 59 Stat. 1544, 1548, 82 UNTS 279, 288.

8 *In re Goering*, 13 Ann. Dig. 203, 208 (Nuremberg, Int'l Mil. Trib. 1946).

9 *In re Ohlendorf*, 15 *ILR* 656 (Nuremberg, U.S. Mil. Trib. 1948).

10 1 B. V. A. Roling and C. F. Ruter eds., *The Tokyo Judgment* 1045–64 [Amsterdam, 1977] (Roling, J., dissenting).

11 See John Finnis, *Natural Law and Natural Rights* [Oxford, 1984].

12 See Mark W. Janis and Carolyn Evans, eds., *Religion and International Law* [2d ed., The Hague, 1999].

13 J. G. Starke, *An Introduction to International Law* 22 [10th ed., London, 1989].

14 Georg Schwarzenberger and E. D. Brown, *A Manual of International Law* 16 [6th ed., rev. 2d impression, Milton, 1976].

15 See Hans Kelsen, *Principles of International Law* 243–44 [2d ed., New York, 1966].

16 See, e.g., H. Krabbe, L'Idee Moderne de l'État, 13 *RCADI* 513 (1926); Leon Duguit, Objective Law (in 3 parts), 20 *Colum. L. Rev.* 816 (1920), 21 id. 17, 125 (1921).

17 See Christian von Wolff, *Jus Gentium Methodo Scientifica Pertractum* (The Law of Nations According to the Scientific Method) (1749) [Carnegie Classics of Int'l Law rep., New York, 1934]; 1 Sir Robert Phillimore, *Commentaries upon International Law* 3 [3d ed., 1879] [rep. 1985].

18 See Anthony Clark Arend, *Legal Rules and International Society* [New York, 1999]; Hedley Bull, *The Anarchical Society: A Study of Order in World Politics* [New York, 1977]; Martin Wight, *Power Politics* [Hedley Bull and Carsten Holbraad, eds., 2d ed., Harmondsworth, 1986].

19 See Charles de Visscher, *Theory and Reality in Public International Law* 17–18 [P. E. Corbett, trans., rev. ed. Princeton, 1968]; Charles G. Fenwick, *International Law* 32–33, 49 [4th ed., New York, 1965].

20 See James Leslie Brierly, *The Basis of Obligation in International Law* 3–9 [Oxford, 1958].

21 See Hersch Lauterpacht, The Grotian Tradition in International Law, 23 *BYBIL* 1, 30–35 (1946).

22 See Friedrich Hegel, *Grundlinien der Philosophie des Rechts* (Philosophy of Right) (1820).

23 See Heinrich Triepel, *Völkerrecht und Landesrecht* (International Law and Municipal Law) (1899).

24 See Kelsen, supra note 15, at 247.

25 Id.

26 Alf Ross, *A Text-Book of International Law* 94 [London, 1947].

27 See Emmerich de Vattel, *Law of Nations* 316 (1758) [Joseph Chitty trans., Philadelphia, 1863].

28 See Fenwick, supra note 19, at 36.

29 See James L. Brierly, *The Law of Nations* 51–52 [Sir Humphrey Waldock ed., 6th ed., Oxford, 1963].

30 Id. at 53.

31 See 1 Lassa F. L. Oppenheim, *International Law* 18–19 [Hersch Lauterpacht ed., 8th ed, London, 1955].

32 See 1 Dionisio Anzilotti, *Corso di Diritto Internazionale* (Lectures on International Law) 43 [3d ed., Rome, 1928].

33 See Oscar Schachter, Towards a Theory of International Obligation, 8 *VJIL* 300, 312 (1968).

34 See Kelsen, supra note 15, at 243–44, 441–42, 557–64.

35 See, e.g., Visscher, supra note 19, at 66–68; Hersch Lauterpacht, *The Function of Law in the International Community* 402 [Oxford, 1933].

36 See Myres S. McDougal, International Law, Power and Policy: A Contemporary Conception, 82 *RCADI* 133 (1953 I); Myres S. McDougal and Florentino P. Feliciano, *Law and Minimum World Public Order* [New Haven, 1961]; Myres S. McDougal and W. Michael Reisman, International Law in Policy-Oriented Perspective, in *The Structure and Process of International Law* 103 [Ronald St. J. MacDonald and Douglas M. Johnston eds., Boston, 1983].

37 See Rosalyn Higgins, *Problems and Process: International Law and How We Use It* 1 [Oxford, 1994].

38 Hans J. Morgenthau, *Politics among Nations: The Struggle for Power and Peace* 3–15 [5th ed., New York, 1978]; George F. Kennan, *American Diplomacy* 95 [expanded ed., New York, 1984].

39 See David Kennedy, *International Legal Structures* [Baden-Baden, 1987]; Martti Koskenniemi, *From Apology to Utopia: The Structure of International Legal Argument* [Helsinki, 1989].

40 See Anne-Marie (Slaughter) Burley, Toward an Age of Liberal Nations, 33 *HILJ* 393 (1992); id., Law among Liberal States: Liberal Internationalism and the Act of State Doctrine, 92 *Colum. L. Rev.* 1907 (1992); id., Liberal

International Relations Theory and International Economic Law, 10 *Am. U. J. Int'l L. & Pol'y* 717 (1995).

41 See 1 Abram Chayes, Thomas Ehrlich, and Andreas Lowenfeld, *International Legal Process* xi [Boston, 1968]; Harold H. Koh, Transnational Legal Process, 75 *Neb. L. Rev.* 181 (1996).

42 Louis Henkin, *How Nations Behave* 47 [New York, 1979].

43 But see Harold J. Berman, Towards an Integrative Jurisprudence: Politics, Morality, History, 76 *Calif. L. Rev.* 779 (1998).

44 See Koskenniemi, supra note 39.

45 See David J. Bederman, The 1871 London Declaration, Rebus Sic Stantibus, and a Primitivist View of the Law of Nations, 82 *AJIL* 1, 35–36 (1988).

46 See Jack L. Goldsmith and Eric A. Posner, A Theory of Customary International Law, 66 *U. Chi. L. Rev.* 1113, 1120–39 (1999); J. Patrick Kelly, The Twilight of Customary International Law, 40 *VJIL* 449 (2000).

47 See Thomas M. Franck, Fairness in the International Legal and Institutional System, 240 *RCADI* 1, 41–61 (1993 III).

48 See *Certain Expenses of the United Nations Opinion, 1962* ICJ 151.

49 See *Asylum Case* (Colom. v. Peru), 1950 ICJ 266.

50 See *Reservations to the Convention on the Prevention and Punishment of the Crime of Genocide* Opinion, 1951 ICJ 15.

51 See *Anglo-Norwegian Fisheries Case* (U.K. v. Nor.), 1951 ICJ 116.

52 See *Corfu Channel Case* (U.K. v. Alb.), 1949 ICJ 4.

2. Sources

1 The Statute of the International Court of Justice, Art. 38, para. 1, June 26, 1945, 59 Stat. 1055, 1066.

2 *Petroleum Development Ltd. v. Sheikh of Abu Dhabi,* 18 *ILR* (No. 37), at 149 (1951).

3 See Anthony Clark Arend, *Legal Rules and International Society* 49–53 [New York, 1999].

4 See Gerrit W. Gong, *The Standard of "Civilization" in International Society* [Oxford, 1984]; Antony Anghie, Finding the Peripheries: Sovereignty and Colonialism in Nineteenth-Century International Law, 40 *HILJ* 1 (1999).

5 *Gentini* (Italy) Claim (Venezuelan Mixed Claims Comm'n 1903), Jackson Ralston, *Venezuelan Arbitrations of 1903,* 720 [Washington, 1904].

6 See Bin Cheng, *General Principles of Law as Applied by International Courts and Tribunals* (1953) [rep., Cambridge, 1987]; A. M. Stuyt, *The General Principles of Law as Applied by International Tribunals to Disputes on Attribution and Exercise of State Jurisdiction* [The Hague, 1946]; Hersch Lauterpacht, *Private Law Sources and Analogies of International Law* [London, 1927].

7 See *Nuclear Test* Cases (Aust./N.Z. v. Fr.), 1974 ICJ 253, 268; *Free Zones of Upper Savoy and the District of Gex* Case (Switz v. Fr.), 1930 PCIJ Ser. A, No. 24, at 12; 1932 PCIJ Ser. A/B, No. 46, at 167.

8 See *Effect of Awards of the UN Administrative Tribunal* Opinion, 1954 ICJ 53; *Mosul Boundary* Opinion, 1925 PCIJ Ser. B, No. 12, at 32.

9 See David J. Bederman, Contributory Fault and State Responsibility, 30 *VJIL* 335 (1990).

10 *Chorzów Factory* (Merits) (Ger. v. Pol.), 1928 PCIJ Ser. A, No. 17, at 29.

11 See *Right of Passage* Case (Port. v. India), 1960 ICJ 6; *South West Africa Case* (Second Phase) (Ethiopia/Liber. v. S. Afr.), 1962 ICJ 6, 47, 319.

12 See *Border and Transborder Armed Actions* Case (Nicar. v. Hond.), 1988 ICJ 69, 105.

13 See John Austin, *The Province of Jurisprudence Determined* 31 (lecture 1) (1832) [rep., London, 1954] ("[C]ustom is transmuted into positive law, when it is adopted as such by the courts of justice, and when the judicial decisions fashioned upon it are enforced by the power of the state.").

14 See Friedrich Karl von Savigny, *System des Heutigen Römischen Rechts* (9 vols., 1840–49) [rep., Aalen, 1981]; id., *Vom Beruf Unsrer Zeit für Gesetzgebung und Rechtswissenschaft* (Of the Vocation of Our Age for Legislation and Jurisprudence) 8–11, 13–14 [3d ed., Heidelberg, 1840].

15 See Michael Byers, *Custom, Power, and the Power of Rules* [Cambridge, 1999]; Clive Parry, *The Sources and Evidences of International Law* [Manchester, 1965]; Karol Wolfke, *Custom in Present International Law* [2d ed., Dordrecht, 1993]; Maurice H. Mendelson, The Formation of Customary International Law, 272 *RCADI* 155 (1998).

16 See Paul Guggenheim, *Traité de Droit International Public* 46–48 (Geneva, 1953).

17 See W. Michael Reisman, The Cult of Custom in the Twentieth Century, 17 *Cal. West. Int'l L. J.* 133 (1987).

18 175 U.S. 677 (1900).

19 1 C. Rob. 20, 165 Eng. Rep. 81 (Adm. 1798) (U.K.).

20 See Jack L. Goldsmith and Eric A. Posner, Understanding the Resem-

blance between Modern and Traditional Customary International Law, 40 *VJIL* 639, 641–54 (2000).

21 See *Anglo-Norwegian Fisheries* Case (U.K. v. Nor.), 1951 ICJ 116, 131, 180–84; *Asylum* Case (Colom. v. Peru), 1950 ICJ 266, 276–77.

22 See *Military and Paramilitary Activities* (Nicar. v. U.S.) (Merits), 1986 ICJ 14, 98.

23 See *North Sea Continental Shelf* Cases (F.R.G. v. Den./Neth.), 1969 ICJ 3, 44.

24 Compare *Gulf of Maine* Case (U.S. v. Can.), 1984 ICJ 246, 293–94; with *Military and Paramilitary Activities* (Nicar. v. U.S.) (Merits), 1986 ICJ 14, 108–9.

25 See Mark E. Villiger, *Customary International Law and Treaties: A Manual on the Theory and Practice of the Interrelation of Sources* [The Hague, 1997]; H. W. A. Thirlway, *International Customary Law and Codification* [Leiden, 1972]; Anthony D'Amato, *The Concept of Custom in International Law* [Ithaca, 1971]; 1 Hans Kelsen, *Principles of International Law* 450 [2d ed., New York, 1966]; Fischer Williams, *Some Aspects of Modern International Law* 44–46 [London, 1939]; Stephen McCaffrey, Is Codification in Decline? 20 *Hastings Int'l & Comp. L. Rev.* 639 (1997).

26 See Jonathan I. Charney, The Persistent Objector Rule and the Development of Customary International Law, 56 *BYBIL* 1 (1986); Ted L. Stein, The Approach of the Different Drummer: The Principle of Persistent Objection in International Law, 26 *HILJ* 457 (1985).

27 See *Anglo-Norwegian Fisheries* (U.K. v. Nor.), 1951 ICJ 116, 131.

28 See *Namibia* Opinion, 1971 ICJ 16.

29 See *Military and Paramilitary Activities* Case (Nicar. v. U.S.) (Merits), 1986 ICJ 14, 100–101.

30 See VCLT, Arts. 53 & 64; [1976] 2 *Y.B. Int'l L. Comm'n* 95, 121. See also Lauri Hannikainen, *Peremptory Norms (Jus Cogens) in International Law: Historical Development, Criteria, Present Status* [Helsinki, 1988]; Christos L. Rozakis, *The Concept of Jus Cogens in the Law of Treaties* [Amsterdam, 1976].

31 See Maurizio Ragazzi, *The Concept of International Obligations* Erga Omnes [Oxford, 1997].

32 See N. C. H. Dunbar, The Myth of Customary International Law, 8 *Austl. Y.B. Int'l L.* 1 (1983); Jack L. Goldsmith and Eric A. Posner, A Theory of Customary International Law, 66 *U. Chi. L. Rev.* 1113, 1120–

39 (1999); J. Patrick Kelly, The Twilight of Customary International Law, 40 *VJIL* 449 (2000).

33 See David P. Fidler, Challenging the Classical Concept of Custom: Perspectives on the Future of Customary International Law, 39 *GYBIL* 198 (1996).

34 See Evangelos Raftopoulos, *The Inadequacy of the Contractual Analogy in the Law of Treaties* [Athens, 1990].

35 *Legal Status of Eastern Greenland* Case (Den. v. Nor.), 1933 PCIJ Ser. A/B, No. 53.

36 *Nuclear Test* Cases (Austl. & N.Z. v. Fr.), 1974 ICJ 253.

37 See Christine Chinkin, The Challenge of Soft Law: Development and Change in International Law, 38 *ICLQ* 850 (1989); Prosper Weil, Towards Relative Normativity in International Law? 77 *AJIL* 413 (1983).

38 But see Dinah Shelton, ed., *Commitment and Compliance: The Role of Non-Binding Norms in the International Legal System* [Oxford, 2000].

39 See VCLT, Arts. 34–36; [1966] 2 *Y.B. Int'l L. Comm'n* 226; *Certain German Interests in Polish Upper Silesia* Case (Ger. v. Pol.), 1926 PCIJ Ser. A, No. 7, at 27–29; *Free Zones of Upper Savoy and the District of Gex* Case (Switz. v. Fr.), 1932 PCIJ Ser. A/B, No. 23, at 19–22.

40 See *Reparation for Injuries Suffered in the Service of the United Nations* Opinion, 1949 ICJ 174.

41 See Oppenheim 1263–65.

42 1969 ICJ 3 (F.R.G. v. Den./Neth.).

43 The SS *China* Incident, [1916] For. Relations of the U.S. Supp. 667.

44 1921 PCIJ Ser. A, No. 1 (Fr./U.K./It./Jap. v. Ger.).

45 See 1 Hersch Lauterpacht, *International Law: Collected Papers* 86–88 [Cambridge, 1970].

46 *Trail Smelter* Case (U.S. v. Can.), 3 RIAA 1905 (1941), reprinted in 35 *AJIL* 684 (1941).

47 Report of the UN Conference on the Human Environment, UN Doc. A/CONF.48/14/Rev.1 (1972), reprinted in 11 *ILM* 1416 (1972).

48 See Edith Brown Weiss, International Environmental Law: Contemporary Issues and the Emergence of a New World Order, 81 *Geo. L. J.* 675 (1993).

3. Methods and Approaches

1 See Henry Wheaton, *Elements of International Law: With a Sketch of the History of the Science* [Philadelphia, 1836]; William Edward Hall, *A*

Treatise on International Law [4th ed., Oxford, 1895]; T. J. Lawrence, *The Principles of International Law* [4th ed., London, 1910].

2 See John Eppstein, *The Catholic Tradition of the Law of Nations* [London, 1935]; Norman De Mattos Bentwich, *The Religious Foundations of Internationalism* [London, 1933]; Robert Francis Wright, *Medieval Internationalism* [London, 1930].

3 See Francisco de Vitoria, *De Indis et de Iure Belli Relectiones* (The Indies and Reflections on the Laws of War) (1557) [Classics of International Law rep., Washington, 1917]; James Brown Scott, *The Spanish Origin of International Law: Francisco de Vitoria and His Law of Nations* [Oxford, 1934]; Antony Anghie, Francisco de Vitoria and the Colonial Origins of International Law, 5 *Soc. & Legal Stud.* 321 (1996).

4 See C. H. Alexandrowicz, *An Introduction to the History of the Law of Nations in the East Indies: (16th, 17th and 18th Centuries)* [Oxford, 1967].

5 Peace Treaty of Paris, Mar. 30, 1856, Art. 7, 15 Martens Nouveau Recueil (Ser. 2) 770, 114 Parry's Consol. T.S. 409. See also Hugh McKinnon Wood, The Treaty of Paris and Turkey's Status in International Law, 37 *AJIL* 262 (1943).

6 See Gerrit W. Gong, *The Standard of "Civilization" in International Society* [Oxford, 1984].

7 Now reflected in the Statute of the ICJ, Art. 9, June 26, 1945, 59 Stat. 1055, 1057.

8 UN Charter, Art. 4, para. 1.

9 Alejandro Alvarez, *Le Droit International Américain* [Paris, 1910]; Alejandro Alvarez, *La Reconstruction du Droit International et Sa Codification en Amérique* [Paris, 1928]; H. B. Jacobin, *A Study of the Philosophy of International Law as Seen in the Work of Latin-American Writers* [The Hague, 1954]; Juan Carlos Puig, *Principios de Derecho Internacional Publico Americano* [Buenos Aires, 1952]. But see Manoel Alvaro de Souza Vianna, *De la Non-Existence d'un Droit International Américain* [Rio de Janeiro, 1912].

10 See Grotius, *De Jure Praedae Commentarius* (Commentary of the Law of Prize and Booty) (1604) [Carnegie Classics of Int'l Law rep., Oxford, 1950]. Part of Grotius's manuscript, entitled *Mare Liberum*, was later published in Amsterdam in 1609 and then reprinted in 1633. See id., *Mare Liberum* (Freedom of the Seas) (1633) [Carnegie Classics of Int'l Law rep., New York, 1916].

11 For the famous counterpoint to Grotius's writing, see John Selden's *Mare Clausum* (Of the Dominion, or Ownership of the Seas) (1652) [New York, 1972].

12 *Church v. Hubbart*, 6 U.S. (2 Cranch) 187, 235 (1804).

13 1951 ICJ 15, 23.

14 See, e.g., *Filartiga v. Peña-Irala*, 630 F.2d 876, 884 & n.15 (2d Cir. 1980).

15 See Martti Koskenniemi, *From Apology to Utopia: The Structure of International Legal Argument* [Helsinki, 1989].

16 See David P. Fidler, Challenging the Classical Concept of Custom: Perspectives on the Future of Customary International Law, 39 *GYBIL* 198 (1996).

17 See W. Michael Reisman, International Incidents: Introduction to a New Genre in the Study of International Law, 10 *YJIL* 1 (1984); Andrew W. Willard, Incidents: An Essay in Method, 10 *YJIL* 21 (1984); W. Michael Reisman and Andre R. Willard, eds., *International Incidents: The Law That Counts in World Politics* [Princeton, 1988].

18 See Derek Bowett, International Incidents: New Genre or New Delusion? 12 *YJIL* 386 (1987).

19 See, e.g., Rosalyn Higgins, *Development of International Law through the Political Organs of the United Nations* [London, 1963]; Ingrid Detter, *Law-Making by International Organizations* [The Hague, 1965]; Obed Y. Asamoah, *The Legal Significance of the Declarations of the General Assembly of the United Nations* [The Hague, 1966].

20 See *Reparations for Injuries Suffered in the Service of the United Nations* Opinion, 1949 ICJ 174.

21 17 U.S. (4 Wheat.) 316 (1819).

22 1962 ICJ 151.

23 See *Lockerbie* Case (Libya v. U.S./U.K.), 1992 ICJ 3, 114 (Provisional Measures).

24 See *Northern Cameroons* Case (Cameroon v. U.K.), 1963 ICJ 15, 32; *Namibia (South West Africa) Legal Consequences* Opinion, 1971 ICJ 7, 50.

25 *Texaco Overseas Petroleum Co. v. Libyan Arab Republic*, 17 *ILM* 1 (Arb. 1978).

26 See Charles Henry Alexandrowicz, *The Law-Making Functions of the Specialized Agencies of the United Nations* [The Hague, 1973]; Thomas Buergenthal, *Law-Making in the International Civil Aviation Organization* [Syracuse, 1969]; R. Michael M'Gonigle and Mark W. Zacher, *Pol-*

lution, Politics, and International Law: Tankers at Sea [Berkeley, 1979]; Kenneth R. Simmonds, *The International Maritime Organization* [London, 1994].

27 For more on this topic, see Richard A. Falk, *The Role of Domestic Courts in the International Legal Order* [Syracuse, 1964]; Richard B. Lillich, The Proper Role of Domestic Courts in the International Legal Order, 11 *VJIL* 9 (1970).

28 See Sir Hersch Lauterpacht, *The Development of International Law by the International Court* [London, 1958]; Edward McWhinney, *The World Court and the Contemporary International Lawmaking Process* [Alphen aan den Rijn, 1979].

29 Oppenheim 41.

30 See *The Maria*, 1 C. Rob. 340, 349a, 165 Eng. Rep. 199, 202 (Adm. 1799) (U.K.).

31 See *Soering v. United Kingdom*, 11 Eur. H.R. Rep. 439 (1989).

32 Oscar Schachter, The Invisible College of International Lawyers, 72 *Nw. U. L. Rev.* 217, 217 (1977–78).

33 Henry Wheaton, *Elements of International Law* § 15 [Philadelphia, 1836].

34 *The Renard*, Hay & M. 222, 165 Eng. Rep. 51 (Adm. 1778) (U.K.).

35 175 U.S. 677, 700 (1900).

36 *Tel-Oren v. Libyan Arab Republic*, 726 F.2d 774, 827 (D.C. Cir. 1984) (Robb, J., concurring) (citations omitted).

37 Jack Goldsmith, Sovereignty, International Relations Theory, and International Law, 52 *Stan. L. Rev.* 959, 982 (2000) (reviewing Stephen D. Krasner, *Sovereignty: Organized Hypocrisy* [Princeton, 1999]).

38 See David J. Bederman, I Hate International Law Scholarship (Sort Of), 1 *Chi. J. Int'l L.* 75 (2000).

39 See Alejandro Alvarez, *Méthodes de la Codification du Droit International Public* [Paris, 1947]; R. P. Dhokalia, *The Codification of Public International Law* [Manchester, 1970].

40 See *The International Law Commission Fifty Years After: An Evaluation* [United Nations, 2000]; *Analytical Guide to the Work of the International Law Commission, 1949–1997* [United Nations, 1998]; Sir Ian Sinclair, *The International Law Commission* [Cambridge, 1987]; Herbert W. Briggs, *The International Law Commission* [Ithaca, 1965].

41 See, e.g., *Toonen*, Communication No. 488/1992, UN Doc. CCPR/C/50/D/488 (1994).

42 See *Velazquez-Rodriguez* Case, Inter-Am. C.H.R., OEA/Ser. C/Case 4 (1988), reprinted in 28 *ILM* 291 (1989); *Soering v. United Kingdom*, 11 Eur. H.R. Rep. 439 (1989).

43 See 28 U.S.C. § 1350.

44 See J. M. Spectar, Saving the Ice Princess: NGOs, Antarctica, and International Law in the New Millennium, 23 *Suffolk Transnat'l L. Rev.* 1 (2000); Chiara Giorgetti, From Rio to Kyoto: A Study of the Involvement of Non-Governmental Organizations in the Negotiations on Climate Change, 7 *N.Y.U. Envtl L. J.* 201 (1999).

45 See William M. Reichert, Resolving the Trade and Environment Conflict: The WTO and NGO Consultative Relations, 5 *Minn. J. Global Trade* 219 (1996).

46 See also Emanuel Adler and Peter M. Haas, Conclusion: Epistemic Communities, World Order, and the Creation of a Reflective Research Program, 46 *Int'l Org.* 367 (1992); Peter M. Haas, Banning Chlorofluorocarbons: Epistemic Community Efforts to Protect Stratospheric Ozone, 46 *Int'l Org.* 187 (1992); M. J. Peterson, Whalers, Cetologists, Environmentalists, and the International Management of Whaling, 46 *Int'l Org.* 147 (1992).

47 See Tsune-Chi Yü, *The Interpretation of Treaties* [New York, 1927]; V. D. Degan, *L'Interprétation des Accords en Droit International* [The Hague, 1963]; György Haraszti, *Some Fundamental Problems of the Law of Treaties* [Budapest, 1973]; Serge Sur, *L'Interprétation en Droit International Public* [Paris, 1974]; David J. Bederman, *Classical Canons: Rhetoric, Classicism, and Treaty Interpretation* [Brookfield, 2001].

48 VCLT, Art. 31.

49 *Interpretation of the 1919 Convention Concerning Employment of Women during the Night*, 1932 PCIJ Ser. A/B, No. 50.

50 VCLT, Art. 32.

51 *Case No. A/18 Concerning the Question of Jurisdiction over Claims of Persons with Dual Nationality*, 5 Iran-U.S. Claims Trib. Rep. 251 (1984-I).

52 VCLT, Art. 31, paras. 1 & 3(c).

53 *Interpretation of Peace Treaties with Bulgaria, Hungary, and Romania* Opinion, 1950 ICJ 65, 221.

54 1950 ICJ 266 (Colom. v. Peru).

55 1960 ICJ 6 (Port. v. India).

56 See Anthony D'Amato, *International Law Anthology* 157 [Cincinnati,

1994]. See also *Temple of Preah Vihear* Case (Camb. v. Thai.), 1962 ICJ 3, 22–31.

57   See Robert Y. Jennings, The Role of the International Court of Justice, 68 *BYBIL* 1 (1998).

58   1927 PCIJ Ser. A, No. 10 (Fr. v. Tur.).

59   1951 ICJ 116 (U.K. v. Nor.).

60   See D'Amato, supra note 56, at 58.

4. Subjects and Objects

1   See Oppenheim 117, 561; Ian Brownlie, *Principles of Public International Law* 57 [5th ed., Oxford, 1998]; David J. Bederman, *International Law Frameworks* 49 [New York, 2001].

2   See 2 J. H. W. Verzijl, *International Law in Historical Perspective* [Leiden, 1969]; Antonio Cassese, *International Law in a Divided World* [Oxford, 1986].

3   See Harold J. Laski, *Studies in the Problem of Sovereignty* [New Haven, 1937]; Johannes Mattern, *Concepts of State Sovereignty and International Law* [Baltimore, 1928]; Arthur Larson and C. Wilfred Jenks, *Sovereignty within the Law* [Dobbs Ferry, 1965].

4   See Hans Kelsen, *Das Problem der Souveränität und die Theorie des Völkkerrechts* [Tübingen, 1920]; James Brierly, *The Basis of Obligation in International Law* 3–9 [Oxford, 1958]; Oppenheim 331.

5   Convention on Rights and Duties of States, Dec. 26, 1933, Art. 1, 49 Stat. 3097, 165 LNTS 21.

6   See Thomas D. Grant, Defining Statehood: The Montevideo Convention and Its Discontents, 37 *CJTL* 403 (1999).

7   See James Crawford, *The Creation of States in International Law* [Oxford, 1979].

8   See John G. Hervey, *The Legal Effects of Recognition in International Law* (1928) [rep., Buffalo, 1974]; Eduardo Jiminiez de Arechaga, *Reconcimento de Gobiernos* [Montevideo, 1947]; Hersch Lauterpacht, *Recognition in International Law* [Cambridge, 1947]; Krystyna Marek, *Identity and Continuity of States* [Geneva, 1954].

9   See *Tinoco Claims* Arbitration (U.K. v. Costa Rica), 1 RIAA 369 (1923).

10   See D. P. O'Connell, *State Succession in Municipal Law and International Law* [Cambridge, 1967]; P. K. Menon, *The Succession of States in Respect to Treaties, State Property, Archives, and Debts* [Lewiston,

1991]; Brigitte Stern, La Succession d'États, 262 *RCADI* 9 [1996]; *La Succession d'États: La Codification à l'Épreuve des Faits* (Hague Academy of International Law) [Dordrecht, 1997].

11 See *Mavromatis Palestine Concessions* (Gr. v. U.K.), 1924 PCIJ Ser. A, No. 2; Edwin M. Borchard, *The Diplomatic Protection of Citizens Abroad; or, The Law of International Claims* (1915) [rep., New York, 1970]; Clyde Eagleton, *The Responsibility of States in International Law* [New York, 1928]; Ian Brownlie, *System of the Law of Nations: State Responsibility (Part 1)* [Oxford, 1983].

12 See Alwyn V. Freeman, *The International Responsibility of States for Denial of Justice* [London, 1938].

13 See *Way* Claim (U.S. v. Mex.), 4 RIAA 391 (1928).

14 See Italian Nationals in New Orleans, John Bassett Moore, *Digest of International Law* 837 [Washington, 1906].

15 See *United States Diplomatic and Consular Staff in Tehran* (U.S. v. Iran), 1980 ICJ 3.

16 See Haig Silvanie, *Responsibility of States for Acts of Unsuccessful Insurgent Governments* [New York, 1939]; Manuel R. Garcia-Mora, *International Responsibility for Hostile Acts of Private Persons against Foreign States* [The Hague, 1962].

17 See David D. Caron, The Basis of Responsibility: Attribution and Other Trans-Substantive Rules, in *Iran–United States Claims Tribunal: Its Contribution to the Law of State Responsibility* [Richard B. Lillich, Daniel B. Magraw, and David J. Bederman eds., New York, 1998].

18 For a summary, see Oppenheim 539–48.

19 But see International Law Commission, State Responsibility: Draft Articles Provisionally Adopted by the Drafting Committee, Arts. 4–11, UN Doc. A/CN.4/l.600 (Aug. 11, 2000).

20 See Thomas M. Franck, *The Power of Legitimacy among Nations* [New York, 1990].

21 Antonio Cassese, *Self-Determination of Peoples: A Legal Reappraisal* [New York, 1995]; Hurst Hannum, *Autonomy, Sovereignty, and Self-Determination: The Accommodation of Conflicting Rights* [Philadelphia, 1996]; Maivân Clech Lâm, *At the Edge of the State: Indigenous Peoples and Self-Determination* [Ardsley, 2000].

22 See Gregory H. Fox and Brad R. Roth, eds., *Democratic Governance and International Law* [Cambridge, 2000]; Thomas M. Franck, The Emerging Right to Democratic Governance, 86 *AJIL* 46 (1992).

23 See International Committee of Jurists, Legal Aspects of the Aaland Islands Question, *League of Nations Official Journal* Special Supplement 3 (1920).

24 See James Crawford, ed., *The Rights of Peoples* [Oxford, 1988].

25 See H. L. A. Hart, *The Concept of Law* 214 [2d ed., Oxford, 1994].

26 See D. W. Bowett, *The Law of International Institutions* [London, 1982]; Felice Morgenstern, *Legal Problems of International Organizations* [Cambridge, 1986]; René-Jean Dupuy ed., *A Handbook of International Organisations* [Dordrecht, 1988].

27 See David J. Bederman, The Souls of International Organizations: Legal Personality and the Lighthouse at Cape Spartel, 36 *VJIL* 275 (1996).

28 See Douglas M. Johnston, Functionalism in the Theory of International Law, 26 *Can. Y.B. Int'l L.* 3 (1988).

29 1949 ICJ 174.

30 Id. at 178.

31 See Guenter Weissberg, *The International Status of the United Nations* [New York, 1961].

32 See Antoine Sottile, *The Problem of the Creation of a Permanent International Criminal Court* [Nendeln, 1966]; M. Cherif Bassiouni, comp., *The Statute of the International Criminal Court: A Documentary History* [Ardsley, 1998].

33 See African [Banjul] Charter on Human and People's Rights, June 27, 1981, OAU Doc. CAB/LEG/67/3 rev. 5, 21 *ILM* 58 (1982); Makau wa Mutua, The Banjul Charter and the African Cultural Fingerprint: An Evaluation of the Language of Duties, 35 *VJIL* 339 (1995).

34 See Giorgos Ténékidès, *L'Individu dans l'Ordre Juridique International* [Paris, 1933]; Peter Pavel Remec, *The Position of the Individual in International Law According to Grotius and Vattel* [The Hague, 1960]; Carl Nørgaard, *The Position of the Individual in International Law* [Copenhagen, 1962].

35 See *Steiner and Gross v. Polish State*, 4 Ann. Dig. Nos. 188, 287 (1927–28). See also Oppenheim 16–17.

36 See *Globocnik-Vojka v. Republic of Austria*, 71 *ILR* 265 (1958). See also Oppenheim 849–50.

37 See W. Paul Gormley, *The Procedural Status of the Individual before International and Supranational Tribunals* [The Hague, 1966].

38 See *Jurisdiction of the Courts of Danzig* Opinion, 1928 PCIJ Ser. B, No. 15.

39 See *Barcelona Traction* Case (Belg. v. Sp.), 1970 ICJ 4; Lucius Caflisch, *La Protection des Sociétés Commerciales et des Intérêts Indirects en Droit International Public* [The Hague, 1969]; Charles N. Brower and Jason D. Brueschke, *The Iran–United States Claims Tribunal* [The Hague, 1998].

40 See Donald Richard Shea, *The Calvo Clause: A Problem of Inter-American and International Law and Diplomacy* [Minneapolis, 1955].

41 See the *Krupp* Trial, 10 Law Reports of Trials of War Criminals 69 (Nuremberg, U.S. Mil. Trib. June 30, 1948); *Doe v. Unocal Corp.*, 963 F. Supp. 880 (C.C.D. Cal. 1997).

42 See, e.g., Michael J. Glennon, Has International Law Failed the Elephant? 84 *AJIL* 1 (1990); Anthony D'Amato and Sudhir K. Chopra, Whales: Their Emerging Right to Life, 85 *AJIL* 21 (1991).

43 See *South West Africa* Cases (Liber. & Eth. v. S. Afr.), 1966 ICJ 51 (Second Phase).

44 See Edith Brown Weiss, *In Fairness to Future Generations: International Law, Common Patrimony, and Intergenerational Equity* [Dobbs Ferry, 1989]; Anthony D'Amato, Do We Owe a Duty to Future Generations to Preserve the Global Environment? 84 *AJIL* 190 (1990).

45 See Derek Parfit, On Doing the Best for Our Children, in *Ethics and Population* 100 [Michael D. Bayles ed., Cambridge, 1976]; id., Future Generations, Further Problems, 11 *Philosophy & Public Affairs* 113 (1982)

46 See Hedley Bull, *The Anarchical Society: A Study of Order in World Politics* [New York, 1977]; Susan Strange, *The Retreat of the State: The Diffusion of Power in the World Community* [New York, 1996]; Thomas M. Franck, Clan and Superclan: Loyalty, Identity, and Community in Law and Practice, 90 *AJIL* 359 (1996).

47 See Anthony Clark Arend, *Legal Rules and International Society* 171–88 [New York, 1999].

5. Coherence and Sophistication

1 For more on the attributes of primitive law, see A. S. Diamond, *Primitive Law Past and Present* [London, 1971]; Max Gluckman, *Politics, Law, and Ritual in Tribal Society* [Chicago, 1965]; E. Adamson Hoebel, *The Law of Primitive Man* [Cambridge, 1964].

2 See Michael Barkun, *Law without Sanctions: Order in Primitive Societies and the World Community* [New Haven, 1968]; Yoram Dinstein, International Law as a Primitive Legal System, 19 *N.Y.U. J. Int'l L. &*

Pol. 1 (1986); A. I. L. Campbell, International Law and Primitive Law, 8 *Oxford J. Leg. Stud.* 169 (1988).

3 H. L. A. Hart, *The Concept of Law* 2 [2d ed., Oxford, 1994].

4 See id. at 92–93, 95–96.

5 See, e.g., Stephen D. Krasner, ed., *International Regimes* [Ithaca, 1983]; Roger D. Masters, World Politics as a Primitive Political System, 16 *World Pol.* 595 (1964); Stephen D. Krasner, Structural Causes and Regime Consequences: Regimes as Intervening Variables, 36 *Int'l Organization* 1 (1982); Anthony Clark Arend, Do Legal Rules Matter? International Law and International Politics, 38 *VJIL* 107, 109–22 (1998).

6 See Maarten Bos, *A Methodology of International Law* 36–47 [Amsterdam, 1984]; Ilmar Tammelo, Zum Aufbau Einer Theorie der Gerechtigkeit, 20 *Österreichische Zeitschrift für Öffentliches Recht* 154 (1970).

7 See Thomas M. Franck, *The Power of Legitimacy among Nations* [New York, 1990].

8 *Barcelona Traction* Case (Belg. v. Sp.), 1970 ICJ 4, 50.

9 See *Effect of Awards of Compensation Made by the United Nations Administrative Tribunal* Opinion, 1954 ICJ 47, 57; *Mavrommatis Palestine Concessions* Case (Gr. v. U.K.), 1924 PCIJ Ser. A, No. 2, at 34 ("The Court, whose jurisdiction is international, is not bound to attach to matters of form the same degree of importance which they might possess in municipal law."). See also Mohamed Shahabuddeen, *Precedent in the World Court* [Cambridge, 1996].

10 *Interpretation of Judgments Nos. 7 and 8 Concerning the Case of the Factory at Chorzów,* 1927 PCIJ Ser. A, No. 13, at 11–12.

11 See *Case Concerning the Interpretation of the Air Transport Services Agreement* (U.S. v. Fr.), 9 RIAA 73 (1964); *Argentine-Chile Frontier* Case, 16 RIAA 109 (1966).

12 3 RIAA 1905, 1964 (1941), reprinted in 35 *AJIL* 684 (1941).

13 See Hersch Lauterpacht, *Private Law Sources and Analogies of International Law* [London, 1927]; Bin Cheng, *General Principles of Law as Applied by International Courts and Tribunals* (1953) [rep., Cambridge, 1987].

14 See Grant Hanessian, General Principles of Law in the Iran-U.S. Claims Tribunal, 27 *CJTL* 309 (1989); John R. Crook, Applicable Law in International Arbitration: The Iran-U.S. Claims Tribunal Experience, 83 *AJIL* 278 (1989).

15 See *Nottebohm* Case (Liecht. v. Guat.) (Second Phase), 1955 ICJ 4, 21–24;

Constitution of the Maritime Safety Committee of the Inter-Govern-mental Maritime Consultative Organization Opinion, 1960 ICJ 150, 171. See also Charles de Visscher, *Problèmes d'Interprétation Judiciare en Droit International Public* [Paris, 1963].

16 1982 ICJ 1, 18.

17 See V. D. Degan, *L'Équité et le Droit International* [The Hague, 1970]; Julius Stone, 'Non Liquet' and the Function of Law in the International Community, 35 *BYBIL* 124 (1959).

18 Oppenheim 13.

19 See Karl Strupp, Le Droit du Juge International de Statuer Selon l'Équité, 33 *RCADI* 351 (1930 III); J. Patrick Kelly, The Twilight of Customary International Law, 40 *VJIL* 449 (2000).

20 ILC Draft Articles on Arbitral Procedure, Art. 12, reprinted in [1958] 2 *Y.B. Int'l L. Comm'n* 8.

21 See PCIJ, Advisory Committee of Jurists, *Procès Verbaux of Proceedings, 16 June–24 July 1920,* 336 [The Hague, 1920].

22 See *Desgranges v. International Labor Organization,* 20 *ILR* 523, 530 (1953).

23 See *Haya de le Torre* Case (Colom. v. Peru), 1951 ICJ 71, 81.

24 1996 ICJ 226, 266 (dispositif ¶ 2(E)).

25 Id. at 279 (Declaration of Judge Vereshchetin).

26 Universal Declaration of Human Rights, Dec. 10, 1948, G.A. Res. 217A (III), UN GAOR, 3d Sess., UN Doc. A/ILO (1948).

27 19 *Dep't State Bull.* 751 (1948).

28 See Hurst Hannum, The Status of the Universal Declaration of Human Rights in National and International Law, 25 *Ga. J. Int'l & Comp. L.* 287 (1995–96).

29 1969 ICJ 3 (F.R.G. v. Den./Neth.).

30 See Malcolm D. Evans, *Relevant Circumstances and Maritime Delimi-tation* [Oxford, 1989].

31 See *Gulf of Maine* Case (Can. v. U.S.), 1984 ICJ 247.

32 See *Tunisia-Libya Continental Shelf* Case, 1982 ICJ 17.

33 See Max Sørensen, Le Problème du Droit Intertemporel dans l'Ordre In-ternational, 1973 *IDIA* 20; T. O. Elias, The Doctrine of Intertemporal Law, 74 *AJIL* 285 (1980); Rosalyn Higgins, Time and the Law: Interna-tional Perspectives on an Old Problem, 46 *ICLQ* 501 (1997).

34 VCLT, Art. 31(3)(c).

35 *Namibia (Legal Consequences)* Opinion, 1971 ICJ 16, 30.

36 Id.

37 See VCLT, Art. 64; Oppenheim 1292–93.

38 *Aegean Sea Continental Shelf* Case (Gr. v. Tur.), 1978 ICJ 3, 32.

39 See *Western Sahara* Opinion, 1975 ICJ 12, 38–40, 67–68.

40 2 RIAA 829 (U.S. v. Neth.) (Perm. Ct. Arb. 1928).

41 *Minquiers and Ecrehos* Case (Fr. v. U.K.), [1953] 2 ICJ Pleadings 64.

42 See 1975 *IDIA* 537; International Law Commission, State Responsibility: Draft Articles Provisionally Adopted by the Drafting Committee, Arts. 13–15, UN Doc. A/CN.4/l.600 (Aug. 11, 2000).

43 For application of the "last in time" rule in U.S. domestic practice, see *Whitney v. Robertson*, 124 U.S. 190 (1888); *Chae Chan Ping v. United States*, 130 U.S. 581 (1889).

44 Oscar Schachter, *International Law in Theory and Practice* 1 [Dordrecht, 1991].

45 See Lauri Hannikainen, *Peremptory Norms (Jus Cogens) in International Law: Historical Development, Criteria, Present Status* [Helsinki, 1988]; Christos L. Rozakis, *The Concept of Jus Cogens in the Law of Treaties* [Amsterdam, 1976].

46 See Maurizio Ragazzi, *The Concept of International Obligations* Erga Omnes [Oxford, 1997].

47 See VCLT, Arts. 34–36.

48 See generally Jean-David Roulet, *Le Caractère Artificiel de l'Abus de Droit en Droit International Public* [Neuchâtel, 1958]; J. F. O'Connor, *Good Faith in International Law* [Aldershot, 1991]; B. O. Iluyomade, The Scope and Content of a Complaint of Abuse of Right in International Law, 16 *HILJ* 47 (1975).

6. Values and Paradoxes

1 See Thomas M. Franck, *The Power of Legitimacy among Nations* [New York, 1990].

2 See Richard Tuck, *On the Rights of War and Peace* [Oxford, 1999].

3 See Immanuel Kant, To Perpetual Peace: A Philosophical Sketch (1795), in *Perpetual Peace and Other Essays* 107 [Ted Humphrey trans., Indianapolis, 1983]; Fernando Tesón, The Kantian Theory of International Law, 92 *Colum. L. Rev.* 53 (1992).

4 Myres S. McDougal, International Law, Power and Policy: A Contemporary Conception, 82 *RCADI* 133 (1953 I); Myres S. McDougal and

Florentino P. Feliciano, *Law and Minimum World Public Order* [New Haven, 1961]; Myres S. McDougal and W. Michael Reisman, International Law in Policy-Oriented Perspective, in *The Structure and Process of International Law* 103 [Ronald St. J. MacDonald and Douglas M. Johnston eds., Boston, 1983].

5 See Charles de Visscher, *Theory and Reality in Public International Law* [P. E. Corbett trans., rev. ed., Princeton, 1968]; Oscar Schachter, *International Law in Theory and Practice* [Dordrecht, 1991]; Rosalyn Higgins, *Problems and Process: International Law and How We Use It* [Oxford, 1994]; Louis Henkin, *International Law: Politics and Values* [Dordrecht, 1995].

6 (U.K. v. Alb.), 1949 ICJ 4, 35. See International Law Commission, Draft Declaration of the Rights and Duties of States, 1949 *Y.B. Int'l L. Comm'n* 286; UN General Assembly Declaration on Principles of International Law Concerning Friendly Relations and Cooperation among States, UN G.A. Res. 2623 (XXV) (1970), reprinted in 9 *ILM* 1292 (1970).

7 See Oppenheim 379–81.

8 Vienna Convention on Diplomatic Relations, opened for signature Apr. 18, 1961, Art. 3(1)(e), 500 UNTS 95.

9 See id., Arts. 22, 30, 31, 45.

10 See David J. Bederman, *International Law in Antiquity* [Cambridge, 2001].

11 See VCLT, Arts. 6–18, 26.

12 Id., Arts. 54–68.

13 See Thomas M. Franck, *Fairness in International Law and Institutions* [Oxford, 1995].

14 See Edwin De Witt Dickinson, *The Equality of States in International Law* (1920) [rep., New York, 1972]; P. H. Kooijmans, *The Doctrine of the Legal Equality of States: An Inquiry into the Foundations of International Law* [Leiden, 1964]; Robert A. Klein, *Sovereign Equality among States: The History of an Idea* [Toronto, 1974].

15 Declaration on Principles of International Law, supra note 6.

16 See [1958] 2 *Y.B. Int'l L. Comm'n* 105; [1961] 2 id. 128.

17 *Genocide Convention* Opinion, 1951 ICJ 15, 23.

18 See Jerzy Makarczyk, *Principles of a New International Economic Order: A Study of International Law in the Making* [Dordrecht, 1988]; Lea Brilmayer, International Justice and International Law, 98 *W. Va. L. Rev.* 611 (1996).

19 See Rüdiger Wolfrum, *The Internationalization of Common Spaces outside National Jurisdiction: The Development of an International Administration for Antarctica, Outer Space, High Seas, and the Deep Sea–Bed* [Berlin, 1984]; Kemal Baslar, *The Concept of the Common Heritage of Mankind in International Law* [The Hague, 1998].

20 1982 ICJ 17.

21 Id. at 256 (quoting *North Sea Continental Shelf* Cases [Ger. v. Neth./Den.], 1969 ICJ 3).

22 See Edith Brown Weiss, *In Fairness to Future Generations: International Law, Common Patrimony, and Intergenerational Equity* [Dobbs Ferry, 1989].

23 See Judith Gail Gardam, Proportionality and Force in International Law, 87 *AJIL* 391 (1993).

24 999 UNTS 171.

25 Opened for signature Dec. 10, 1982, UN Doc. A/CONF.62/122 (1992), reprinted in 21 *ILM* 1261 (1982).

26 See Theodor Meron, *Henry's Wars and Shakespeare's Laws: Perspectives on the Law of War in the Later Middle Ages* [Oxford, 1993]; id., *Bloody Constraint: War and Chivalry in Shakespeare* [New York, 1998].

27 See *Brown v. United States*, 12 U.S. (8 Cranch) 110, 128 (1814) (Marshall, C.J.).

28 For more on Martens, see V. V. Pustogarov, *Our Martens: F. F. Martens, International Lawyer and Architecht of Peace* [W. E. Butler trans., The Hague, 2000].

29 Agreement for the Prosecution and Punishment of the Major War Criminals of the European Axis, Aug. 8, 1945, Art. 6, 59 Stat. 1544, 1548, 82 UNTS 279, 288.

30 1949 ICJ 4 (U.K. v. Albania).

31 ILC Draft Declaration on Rights and Duties of States, supra note 6, Art. 1; Declaration on Principles of International Law, supra note 6.

32 See *In re Pavelic*, [1933–34] Ann. Dig. No. 158 (Turin Ct. App. 1934) (Italy).

33 *Underhill v. Hernandez*, 168 U.S. 250, 252 (1897).

34 See Burleigh Cushing Rodick, *The Doctrine of Necessity in International Law* [New York, 1928].

35 The *Caroline* Incident, 2 John Bassett Moore, *Digest of International Law* 412 [Washington, 1906].

36 See Hersch Lauterpacht, Angary and Requisition of Neutral Property, 27 *BYBIL* 455 (1950).

37 See Oppenheim 739–41; Nicholas M. Poulantzas, *The Right of Hot Pursuit in International Law* (Leiden, 1969); The Red Crusader, 35 *ILR* 485 (Comm'n Inquiry 1962).

38 See Instructions for the Government of Armies of the United States in the Field, April 24, 1863, reprinted in Dietrich Schindler and Jiri Toman eds., *The Laws of Armed Conflicts: A Collection of Conventions, Resolutions, and Other Documents* 3 [Dordrecht, 1988].

39 See Manfred Lachs, Science, Technology, and World Law, 86 *AJIL* 673 (1992).

40 See John Rawls, *A Theory of Justice* 127–30 [Cambridge, 1971]. See also Franck, supra note 13, at 27–40.

41 See Jack L. Goldsmith and Eric A. Posner, A Theory of Customary International Law, 66 *U. Chi. L. Rev.* 1113 (1999).

42 See Ronald H. Coase, The Problem of Social Costs, 3 *J. L. & Econ.* 1 (1960).

43 See, e.g., Jeffrey L. Dunoff and Joel P. Trachtman, Economic Analysis of International Law, 24 *YJIL* 1 (1999).

44 See *Lac Lanoux* Case, 12 RIAA 281 (Fr. v. Sp.) (1957).

45 See Philippe Sands, *Principles of International Environmental Law* [Manchester, 1995].

46 *Nuclear Test* Cases (Austl. & N.Z. v. Fr.), 1974 ICJ 253, 267.

47 *Mosul Frontier* Opinion, 1925 PCIJ Ser. B, No. 12, at 25.

48 See *Reference Re Secession of Québec*, [1998] 2 S.C.R. 217 (Can.), reprinted in 37 *ILM* 1340 (1998).

49 See S. James Anaya, *Indigenous Peoples in International Law* [New York, 1996].

50 See Edwin M. Borchard, *The Diplomatic Protection of Citizens Abroad; or, The Law of International Claims* (1915) [rep., New York, 1970].

51 *Harry Roberts* Claim (U.S. v. Mex.), 4 RIAA 77 (1926), reprinted in 21 *AJIL* 357 (1927).

52 See Garrett Hardin, The Tragedy of the Commons, 162 *Science* 1243 (1968).

53 Mar. 3, 1973, 993 UNTS 243.

54 See *GATT Panel Decision—Restriction on Imports of Tuna*, 30 *ILM* 1594 (1991); *United States—Import Prohibition of Certain Shrimp and Shrimp Products* (WTO App. Oct. 12, 1998), 38 id. 118, 174 (1999).

55 See Mancur Olson Jr., *The Logic of Collective Action* [Cambridge, 1971].

56 See Intellectual Property and Human Rights, UN Commission on Hu-

man Rights, Sub-Commission on the Promotion and Protection of Human Rights (Aug. 17, 2000).

57 See Fernando Tesón, *Humanitarian Intervention: An Inquiry into Law and Morality* [Dobbs Ferry, 1988]; Sean D. Murphy, *Humanitarian Intervention: The United Nations in an Evolving World Order* [Philadelphia, 1996].

7. Confines

1 [1887] U.S. Foreign Rel. 751.

2 See, e.g., *Case Concerning Certain German Interests in Polish Upper Silesia* (Ger. v. Pol.) (Merits), 1926 PCIJ Ser. A, No. 17; *Case Concerning the Rights of Nationals of the United States of America in Morocco* (Fr. v. U.S.), 1952 ICJ 176.

3 1929 PCIJ Ser. A, No. 21 (Fr. v. Braz.).

4 See Ruth D. Masters, *International Law in Domestic Courts* [New York, 1932]; Richard Falk, *The Role of Domestic Courts in the International Legal Order* [Syracuse, 1964].

5 See Oppenheim 53–55.

6 See id. 82–86.

7 See *Treatment of Polish Nationals in Danzig* Opinion, 1932 PCIJ Ser. A/B, No. 44.

8 *Greek and Bulgarian Communities* Case (Gr. v. Bul.), 1930 PCIJ Ser. B, No. 17, at 32; see also *Applicability of the Obligation to Arbitrate under Section 21 of the United Nations Headquarters Agreement*, 1988 ICJ 12, 34.

9 159 U.S. 113, 163–64 (1895).

10 See *Lawless v. Ireland*, Eur. Ct. H.R., Ser. A, No. 1 (1961); *Lithgow v. United Kingdom*, 8 Eur. H.R. Rep. 329 (1986). See also Michael R. Hutchinson, The Margin of Appreciation and the European Court of Human Rights, 48 *ICLQ* 638 (1999).

11 1955 ICJ 4 (Liechtenstein v. Guatemala).

12 See Oppenheim 851–56.

13 *Nationality Decrees Issued in Tunis and Morocco (French Zone)* Opinion, 1923 PCIJ Ser. B, No. 4, at 24.

14 See A. A. Cançado Trindade, *The Application of the Rule of Exhaustion of Local Remedies in International Law* [Cambridge, 1983]; C. F. Amerasinghe, *Local Remedies in International Law* [Cambridge, 1990].

15 See *Finnish Shipowners* Claim (Finland v. U.K.), 3 RIAA 1479 (1934); *Panevezys-Saldutiskis Ry.* Case (Estonia v. Lithuania), 1939 PCIJ Ser. A/B, No. 76.

16 See *Interhandel* Case (Switz. v. U.S.), 1959 ICJ 6, 27.

17 1989 ICJ 15 (U.S. v. It.).

18 See Sompong Sucharitkul, *State Immunities and Trading Activities in International Law* [New York, 1959]; Gamal Moursi Badr, *State Immunity* [The Hague, 1984]; Christophe Schreuer, *State Immunity* [Cambridge, 1988].

19 See *The Schooner Exchange v. M'Faddon*, 11 U.S. (7 Cranch) 116 (1812).

20 See, e.g., *Dralle v. Republic of Czechoslovakia*, 1950 ILR 155 (Austrian S.Ct. 1950).

21 26 *Dep't of State Bulletin* 984 (1952).

22 See Oppenheim 456–58.

23 1927 PCIJ Ser. A, No. 10 (Fr. v. Tur.).

24 Id. at 34 (Loder, J., dissenting).

25 *Restatement (Third) Foreign Relations Law of the United States* § 403 (American Law Institute) [St. Paul, 1987].

26 See also *Timberlane Lumber Co. v. Bank of America*, 549 F.2d 597 (9th Cir. 1976).

27 See 44 [1] *IDIA* 167; 45 [2] id. 292, 299; M. S. Rajan, *United Nations and Domestic Jurisdiction* [2d ed., New York, 1961]; Ian Brownlie, *Principles of Public International Law* [5th ed., Oxford, 1998].

28 Oppenheim 6–7; see also W. E. Beckett, What Is Private International Law? 7 *BYBIL* 73 (1926).

29 Joseph Story, *Commentaries on the Conflict of Laws* 24, 33 [1st ed., Boston, 1834].

30 See Alan Watson, *Joseph Story and the Comity of Errors: A Case Study in Conflict of Laws* [Athens, 1992].

31 See David J. Bederman, Compulsory Pilotage, Public Policy, and the Early Private International Law of Torts, 64 *Tul. L. Rev.* 1033 (1990).

32 But see *Guardianship of Infants* Case (Neth v. Swe.), 1958 ICJ 55.

33 See *Anglo-Iranian Oil Co.* Case (U.K. v. Iran), 1952 ICJ 93, 111–13; *Barcelona Traction* Case (Belg. v. Sp.), 1970 ICJ 4, 50.

34 See *Folliott v. Ogden*, 1 H.L.C. 123; 126 Eng. Rep. 75 (1789); *The Antelope*, 23 U.S. (10 Wheat.) 66 (1825).

35 See Oppenheim 488–98.

36 See Stephen J. Toope, *Mixed International Arbitration* [Cambridge, 1990].

37 (Eth./Lib. v. S. Afr.) (Jurisdiction), 1962 ICJ 319, 466 (Fitzmaurice, J., dissenting).
38 See *South West Africa* Cases (Eth./Lib. v. S. Afr.) (Merits), 1966 ICJ 4.
39 Dean Acheson, Panel: Cuban Quarantine: Implications for the Future, 57 *Proc. Am. Soc'y Int'l L.* 14 (1963).
40 1996 ICJ 226, 266 (dispositif ¶ 2(E)).
41 Opened for signature Dec. 10, 1982, Arts. 57, 83, UN Doc. A/CONF.62/122 (1992), reprinted in 21 *ILM* 1261 (1982).
42 Gilbert Gidel, *Le Régime des Fleuves Internationaux* [Paris, 1948]; Richard Baxter, *The Law of International Waterways* [Cambridge, 1964].
43 See *International Commission of the River Oder* Opinion, 1929 PCIJ Ser. A, No. 23 (1929).
44 12 RIAA 281 (Fr. v. Sp.) (1957).
45 Alexandra Merle Post, *Deep Sea Mining and the Law of the Sea* [The Hague, 1983]; Wolfgang Hauser, *The Legal Regime for Deep Seabed Mining under the Law of the Sea Convention* [Deventer, 1983].
46 Apr. 18, 1961, Art. 9(1), 500 UNTS 95.
47 See VCLT, Art. 20.
48 See *Air Services Agreement* Arbitration (U.S. v. Fr.), 18 RIAA 417 (1978).
49 But see Oscar Schachter, *International Law in Theory and Practice* 192–99 [Dordrecht, 1991].
50 See 1974 ICJ 253 (Austl./N.Z. v. Fr.).
51 See *Electricity Company of Sofia and Bulgaria* (Bulg. v. Belg.), 1939 PCIJ Ser. A/B, No. 77.
52 See *Monetary Gold Removed from Rome in 1943* (Italy v. Fr./U.K./U.S.), 1954 ICJ 19.
53 See *Nicaragua* Case, 1984 ICJ 392 (Jurisdiction).

8. Formalism and Pragmatism

1 See Kenneth W. Abbott, Modern International Relations Theory: A Prospectus for International Lawyers, 14 *YJIL* 335 (1989).
2 See Benedict Kingsbury, Confronting Difference: The Puzzling Durability of Gentili's Combination of Pragmatic Pluralism and Normative Judgment, 92 *AJIL* 713 (1998).
3 Wolfgang Friedman, The Reality of International Law—A Reappraisal, 10 *CJTL* 59, 60 (1971).
4 See Alexandre Charles Kiss and Dinah Shelton, Systems Analysis of

International Law: A Methodological Inquiry, 17 *Neth. Y.B. Int'l L.* 45 (1986).

5 Harold G. Maier, The Authoritative Sources of Customary International Law in the United States, 10 *Mich. J. Int'l L.* 450, 480 (1989).

6 (Gr. v. U.K.), 1924 PCIJ Ser. A, No. 2, at 34.

7 See Robert S. Summers, Theory, Formality, and Practical Legal Criticism, 107 *L.Q. Rev.* 407 (1990); Frederick Schauer, Formalism, 97 *Yale L. J.* 509 (1988); James G. Wilson, The Morality of Formalism, 33 *UCLA L. Rev.* 431 (1985).

8 See Frank I. Michelman, A Brief Anatomy of Adjudicative Rule-Formalism, 66 *U. Chi. L. Rev.* 934 (1999); Richard H. Pildes, Forms of Formalism, id. 607.

9 See Oppenheim xi–xii (indicating that earlier editions of the treatise were split between the international law of peace and of war); Axel Möller, *International Law in Peace and War* [London, 1935].

10 See Philip C. Jessup, *Neutrality, Its History, Economics, and Law* [New York, 1935].

11 VCLT, Art. 73 & pmblr. para. 8.

12 See id., Arts. 7–17, 24–25.

13 See id., Arts. 28, 29.

14 See id., Arts. 46–64.

15 Ian Brownlie, *Principles of Public International Law* 129 [5th ed., Oxford, 1998].

16 See D. P. O'Connell, *State Succession in Municipal Law and International Law* [Cambridge, 1967]; Brigitte Stern, La Succession d'États, 262 *RCADI* 9 (1996).

17 Aug. 23, 1978, UN Doc. A/CONF.80/31 (1978).

18 Apr. 8, 1983, UN Doc. A/CONF.117/14 (1983).

19 Oppenheim 209.

20 See 1986 ICJ 14, 113–14.

21 Protocol Additional to the Geneva Conventions Relating to the Protection of Victims of Non-International Armed Conflicts, June 8, 1977, art. 1(2), 16 *ILM* 1442 (1977).

22 UN Doc. S/Res/808 (1993).

23 *Prosecutor v. Tadič*, 35 ILM 32 (1996) (ICTFY App. 1995).

24 See Oppenheim 1031–1178.

25 See Philip C. Jessup, *The Law of Territorial Waters and Maritime Jurisdiction* [New York, 1927]; Gilbert Gidel, *Le Droit International Public*

de la Mer [Paris, 1932–34]; D. P. O'Connell, *The International Law of the Sea* [2d ed., Oxford, 1984].

26 See Oppenheim 602–11.

27 See Alwyn V. Freeman, *The International Responsibility of States for Denial of Justice* [London, 1938].

28 4 RIAA 282 (1927).

29 4 id. 632 (1927).

30 *Emanuel Too v. United States,* 23 *Iran-U.S. Claims Trib. Rep.* 378 (1989).

31 See Douglas M. Johnston, Functionalism in the Theory of International Law, 26 *Can. Y.B. Int'l L.* 3 (1988).

32 See Brian Z. Tamanaha, *Realistic Socio-Legal Theory: Pragmatism and a Social Theory of Law* [Oxford, 1997]; Richard Posner, Pragmatic Adjudication, 8 *Cardozo L. Rev.* 1 (1996); Steven D. Smith, The Pursuit of Pragmatism, 100 *Yale L. J.* 409 (1990); Richard Rorty, The Banality of Pragmatism and the Poetry of Justice, 63 *So. Cal. L. Rev.* 1811 (1990); Patrick S. Atiyah, *Pragmatism and Theory in English Law* [Oxford, 1987].

33 (Nicar. v. U.S.) (Merits), 1986 ICJ 14, 98.

34 See *Reparations for Injuries Suffered in the Service of the United Nations* Opinion, 1949 ICJ 174; VCLT, Arts. 34–38. See also Ronald Francis Roxburgh, *International Conventions and Third States* [London, 1917]; Oppenheim 1260–66.

35 VCLT, Art. 18.

36 See Athanassios Vamvoukos, *Termination of Treaties in International Law: The Doctrines of* Rebus Sic Stantibus *and* Desuetude [Oxford, 1985]; Oppenheim 1304–9.

37 League Covenant, Art. 19. See also Aladar Goellner, *La Revision des Traités sous le Régime de la Société des Nations* [Paris, 1925].

38 *Fisheries Jurisdiction* Case (U.K. v. Ice.), 1973 ICJ 3.

39 1951 ICJ 15.

40 See VCLT, Art. 19(c).

41 Compare *Belilos,* 132 Eur. Ct. H.R. (Ser. A.) (1988) and *Advisory Opinion on Restriction to the Death Penalty,* Adv. Op. No. OC-3 (Ser. A) No. 3 (Inter-Am. Ct. H.R. 1983), reprinted in 23 *ILM* 320 (1984).

42 See Roberto Ago, *Il Requisto dell'Effetività dell'Occupazione in Diritto Internationale* [Rome, 1934]; Arthur S. Keller, Oliver J. Lissitzyn, and Frederick J. Mann, *Creation of Rights of Sovereignty through Symbolic Acts, 1400–1800* [New York, 1938].

43 See *Clipperton Island* Case (Fr. v. Mex.), 2 RIAA 1105 (1931); *Legal Sta-*

tus of Eastern Greenland Case (Den. v. Nor.), 1933 PCIJ Ser. A/B, No. 53.

44 See 1 Green Hackworth, *Digest of International Law* 458 [Washington, 1940].

45 402 UNTS 71.

46 See 1962 ICJ 151.

47 See *Namibia (Legal Consequences)* Opinion, 1971 ICJ 16, 21–27.

48 *The Case of B.*, 20 *Entscheidungen des Reichgerichts in Strafsachen* 148 (1889), 17 *Journal du Droit International Privé* (Clunet) 498 (1890).

49 See *Re Wood Pulp Cartel: A. Ahlstrom Osakeyhtio v. E.C. Commission,* [1988] 4 C.M.L.R. 901; *Re The LdPE Cartel: The Community v. Atochem SA,* [1990] 4 C.M.L.R. 382.

50 Opened for signature Dec. 10, 1982, Arts. 74, 83, UN Doc. A/CONF.62/122 (1992), reprinted in 21 *ILM* 1261 (1982).

51 See *Delimitation of the Continental Shelf in the Western Approaches* (Gr. Brit. v. Fr.), 18 *ILM* 397 (1978).

52 999 UNTS 171.

53 213 UNTS 222.

54 Eur. Ct. H.R., Ser. A, No. 1 (1961).

55 Gilbert Gidel, *Le Régime des Fleuves Internationaux* [Paris, 1948]; Richard Baxter, *The Law of International Waterways* [Cambridge, 1964]; Oppenheim 582–89.

56 *International Commission of the River Oder* Opinion, 1929 PCIJ Ser. A, No. 23 (1929).

57 International Law Association, *Report of the 52nd Conference,* Helsinki (1966).

58 See *Gabčikovo-Nagymaros Project* Case (Hungary v. Slovakia), 1994 ICJ 151.

59 See GATT, 55 UNTS 308, Art. XVIII.

60 See *United States (Mergé) v. Italy,* 14 RIAA 236 (Italy-U.S. Conciliation Comm'n 1955).

61 See *A/18* Case, 5 *Iran-U.S. Claims Trib. Rep.* 251 (1984).

62 See *Case Concerning the Barcelona Traction, Light and Power Co., Ltd.* (Belgium v. Spain) (Second Phase), 1970 ICJ 3.

63 19 *Dep't of State Press Releases* 50–52, 136–37, 140, 143–44 (1938).

64 See *Kügele v. Polish State,* 6 Ann. Dig. 69 (Upper Silesian Arb. Trib. 1930).

9. Enforcement and Compliance

1 See Lori Fisler Damrosch, Enforcing International Law through Non-Forcible Measures, 269 *RCADI* 9 (1997).

2 See Elisabeth Zoller, *Peaceful Unilateral Remedies: An Analysis of Countermeasures* [Dobbs Ferry, 1984].

3 VCLT, Art. 60(3)(b). See also *Tacna-Arica* Arbitration (Chile v. Peru), 2 RIAA 929 (1925); *Namibia* Opinion, 1971 ICJ 16, 47; Shabtai Rosenne, *Breach of Treaty* [Cambridge, 1985].

4 18 RIAA 417 (1978).

5 See *United States Diplomatic and Consular Staff in Tehran* Case (U.S. v. Iran), 1980 ICJ 3.

6 See generally Terry D. Gill, *Litigation Strategy at the International Court: A Case Study of the* Nicaragua v. United States *Dispute* [The Hague, 1989].

7 1986 ICJ 14 (Merits Phase).

8 *Handel v. Artukovic*, 601 F. Supp. 1421, 1428 (C.D. Cal. 1985).

9 See 28 U.S.C. §§ 1601–11. See also Joseph W. Dellapenna, *Suing Foreign Governments and Their Corporations* [Washington, 1988].

10 See *Letelier v. Republic of Chile*, 748 F.2d 790, 799 (2d Cir. 1984).

11 See Christine D. Gray, *Judicial Remedies in International Law* [Oxford, 1987].

12 See Jackson H. Ralston, *The Law and Procedure of International Tribunals* [rev. ed., Stanford, 1926]; Yves Dezalay and Bryant G. Garth, *Dealing in Virtue: International Commercial Arbitration and the Construction of a Transnational Legal Order* [Chicago, 1996]; J. G. Merrills, *International Dispute Settlement* [3d ed., Cambridge, 1998].

13 See Jonathan I. Charney, Is International Law Threatened by Multiple International Tribunals? 271 *RCADI* 101 (1998).

14 See Jean-Pierre Cot, *La Conciliation Internationale* [Paris, 1968]; Nissim Bar-Yaacov, *The Handling of International Disputes by Means of Inquiry* [London, 1974].

15 See UN Secretary-General: Ruling Pertaining to the Differences between France and New Zealand Arising from The Rainbow Warrior Affair, 26 *ILM* 1346 (1987); *Rainbow Warrior* Arbitration (N.Z. v. Fr.), 82 *ILR* 499 (1990); *Request for an Examination of the Situation in Accordance with Paragraph 3 of the Court's Judgment of 20 December 1974* Case (Austl./N.Z. v. Fr.), 1995 ICJ 288.

16 See ICJ Statute, Art. 36.

17 See Marjorie M. Whiteman, *Damages in International Law* [Washing-

ton, 1937]; Dinah Shelton, *Remedies in International Human Rights Law* [Oxford, 1999].

18 See Emanuel Adler and Peter M. Haas, Conclusion: Epistemic Communities, World Order, and the Creation of a Reflective Research Program, 46 *Int'l Org.* 367 (1992); Abram Chayes and Antonia Handler Chayes, *The New Sovereignty: Compliance with International Regulatory Agreements* [Cambridge, 1995].

19 See Maurizio Ragazzi, *The Concept of International Obligations* Erga Omnes [Oxford, 1997].

20 *South West Africa* Case (Lib./Eth. v. S. Afr.)(Second Phase), 1966 ICJ 6, 47.

21 International Law Commission, State Responsibility: Draft Articles Provisionally Adopted by the Drafting Committee, Art. 34, para. 1, UN Doc. A/CN.4/l.600 (Aug. 11, 2000). See also id., Art. 49.

22 Louis Henkin, *How Nations Behave* 47 [2d ed., New York, 1979].

23 See, e.g., Roger Fisher, *Improving Compliance with International Law* [Charlottesville, 1981]; Oran Young, *Compliance and Public Authority* [Baltimore, 1979]; Benedict Kingsbury, The Concept of Compliance as a Function of Competing Conceptions of International Law, 19 *Mich. J. Int'l L.* 345 (1998); Harold Hongju Koh, Why Do Nations Obey International Law? 106 *Yale L. J.* 2599 (1997).

10. Rectitude and Ambition

1 See VCLT, Art. 62.

2 Cicero, *De Oficiis* i.10.33.

3 1927 PCIJ Ser. A, No. 10, at 34 (Loder, J., dissenting).

4 See Andreas F. Lowenfeld, *International Litigation and the Quest for Reasonableness* [Oxford, 1996]; *Restatement (Third) Foreign Relations Law of the United States* § 403 [St. Paul, 1987]; *Timberlane Lumber Co. v. Bank of America,* 549 F.2d 597 (9th Cir. 1976).

5 *Case Concerning the Frontier Dispute* (Burkino Faso v. Mali), 1986 ICJ 554 (at ¶ 25).

6 See *Wildenhus'* Case, 120 U.S. 1 (1887); *Lauritzen v. Larsen,* 345 U.S. 571 (1953).

7 See Oppenheim 622–24.

8 See id. at 734–35, 741–44.

9 See Myres S. McDougal and William T. Burke, *The Public Order of the Oceans* [New Haven, 1986]; René-Jean Dupuy and Daniel Vignes, *Traité du Nouveau Droit de la Mer* 337–74 [Paris, 1985].

10 See 3 RIAA at 1965.

11 1949 ICJ 4 (U.K. v. Alb.).

12 See Hay-Hull Correspondence, 19 *Dep't of State Press Releases* 50–52, 136–37, 140, 143–44 (1938).

13 See 1949 ICJ at 195 (Hackworth, J., dissenting).

14 See *Lockerbie* Case (Libya v. U.S./U.K.), 1992 ICJ 3, 114 (Provisional Measures).

15 ICJ Statute, Art. 31.

16 See ICJ Statute, Arts. 62 & 63.

17 See 11 J. H. W. Verzijl, W. P. Heere and J. P. S. Offerhaus, *International Law in Historical Perspective: The Law of Maritime Prize* [Dordrecht, 1992]; David J. Bederman, The Feigned Demise of Prize, 9 *Emory Int'l L. Rev.* 31 (1995).

18 See Thomas S. Kuhn, *The Structure of Scientific Revolutions* [3d ed., Chicago, 1996].

19 See League of Nations Covenant, Art. 22.

20 See Oppenheim 227–34.

21 See Rome Statute of the International Criminal Court, July 17, 1998, 37 *ILM* 999 (1998), UN Doc. A/CONF.183/9* (1999).

22 *R. v. Bow Street Magistrate, Ex Parte Pinochet Ugarte* (No. 3), [1999] 2 W.L.R. 827 (H.L.) (U.K.).

23 See League of Nations Covenant, Art. 18; UN Charter, Art. 102(1).

11. Skepticism and Exuberance

1 See, e.g., Rosalyn Higgins, *Problems and Process: International Law and How We Use It* [Oxford, 1994]; Louis Henkin, *International Law: Politics and Values* [Dordrecht, 1995].

2 See Hedley Bull, *The Anarchical Society: A Study of Order in World Politics* [New York, 1977]; Susan Strange, *The Retreat of the State: The Diffusion of Power in the World Community* [New York, 1996]; Thomas M. Franck, Clan and Superclan: Loyalty, Identity, and Community in Law and Practice, 90 *AJIL* 359 (1996).

3 See H. L. A. Hart, *The Concept of Law* 214 [2d ed., Oxford, 1994].

4 See Thomas S. Kuhn, *The Structure of Scientific Revolutions* [3d ed., Chicago, 1996].

5 1 Charles Louis Montesquieu, *The Spirit of the Laws* 8 (1748) [Ann M. Cohler, Basia Carolyn Miller and Harold Samuel Stone trans. and eds., Cambridge, 1989].

INDEX

recognized as, 86–88; involved
in international lawmaking,
54–70; *La Jeune Eugénie*
decision on natural overlaw
and, 6–7; necessity, cooperation,
rationality motivations of, 125–29;
neomedievalism and, 92–93;
positivism vs. naturalist rules for,
5–6; remedial defect for nonstate,
198–99; self-interest compliance
by, 20–21; state immunities for
individual, 168; treatment of
customary law by, 48. *See also*
nation-states
International Atomic Energy Agency
(Vienna), 156
international claims tribunals, 63
international community: *actio
populari s* violations and, 109,
201; defining, 49–54, 204; "family
of nations" metaphor used
for, 50–51; League of Nations
Covenant on peaceful change by,
205; moderate scarcity condition
and, 128; state membership in,
81–82; state self-determination
and, 86; universalism standard
embraced by, 51; UN Security
Council inaction and, 189. *See
also* international society
international institutions:
coordinating legal demands
of, 196–97; exhaustion rule
limiting individual relief from,
145–46; international lawmaking
by, 67–68; pragmatism used
to promote, 175; recognized
as international actors, 86–87;

Reparations for Injuries case on
status of, 87–88
International Labor Organization
Convention on the Employment
of Women during the Night (1919),
71
international law: analogy tool
and, 96–98; Austinian critique
of, 25–26; birth and historic
development of, 3–10; codified
structure of, 27–28; conflict
management domain of, 107,
202–3; consent vs. principle
basis of rules, 19; conservatism
of, 205–12; defining relevant
community for, 49–54; domestic
and, 21–23, 140–50; growing
autonomy of, 25–26; as horizontal
enforcement system, 190; lacunae
and, 98–100; monism vs. dualism
regarding domestic and, 141–42,
149–50; nature and influence of,
1; obedience or compliance with,
20–21; organizing principles of
authority of, 17–23; politics and,
18–19, 154–61; preference of state
position over practice by, 58; as
primitive legal system, 94–95;
progressivism of achievements
of, 212–20; promoting coherence/
sophistication in, 106–9; public
and private, 13–14, 150–54; as
rules or process, 23; skepticism
and exuberance on, 221–25;
sources of, 27–48; subjects and
objects of, 79–93; success in
conflict management by, 186–87.
See also international lawmaking

27; neutrality/predictability
criteria of, 48; pragmatic nature
of, 171–72; as primitive, 94;
structural formalisms and, 165;
subject/objects discourse and, 80;
synergies among, 45–48; treaties
as, 40–45
international law subjects:
distinction between objects and,
79–80; international institutions
and individuals as, 88–91; nation-
states as, 80–87; people not yet
born as, 92; recent challenges to
traditional, 91–93
international law theory: on bases
of international obligation, 3,
11–17; consent theory approach
to, 14–15, 38–39, 101–2, 197,
210–11; international conduct
validating, 25–26; neopositivist
approach to, 16–17; New Haven
school approach to, 16, 23,
112; New Stream scholarship
approach to, 17, 222. See also
naturalist approach; positivist
approach
international law values: certainty,
204; challenge of group rights
to, 131–32; challenges to
Eurocentric character of, 111–13;
competing fairness, humanity, and
democracy, 116–25, 133; during
European colonial imperialism,
7–8; necessity, cooperation, and
rationality, 125–29, 134, 135;
neutrality of diverse, 113–29;
pragmatism and conflict in,
178–84; reconciling paradoxes

of, 129–38; regarding common
resource management, 133–35;
sovereignty and peace, 113–16;
watershed (1945) for, 111. See also
international law rules
international legal personality:
Reparations for Injuries decision,
establishment of, 87–89; rights
and duties paradigm of, 89–90
international legal technique:
defining, 70; for identifying
emerging custom, 73–77;
intentionalist approach as,
71–72; teleological approach as,
72; textualism as, 71; for treaty
interpretation, 70–73; varying
levels of, 77–78
international relations: achieving
openness of, 219; autonomous vs.
dependence on politics of, 18–19;
conservatism to promote stability
in, 206–7; difficulties with UN
lawmaker role in, 59–62; impact
of state self-determination on, 86;
obedience or compliance approach
to, 20–21; obligation understood
through examining, 24; positivism
approach (1848–1919) to, 7–8;
respect for sovereignty foundation
for, 114; slavery/slave trade and,
6–7; sovereignty or cooperation
paradigm for, 19–20; UN Charter
ordering of, 216
International Sea Bed Authority, 158
international society: defining
community of, 49–54; emergence
of democracy as standard of, 54;
organizing principles of authority

The Spirit of the Laws

Alan Watson, General Editor

David J. Bederman, *The Spirit of International Law*
John Owen Haley, *The Spirit of Japanese Law*
Bernard G. Weiss, *The Spirit of Islamic Law*
Calum Carmichael, *The Spirit of Biblical Law*
R. H. Helmholz, *The Spirit of Classical Canon Law*
Geoffrey MacCormack, *The Spirit of Traditional Chinese Law*
Alan Watson, *The Spirit of Roman Law*